CU00664985

Barclay o
Matthew: Year A

THE NEW DAILY STUDY BIBLE

Barclay on the Lectionary

Matthew: Year A

William Barclay

SAINT ANDREW PRESS

Edinburgh

First published in 2013 by
SAINT ANDREW PRESS
121 George Street
Edinburgh EH2 4YN

Copyright © The William Barclay Estate, 1975, 2001
Layout and Publisher's Introduction copyright © Saint Andrew Press 2013

ISBN 978 0 7152 0972 1

All rights reserved. No part of this publication may be reproduced
or stored or transmitted by any means or in any form, electronic or
mechanical, including photocopying, recording, or any information
storage and retrieval system without permission in writing from the
publisher. This book is sold subject to the condition that it shall not,
by way of trade or otherwise, be lent, resold, hired out or otherwise
circulated without the publisher's prior consent.

The right of William Barclay to be identified as author of this work
has been asserted in accordance with the Copyright Designs and
Patents Act 1988.

British Library Cataloguing in Publication Data
A catalogue record for this book is available from the British Library.

It is the publisher's policy to only use papers that are natural and
recyclable and that have been manufactured from timber grown in
renewable, properly managed forests. All of the manufacturing processes
of the papers are expected to conform to the environmental regulations
of the country of origin.

Typeset by Manila Typesetting Company
Printed in the United Kingdom by
CPI Group (UK) Ltd, Croydon

Contents

Publisher's Introduction

William Barclay was a biblical scholar who possessed a remarkable gift of communication. His belief that the results of biblical scholarship should not be the preserve of academics but should be made available and accessible to the ordinary reader resulted in the now famous series of commentaries, The Daily Study Bible.

Those commentaries are full of colourful stories and numerous quotations from poetry and hymnody which bring the text alive, but Barclay was not afraid to challenge the reader by going straightforwardly and fascinatingly into more academic topics. His talent for enthralling communication enabled him to delve in a highly accessible way into the root of language and explain the meaning of the original Greek words or explore the complex background of Judaism and the Roman world.

William Barclay was Professor of Biblical Criticism, but he was also a minister of the Church of Scotland and he makes it very clear in his Introduction to the series that the primary aim of the Daily Study Bible series has never been academic. He explains that the aim 'could be summed up in the famous words of Richard of Chichester's prayer – to enable men and women to know Jesus Christ more clearly, to love him more dearly, and to follow him more nearly'.

It is therefore appropriate that William Barclay's commentary, now taken from The New Daily Study Bible (revised in c. 2001), should be set alongside the readings from the Common Worship

Lectionary, offering readers a chance to engage with Barclay's unique guide to reading the scriptures in a new pattern of daily readings.

The readings in Barclay on the Lectionary are those chosen for the Principal Sunday services and, as the Lectionary follows a three-year cycle, with concentration each year on the readings in one particular Gospel, readers have the opportunity to follow a single narrative throughout the year. In this volume, Barclay on the Lectionary follows Year A – the Gospel of Matthew. In subsequent volumes, Year B (the Gospel of Mark) and Year C (the Gospel of Luke) will be followed. In each volume, some readings from John's Gospel are also included.

As you read, you may develop a wish to engage further with Barclay's writing. It should be remembered that when Barclay wrote he was not following any lectionary but working his way through each book of the New Testament in sequence. So, in a few cases, you will find that his commentary is relatively brief and, in many more instances it has been necessary to edit texts to accommodate a more uniform length for each day's selection. However, those who wish to see the full commentary (which often includes more examples and stories used as illustration or further examination of a particular passage) and take exploration further can turn to the full text in The New Daily Study Bible series.

In bringing together commentary and lectionary in this way, it is hoped that new readers will discover William Barclay's special ways of drawing meaning from the biblical text, and that those already familiar with his work will find new inspiration for their Bible reading, so fulfilling his own expressed prayer that 'God will continue to use The Daily Study Bible to enable men and women better to understand his word'.

The First Sunday of Advent
The Threat of Time *and* The Coming of the King

Romans 13:11–14

Like so many great men, Paul was haunted by the shortness of time. In 'To My Coy Mistress', Andrew Marvell spoke of hearing 'time's winged chariot hurrying near'. In 'When I Have Fears', Keats expressed a similar anxiety, that he might 'cease to be before my pen has gleaned my teaming brain'. In his *Songs of Travel*, Robert Louis Stevenson wrote:

> The morning drum-call on my eager ear
> Thrills unforgotten yet; the morning dew
> Lies yet undried along my fields of noon.
> But now I pause at whiles in what I do
> And count the bell, and tremble lest I hear
> (My work untrimmed) the sunset gun too soon.

But there was more in Paul's thought than simply the shortness of time. He expected the second coming of Christ. The early Church expected it at any moment, and therefore it had the urgency to be ready. That expectancy has grown dim and faint, but one permanent fact remains: not one of us knows when God will rise and bid us to go. The time grows ever shorter, for we are every day one day nearer that time. We too, must have all things ready.

The last verses of this passage have achieved a lasting fame, for it was through them that Augustine found conversion. He tells the story in his *Confessions* (C. H. Dodd's translation). He was walking in the garden. His heart was in distress, because of his failure to live the good life. He kept exclaiming miserably. 'How long? How Long? Tomorrow and tomorrow – why not now? Why not this hour an end to my depravity?' Suddenly he heard a voice saying, 'Take and read.' It sounded like a child's voice; and he racked his mind to try to remember any child's game in which these words occurred, but could think of none. He hurried back to the seat where his friend Alypius was sitting, for he had left there a volume of Paul's writings. 'I snatched it up and read silently the first passage my eyes fell upon: "Let us not walk in revelry or drunkenness, in immorality and in shamelessness, in contention and in strife. But put on the Lord Jesus Christ, as a man puts on a garment, and stop living a life in which your first thought is to gratify the desires of Christless human nature." I neither wished nor needed to read further. With the end of the sentence, as though the light of assurance had poured into my heart, all the shades of doubt were scattered. I put my finger in the page and closed the book. I turned to Alypius with a calm countenance and told him.' Out of his word, God had spoken to Augustine. It was Samuel Taylor Coleridge who said that he believed the Bible to be inspired because, as he put it, 'It finds me.' God's word can always find the human heart.

It is interesting to look at the six sins which Paul selects as being, as it were, typical of the Christless life.

(1) There is *revelry* (*kōmos*). This is an interesting word. Originally, *kōmos* was the band of friends who accompanied a victor home from the games, singing his praises and celebrating his triumph as they went. Later, it came to mean a noisy band of revelers who swept their way through the city streets at night – what, in the first decade of the nineteenth century in Regency England, would have been called a *rout*. It describes the kind of revelry which is undignified and which is a nuisance to others.

(2) There is *drunkenness* (*methē*). To the Greeks, drunkenness was a particularly disgraceful thing. They were a wine-drinking people. Even children drank wine. Breakfast was called *akratisma*, and

consisted of a slice of bread dipped in wine. For all that, drunkenness was considered specially shameful, for the wine the Greeks drank was much diluted, and was drunk because the water supply was inadequate and dangerous. This was a vice which not just Christians but any respectable person would have condemned.

(3) There was *immorality* (*koitē*). *Koitē* literally means a bed and has in it the meaning of the desire for the forbidden bed. The word brings to mind people who set no value in fidelity and who take pleasure when and where they will.

(4) There is *shamelessness* (*aselgeia*). *Aselgeia* is one of the ugliest words in the Greek language. It describes not only immorality; it describes those who are lost in shame. Most people seek to conceal their evil deeds, but people in whose hearts there is *aselgeia* are long past that. They do not care how much of a public exhibition they make of themselves; they do not care what people think of them. *Aselgeia* is the quality of those who dare publicly to do the things which are unbecoming for anyone to do.

(5) There is *contention* (*eris*). *Eris* is the spirit that is born of uncontrolled and unholy competition. It comes from the desire for place, power and prestige, and from the hatred of being bettered. It is essentially the sin which places self in the foreground and is the entire negation of Christian love.

(6) There is *envy* (*zēlos*). *Zēlos* need not be a bad word. It can describe the noble attempt to emulate by those who, when confronted with greatness of character, wish to attain to it. But it can also mean that envy which grudges others their nobility and their superiority. It describes here the spirit which cannot be content with what it has and looks with jealous eye on every blessing given to someone else and denied to itself.

Matthew 24:36–44

These verses refer to the second coming and they tell us certain most important truths.

(1) They tell us that the hour of that event is known to God and to God alone. It is, therefore, clear that speculation regarding the time of the second coming is nothing less than blasphemy, for anyone who so speculates is seeking to wrest from God secrets which belong to God alone. It is no one's duty to speculate; it is our duty to prepare ourselves, and to watch.

(2) They tell us that the time will come with shattering suddenness on those who are immersed in material things. In the old story, Noah prepared himself in the calm weather for the flood which was to come, and when it came he was ready. But the rest of humanity was lost in its eating and drinking and marrying and giving in marriage, and was caught completely unawares, and was therefore swept away. These verses are a warning never to become so immersed in time that we forget eternity, never to let our concern with worldly affairs, however necessary, completely distract us from remembering that there is a God, that the issues of life and death are in his hands, and that whenever his call comes, at morning, at midday or at evening, it must find us ready.

(3) They tell us that the coming of Christ will be a time of separation and judgement, when he will gather to himself those who are his own.

So this section says quite definitely that no one knows the time of the second coming, not the angels, not even Jesus himself, but only God; and that it will come upon men and women with the suddenness of a rainstorm out of the sky. Beyond these things we cannot go – for God has kept the intimate knowledge to himself and his wisdom.

4

There is a practical outcome of all this. If the day and the hour of the coming of Christ are known to none save God, then life must be constant preparation for that coming.

To live without watchfulness invites disaster. Thieves do not send a letter saying they are going to burgle a house; the principal weapon of their wicked undertakings is surprise; therefore a householder who has valuables in the house must maintain constant guard. But to get this picture right we must remember that the watching of the Christian for the coming of Christ is not that of terror-stricken fear and shivering apprehension; it is the watching of eager expectation for the coming of glory and joy.

The Second Sunday of Advent
The Inclusive Church *and*
The Emergence of John the Baptizer

Romans 15:4–13

Paul makes an appeal that all people within the Church should be bound into one, that those who are weak in the faith and those who are strong in the faith should be one united body, that Jew and Gentile should find a common fellowship. There may be many differences, but there is only one Christ, and the bond of unity is a common loyalty to him. Christ's work was for Jew and Gentile alike. He was born a Jew and was subject to the Jewish law. This was in order that all the great promises given to the ancestors of the Jewish race might come true and that salvation might come first to the Jews. But he came not only for the Jews, but also for the Gentiles.

To prove that this is not his own novel and heretical idea, Paul cites four passages from the Old Testament; he quotes them from the Septuagint, the Greek version of the Old Testament, which is why they vary from the translation of the Old Testament as we know it. The passages are Psalm 18:50, Deuteronomy 32:43, Psalm 117:1 and Isaiah 11:10. In all of them, Paul finds ancient forecasts of the reception of the Gentiles into the faith. He is convinced that, just as Jesus Christ came into this world to save all people, so the Church must welcome all men and women, no matter what their differences may be. Christ was an inclusive Saviour, and therefore his Church must be an inclusive Church.

Then Paul goes on to sound the notes of the Christian faith. The great words of the Christian faith flash out one after another.

(1) There is *hope*. It is easy in the light of experience to despair of oneself. It is easy in the light of events to despair of the world. The story is told of a meeting in a certain church at a time of emergency. The meeting was opened with prayer by the chairman. He addressed God as 'Almighty and eternal God, whose grace is sufficient for all things.' When the prayer was finished, the business part of the meeting began; and the chairman introduced the business by saying: 'Friends, the situation in this church is completely hopeless, and nothing can be done.' Either his prayer was composed of empty and meaningless words, or his statement was untrue. It has long ago been said that there are no hopeless situations; there are only men and women who have grown hopeless about them.

There is something in Christian hope that not all the shadows can quench – and that something is the conviction that God is alive. No individual is hopeless as long as there is the grace of Jesus Christ; and no situation is hopeless as long as there is the power of God.

(2) There is *joy*. There is all the difference in this world between pleasure and joy. The Cynic philosophers declared that pleasure was unmitigated evil. Antisthenes made the strange statement that he would 'rather be mad than pleased'.

Their argument was that 'pleasure is only the pause between two pains'. You have longing for something, that is the pain; you get it, the longing is satisfied and there is a pause in the pain; you enjoy it and the moment is gone; and the pain comes back. Indeed, that is the way pleasure works. But Christian joy is not dependent on things outside us; its source is in our consciousness of the presence of the living Lord, the certainty that nothing can separate us from the love of God in him.

(3) There is *peace*. The ancient philosophers sought for what they called *ataraxia*, the untroubled life. They wanted all that serenity

7

which is proof both against the shattering blows and against the petty pinpricks of this life. One would almost say that, today, serenity is a lost possession. There are two things which make it impossible.

(a) There is *inner tension*. People live a distracted life, for the word *distract* literally means *to pull apart*. As long as someone is a walking civil war and a split personality, there can obviously be for that person no such thing as serenity. There is only one way out of this, and that is for self to hand control to Christ. When Christ controls, the tension is gone.

(b) There is *worry about external things*. Many are haunted by the chances and the changes of life. The writer H. G. Wells tells how in New York harbour he was once on a liner. It was foggy, and suddenly out of the fog loomed another liner, and the two ships slid past each other with only yards to spare. He was suddenly face to face with what he called the general large dangerousness of life. It is hard not to worry, for human beings are characteristically creatures who look forward to uncertainty and fear. The only end to that worry is the utter conviction that, whatever happens, God's hand will never cause his children a needless tear. Things will happen that we cannot understand; but, if we are sure enough of God's love, we can accept with serenity even those things which wound the heart and baffle the mind.

(4) There is *power*. Here is the supreme human need. It is not that we do not know the right thing; it is not that we do not recognize the fine thing; the trouble is doing it. The trouble is to cope with and to conquer things, to make what H. G. Wells called 'the secret splendour of our intentions' into actual facts. That we can never do alone. Only when the surge of Christ's power fills our weakness can we have control of life as we ought. By ourselves, we can do nothing; but, with God, all things are possible.

Matthew 3:1–12

The emergence of John was like the sudden sounding of the voice of God. At this time, the Jews were sadly conscious that the voice of the prophets spoke no more. They said that for 400 years there had been no prophet. Throughout long centuries, the voice of prophecy had been silent. As they put it themselves, 'There was no voice, nor any that answered.' But in John the prophetic voice spoke again. What then were the characteristics of John and his message?

(1) He fearlessly denounced evil wherever he might find it. If Herod the king sinned by contracting an evil and unlawful marriage, John rebuked him. If the Sadducees and Pharisees, the leaders of orthodox religion, the 'church' leaders of their day, were sunk in ritualistic formalism, John never hesitated to say so. If the ordinary people were living lives which were unaware of God, John would tell them so.

Wherever John saw evil – in the state, in the religious establishment, in the crowd – he fearlessly rebuked it. He was like a light which lit up the dark places; he was like a wind which swept from God throughout the country. It was said of a famous journalist who was great, but who never quite fulfilled the work he might have done, 'He was perhaps not easily enough disturbed.' There is still a place in the Christian message for warning and denunciation. 'The truth', said Diogenes, 'is like the light to sore eyes.' 'He who never offended anyone', he said, 'never did anyone any good.'

It may be that there have been times when the Church was too careful not to offend. There come occasions when the time for smooth politeness has gone, and the time for blunt rebuke has come.

(2) He urgently summoned men and women to righteousness. John's message was not a mere negative denunciation; it was a positive erecting of the moral standards of God. He not only denounced people for what they had done; he summoned them to what they ought to do. He not only condemned them for what they were; he challenged them to be what they could be. He was like a voice calling people to higher things. He not only rebuked evil, he also set before men and women the good. It may well be that there have been times when the Church was too occupied in telling people what not to do, and too little occupied in setting before them the height of the Christian ideal.

(3) John came from God. He came out of the desert. He came among the people only after he had undergone years of lonely preparation by God. As the Baptist minister Alexander Maclaren said, 'John leapt, as it were, into the arena full-grown and full-armed.' He came, not with some opinion of his own, but with a message from God. For a long time before he spoke to the world, he had kept company with God. The preacher, the teacher with the prophetic voice, must always come into the presence of others out of the presence of God.

(4) John pointed beyond himself. The man was not only a light to shine on all that was evil, a voice to rebuke sin, he was also a signpost to God. It was not himself whom he wished people to see; he wished to prepare them for the one who was to come.

John was preparing the way for the king. Preachers, teachers with prophetic voices, point not at themselves, but at God. Their aim is not to focus their eyes on their own cleverness, but on the majesty of God. True preachers are obliterated in their message.

The Third Sunday of Advent
Waiting for the Coming of the Lord *and* Confidence and Admiration in the Voice of Jesus

James 5:7–10

The early Church lived in expectation of the immediate second coming of Jesus Christ, and James encourages his people to wait with patience for the few years which remain. The farmer has to wait for the crops until the early and the late rains have come. The early and the late rains are often spoken of in Scripture, for they were all-important to the farmer of Palestine (Deuteronomy 11:14; Jeremiah 5:24; Joel 2:23). The early rain was the rain of late October and early November, without which the seed would not germinate. The late rain was the rain of April and May, without which the grain would not mature. The farmer needs to wait patiently for the working of nature; and Christians need to wait patiently until Christ comes.

During that waiting, they must confirm their faith. They must not blame one another for the troubles of the situation in which they find themselves – for, if they do, they will be breaking the commandment which forbids Christians to judge one another (Matthew 7:1); and if they break that commandment, they will be condemned. James has no doubt of the nearness of the coming of Christ. The judge is at the door, he says, using a phrase which Jesus himself had used (Mark 13:29; Matthew 24:33).

We may now gather up briefly the teaching of the New Testament about the second coming and the various uses it makes of the idea.

(1) The New Testament is clear that no one knows the day or the hour when Christ will come again. So secret, in fact, is that time that Jesus himself does not know it; it is known only to God (Matthew 24:36; Mark 13:32). From this basic fact, one thing is clear. Human speculation about the time of the second coming is not only useless, it is blasphemous – for surely no one should seek to gain a knowledge which is hidden from Jesus Christ himself and exists only in the mind of God.

(2) The one thing that the New Testament does say about the second coming is that it will be as sudden as the lightning and as unexpected as a thief in the night (Matthew 24:27, 37, 39; 1 Thessalonians 5:2; 2 Peter 3:10). We cannot wait to get ready when it comes; we must be ready for its coming. So, the New Testament urges certain duties upon Christians.

(a) They must be constantly on the watch (1 Peter 4:7). They are like servants whose master has gone away and who, not knowing when he will return, must have everything ready for his return, whether it comes in the morning, at midday or in the evening (Matthew 24:36–51).

(b) Long delay must not produce despair or forgetfulness (2 Peter 3:4). God does not see time as human beings do. To him, 1,000 years are just the same as a period on watch in the night; and, even if the years pass on, it does not mean that he has either changed or abandoned his design.

(c) The time given to prepare for the coming of the King must be used. Christians must be sober (1 Peter 4:7). They must strengthen themselves in holiness (1 Thessalonians 3:13). By the grace of God, they must become blameless in body and in spirit (1 Thessalonians 5:23). They must put off the works of darkness and put on the armour of light now that the night is far gone and the day is near (Romans 13:11– 14). They must use the time given to them to make themselves such that they can greet the coming of the King with joy and without shame.

(d) When that time comes, they must be found in fellowship. Peter uses the thought of the second coming to urge people to love and mutual hospitality (1 Peter 4:8–9). Paul commands that all things be done in love – *Maran atha* – the Lord is at hand (1 Corinthians 16:14, 16:22). He says that our *forbearance* must be known to all because the Lord is at hand (Philippians 4:5). The word translated as *forbearance* is *epieikēs*, which means the spirit that is more ready to offer forgiveness than to demand justice. The writer to the Hebrews demands mutual help, mutual Christian fellowship and mutual encouragement because the day is coming near (Hebrews 10:24–5). The New Testament is sure that in view of the coming of Christ we must have our personal relationships right with our neighbours and would urge that we should never end a day with an unhealed rift between ourselves and another person, in case Christ should come in the night.

(5) John uses the second coming as a reason for urging people to abide in Christ (1 John 2:28). Surely the best preparation for meeting Christ is to live close to him every day.

Much of the imagery attached to the second coming is Jewish and is part of the traditional apparatus of the last things in ancient Jewish thought. There are many things which we are not meant to take literally. But the great truth behind all the temporary pictures of the second coming is that this world is not purposeless but that it is going somewhere, that there is one divine far-off event to which the whole creation moves.

Matthew 11:2–11

The career of John had ended in disaster. It was not John's habit to soften the truth for anyone; and he was incapable of seeing evil without rebuking it. He had spoken too fearlessly *and too definitely for his own safety*. Herod Antipas of Galilee had paid a visit to his brother in Rome. During that visit, he seduced his brother's wife. He came home again, dismissed his own wife and married the sister-in-law whom he had lured away from her husband. Publicly and sternly, John rebuked Herod. It was never safe to rebuke a despot, and Herod took his revenge; John was thrown into the dungeons of the fortress of Machaerus in the mountains near the Dead Sea.

For any human being, that would have been a terrible fate; but for John the Baptist, it was worse than for most. He was a child of the desert; all his life he had lived in the wide-open spaces, with the clean wind on his face and the spacious vault of the sky for his roof. And now he was confined within the four narrow walls of an underground dungeon. For someone like John, who had perhaps never lived in a house, this must have been agony. There is nothing to wonder at, and still less to criticize, in the fact that questions began to take shape in John's mind. He had been so sure that Jesus was the one who was to come. That was one of the most common titles of the Messiah for whom the Jews waited with such eager expectation (Mark 11:9; Luke 13:35, 19:38; Hebrews 10:37; Psalm 118:26). Those who face death cannot afford to have doubts; they must be sure; and so John sent his disciples to Jesus with the question: 'Are you he who is to come, or shall we look for another?'

In Jesus' answer we hear the *accent of confidence*. Jesus' answer to John's disciples was: 'Go back, and don't tell John what I am saying; *tell him what I am doing.* Don't tell John what I am claiming; *tell him what is happening.*' Jesus demanded that there should be applied to him the most acid of tests, that of deeds. Jesus was the only person who could ever demand without qualification to be judged not by what he said but by what he did. The challenge of Jesus is still the same. He does not so much say 'Listen to what I have to tell you' as 'Look what I can do for you; see what I have done for others.'

14

There are few to whom Jesus paid so tremendous a tribute as he did to John the Baptizer. He begins by asking the people what they went into the desert to see when they streamed out to John.

Did they go out to see a prophet? Prophets are the *forthtellers* of the truth of God. Prophets are those who are in God's confidence. 'Surely the Lord God does nothing, without revealing his secret to his servants the prophets' (Amos 3:7). Prophets are two things – they are people with a message from God, and they are people with the courage to deliver that message. Prophets are people with God's wisdom in their minds, God's truth on their lips and God's courage in their hearts. And most certainly John had all those characteristics.

But John was something more than a prophet. The Jews had, and still have, one settled belief. They believed that before the Messiah came, Elijah would return to herald his coming. To this day, when the Jews celebrate the Passover Feast, a vacant chair is left for Elijah. 'Lo, I will send you the prophet Elijah before the great and terrible day of the Lord comes' (Malachi 4:5). Jesus declared that John was nothing less than the divine herald whose duty and privilege it was to announce the coming of the Messiah. John was nothing less than the herald of God, and no one could have a greater task than that.

Such was the tremendous tribute of Jesus to John, spoken with the accent of admiration. There had never been a greater figure in all history; and then comes the startling sentence: 'But the least in the kingdom of heaven is greater than he.'

Here, there is one quite general truth. With Jesus, there came into the world something absolutely new. The prophets were great; their message was precious; but with Jesus there emerged something still greater, and a message still more wonderful.

So John had the destiny which sometimes falls to an individual; he had the task of pointing men and women to a greatness into which he himself did not enter. It is given to some people to be the signposts of God. They point to a new ideal and a new greatness which others will enter into, but into which they will not come. It is very seldom that any great reformer is the first person to toil for the reform with which his or her name is connected. Many who went before glimpsed the glory, often laboured for it, and sometimes died for it. Someone tells how from the windows of his house every evening he used to watch the lamp-lighter go along the streets lighting the lamps – *and the lamp-lighter was himself a blind man.* He was bringing to others the light which he himself would never see. We should never be discouraged in the church or in any other walk of life, if the dreams we have dreamed and for which we have toiled are never worked out before the end of the day. God needed John; God needs his signposts who can point others on the way, although they themselves cannot ever reach the goal.

The Fourth Sunday of Advent
A Call, a Gospel and a Task *and*
Born of the Holy Spirit

Romans 1:1–7

When Paul wrote his letter to the Romans, he was writing to a church which he did not know personally and to which he had never been. He was writing to a church which was situated in the greatest city in the greatest empire in the world. Because of that, he chose his words and thoughts with the greatest care.

He begins by giving his own credentials.

(1) He calls himself the slave (*doulos*) of Jesus Christ. In this word 'slave', there are two backgrounds of thought.

(a) Paul's favourite title for Jesus is *Lord* (*kurios*). In Greek, the word *kurios* describes someone who has undisputed possession of a person or a thing. It means *master* or *owner* in the most absolute sense. The opposite of *Lord* (*kurios*) is *slave* (*doulos*). Paul thought of himself as the slave of Jesus Christ, his Master and his Lord. Jesus had loved him and given himself for him, and therefore Paul was sure that he belonged no longer to himself but entirely to Jesus. On the one side, *slave* describes the utter obligation of love.

(b) But *slave* (*doulos*) has another side to it. In the Old Testament, it is the word used regularly to describe the great men of God. Moses was the *doulos* of the Lord (Joshua 1:2). Joshua was the *doulos* of God (Joshua 24:29). The proudest title of the prophets, the title which distinguished them from others, was that they were the slaves of God (Amos 3:7; Jeremiah 7:25). When Paul calls himself the slave of Jesus Christ, he is setting himself in the succession of the prophets. Their greatness and their glory lay in the fact that they were slaves of God; and so did his. So, *the slave of Jesus Christ* describes at one and the same time the obligation of a great love and the honour of a great office.

(2) Paul describes himself as *called to be an apostle*. In the Old Testament, the great figures were those who heard and answered the call of God. Abraham heard the call of God (Genesis 12:1–3). Moses answered God's call (Exodus 3:10). Jeremiah and Isaiah were prophets because, almost against their will, they were compelled to listen to and to answer the call of God (Jeremiah 1:4–5; Isaiah 6:8–9). Paul never thought of himself as a man who had aspired to an honour; he thought of himself as a man who had been given a task. Jesus said to his disciples: 'You did not choose me but I chose you' (John 15:16). Paul thought of life not in terms of what he wanted to do but in terms of what God meant him to do.

(3) Paul describes himself as *set apart to serve the good news of God*. He was conscious of a double setting apart in his life. Twice in his life, this very same word (*aphorozein*) is used of him.

(a) He was set apart *by God*. He thought of God as separating him for the task he was to do even before he was born (Galatians 1:15). For each one of us, God has a plan; no one's life is purposeless. God sent us into the world to do some definite thing.

(b) He was set apart *by the Church*, when the Holy Spirit told the leaders of the church at Antioch to separate him and Barnabas for the special mission to the Gentiles (Acts 13:2). Paul was conscious of having a task to do for God and for the Church of God.

(4) In this setting apart, Paul was aware of having received two things. In verse 5, he tells us what these two things were.

(a) He had received *grace*. *Grace* always describes some gift which is absolutely free and absolutely unearned. In his pre-Christian days, Paul had sought to earn glory in the eyes of others and merit in the sight of God by meticulous observance of the works of the law, and he had found no peace that way. Now, he knew that what mattered was not what he could do but what God had done.

He saw that salvation depended not on what human effort could do but on what God's love had done. All was of grace, free and undeserved.

(b) He had received *a task*. He was set apart to be the apostle to the Gentiles. Paul knew himself to be chosen not for special honour but for special responsibility. He knew that God had set him apart, not for glory but for toil. Once, Paul had been a Pharisee (Philippians 3:5). He had felt himself *separated* in such a way as to have nothing but contempt for all ordinary men and women. Now he knew himself to be *separated* in such a way that he must spend all his life in bringing the news of God's love to every individual of every race. Christianity always separates us, but it separates us not for privilege and self-glory and pride but for service and humility and love for all people.

(5) Besides giving his own credentials, Paul, in this passage, sets out in its most essential outline the gospel which he preached. It was a gospel which centred in Jesus Christ (verses 3–4). In particular, it was a gospel of two things.

(a) It was a gospel of the *incarnation*. He told of a Jesus who was really and truly a man. The second-century Bishop of Lyons, Irenaeus, summed it up when he said of Jesus: 'He became what we are, to make us what he is.' Paul preached of someone who was not a legendary figure in an imaginary story, not a demi-god, half-god and half-man. He preached about one who was really and truly one with those he came to save.

(b) It was a gospel of the *resurrection*. If Jesus had lived a lovely life and died a heroic death, and if that had been the end of him, he might have been numbered with the great and the heroic; but he would simply have been one among many. His uniqueness is guaranteed forever by the fact of the resurrection. The others are dead and gone, and have left a memory. Jesus lives on and gives us a presence, still mighty with power.

Matthew 11:18–25

This passage tells us how Jesus was born by the action of the Holy Spirit. It tells us of what we call the virgin birth. If we come to this passage with fresh eyes, and read it as if we were reading it for the first time, we will find that what it stresses is not so much that Jesus was born of a woman who was a virgin, as that the birth of Jesus is the work of the Holy Spirit. Mary 'was found to be with child from the Holy Spirit'. 'The child conceived in her is from the Holy Spirit.' It is as if these sentences were underlined, and printed large. That is what Matthew wishes to say to us in this passage. What then does it mean to say that in the birth of Jesus the Holy Spirit of God was specially operative?

In Jewish thought, the Holy Spirit had certain very definite functions. We cannot bring to this passage the *Christian* idea of Holy Spirit in all its fullness, because Joseph would know nothing about that. We must interpret it in the light of the *Jewish* idea of the Holy Spirit, for it is that idea that Joseph would inevitably bring to this message, for that was all he knew.

(1) According to the Jewish idea, *the Holy Spirit was the person who brought God's truth to men and women*. It was the Holy Spirit who taught the prophets what to say; it was the Holy Spirit who taught people of God what to do; it was the Holy Spirit who, throughout the ages and the generations, brought God's truth to men and women. So, Jesus is the one person who brings God's truth to them.

(2) The Jews believed that the Holy Spirit not only brought God's truth to men and women, but also *enabled them to recognize that truth when they saw it*. So Jesus opens people's eyes to the truth. We are often blinded by our own ignorance; we are led astray by our own prejudices; our minds and eyes are darkened by our own sins and our own passions. Jesus can open our eyes until we are able to see the truth.

(3) The Jews specially *connected the Spirit of God with the work of creation*. It was through his Spirit that God performed his creating work. In the beginning, the Spirit of God moved upon the face of the waters, and chaos became a world (Genesis 1:2). 'By the word of the Lord the heavens were made,' said the psalmist, 'and all their host by the breath of his mouth' (Psalm 33:6). (Both in Hebrew, *ruach*, and in Greek, *pneuma*, the word for *breath* and *spirit* is the same word.) 'When you send forth your spirit, they are created' (Psalm 104:30). 'The spirit of God has made me,' said Job, 'and the breath of the Almighty gives me life' (Job 33:4). The Spirit is the Creator of the World and the Giver of Life. So, in Jesus there came into the world God's life-giving and creating power. That power, which reduced the primal chaos to order, came to bring order to our disordered lives. That power, which breathed life where there was no life, has come to breathe life into our weaknesses and frustrations. We could put it this way – we are not really alive until Jesus enters into our lives.

(4) The Jews specially connected the Spirit not only with the work of creation but *with the work of re-creation*. Ezekiel draws his grim picture of the valley of dry bones. He goes on to tell how the dry bones came alive; and then he hears God say: 'I will put my spirit within you, and you shall live' (Ezekiel 37:14). The Rabbis had a saying: 'God said to Israel: "In this world my Spirit has put wisdom in you, but in the future my Spirit will make you to live again."' When people are dead in sin and in lethargy, it is the Spirit of God which can waken them to life anew. So, in Jesus there came to this world the power which can re-create life. He can bring to life again the soul which is dead in sin and revive again the ideals which have died. He can make strong again the will to goodness which has perished and renew life when people have lost all that life means.

There is much more in this chapter than the crude fact that Jesus Christ was born of a virgin mother. The essence of Matthew's story is that in the birth of Jesus the Spirit of God was operative as never before in this world. It is the Spirit who brings God's truth to men and women and who enables them to recognize that truth when they see it. It is the Spirit who was God's agent in the creation of the world and who alone can re-create the human soul when it has lost the life it ought to have. Jesus enables us to see what God is and what we ought to be, opening the eyes of our minds so that we can see the truth of God for us. Jesus is the creating power come among us, the re-creating power which can release the souls of men and women from the death of sin.

The First Sunday of Christmas
The Essential Suffering *and* Escape to Egypt

Hebrews 2:10–18

Here, the writer to the Hebrews uses one of the great titles of Jesus. He calls him *the pioneer (archēgos) of glory*. The same word is used of Jesus in Acts 3:15, 5:31; Hebrews 12:2. At its simplest, it means *head* or *chief*. So, Zeus is the *head* of the gods and a general is the *head* of his army. It can mean a *founder* or *originator*. So, it is used of the founder of a city or of a family or of a philosophic school. It can be used in the sense of *source* or *origin*. So, a good governor is said to be the *archēgos* of peace and a bad governor the *archēgos* of confusion.

One basic idea clings to the word in all its uses. An *archēgos* is someone who begins something in order that others may enter into it. The word is used to describe the person who begins a family so that some day others may be born into it, who founds a city in order that others may some day live in it, who founds a philosophic school so that others may follow into the truth and the peace that that person has already discovered; someone who is the author of blessings into which others may also enter. An *archēgos* is the one who blazes a trail for others to follow. Let us take an analogy. Suppose a ship is on the rocks, and the only way to safety is for someone to swim ashore with a line so that, once the line is secured, others might follow. The one who is first to swim ashore will be the *archēgos* of the safety of the others. This is what the writer to the Hebrews means when he says that Jesus is the *archēgos* of our salvation. Jesus has blazed the trail to God for us to follow.

How was Jesus enabled to take on this role? The Authorized and Revised Standard Versions say that God made him *perfect* through suffering. The verb translated as *make perfect* is *teleioun*, which comes from the adjective *teleios*, which is usually translated as *perfect*. But, in the New Testament, *teleios* has a very special meaning. It has nothing to do with abstract, metaphysical and philosophic perfection. It is used, for instance, of an animal which is unblemished and fit to be offered as a sacrifice; of a scholar who is no longer at the elementary stage but is mature; of a human being or an animal who is fully grown; of a Christian who is no longer on the fringe of the Church but who is baptized. The basic meaning of *teleios* in the New Testament is always that the thing or person described in this way *fully carries out the purpose for which he or she is designed*. Therefore, the verb *teleioun* will mean not so much *to make perfect* as *to make fully adequate for the task for which designed*. So, what the writer to the Hebrews is saying is that, through suffering, Jesus was made fully able to complete the task of being the pioneer of our salvation. Why should that be?

(1) It was through his sufferings that he was really *identified* with us. The writer to the Hebrews quotes three Old Testament texts as forecasts of this identity with men and women – Psalm 22:22; Isaiah 8:17, 8:18. If Jesus had come into this world in a form in which he could never have suffered, he would have been quite different from us and so no Saviour for us. As Jeremy Taylor, the seventeenth-century churchman, said: 'When God would save men, he did it by way of a man.' It is, in fact, this identification with us which is the essence of the Christian idea of God. When the Greeks thought of their gods, they thought of them as Tennyson pictures them in 'The Song of the Lotos-Eaters':

For they lie beside their nectar, and the bolts are hurl'd
Far below them in the valleys, and the clouds are lightly curl'd
Round their golden houses, girdled with the gleaming world:
Where they smile in secret, looking over wasted lands,

Blight and famine, plague and earthquake, roaring deeps and
  fiery sands,
Clanging fights, and flaming towns, and sinking ships, and
  praying hands.

The basis of the Greek idea of God was *detachment*; the basis of
the Christian idea is *identity*. Through his sufferings, Jesus Christ
identified himself with us.

(2) Through this identity, Jesus Christ *sympathizes* with us. He literally *feels* with us. It is almost impossible to understand another person's sorrows and sufferings unless we have been through them. A
person without a trace of nerves has no conception of the tortures of
nervousness. A person who is perfectly physically fit has no conception of the weariness of the person who is easily tired or the suffering
of the person who is never free from pain. A person who learns easily often cannot understand why someone who is slow finds things so
difficult. A person who has never known sorrow cannot understand
the pain at the heart of the person into whose life grief has come. A
person who has never loved can never understand either the sudden
glory or the aching loneliness in the lover's heart. Before we can have
sympathy, we must go through the same things that the other person
has gone through – and that is precisely what Jesus did.

(3) Because he sympathizes, Jesus can really *help*. He has met
our sorrows; he has faced our temptations. As a result, he knows
exactly what help we need; and he can give it.

Matthew 2:13–23

The ancient world had no doubt that God sent his messages to
men and women in dreams. So Joseph was warned in a dream to
flee into Egypt to escape Herod's murderous intentions. The flight
into Egypt was entirely natural. Often, throughout the troubled

centuries before Jesus came, when some peril and some tyranny and some persecution made life intolerable for the Jews, they sought refuge in Egypt. The result was that every city in Egypt had its colony of Jews; and in the city of Alexandria there were actually more than 1,000,000 Jews, and certain districts of the city were entirely handed over to them. Joseph in his hour of peril was doing what many Jews had done before; and when Joseph and Mary reached Egypt they would not find themselves altogether among strangers, for in every town and city they would find Jews who had sought refuge there.

One of the loveliest New Testament legends is connected with the flight into Egypt. It is about the penitent thief. Legend calls the penitent thief Dismas, and tells that he did not meet Jesus for the first time when they both hung on their crosses on Calvary. The story runs like this. When Joseph and Mary were on their way to Egypt, they were waylaid by robbers. One of the robber chiefs wished to murder them at once and to steal their little store of goods. But something about the baby Jesus went straight to Dismas' heart, for Dismas was one of these robbers. He refused to allow any harm to come to Jesus or his parents. He looked at Jesus and said: 'O most blessed of children, if ever there come a time for having mercy on me, then remember me, and forget not this hour.' So, the legend says, Jesus and Dismas met again at Calvary, and Dismas on the cross found forgiveness and mercy for his soul.

The last words of this passage introduce us to a custom which is characteristic of Matthew. He sees in the flight to Egypt a fulfilment of the word spoken by Hosea. He quotes it in the form: 'Out of Egypt I have called my son.' That is a quotation from Hosea 11:1, which reads: 'When Israel was a child, I loved him, and out of Egypt I called my son.' It can be seen at once that in its original form this saying of Hosea had nothing to do with Jesus, and nothing to do with the flight to Egypt. It was nothing more than a simple statement of how God had delivered the nation of Israel from slavery and from bondage in the land of Egypt. This is typical of Matthew's use of the Old Testament. He is prepared to use as a prophecy about Jesus any text at all which can be made verbally to fit, even though originally it had nothing to do with the question in hand, and was never meant to have anything to do with it. Matthew knew that almost the only way to convince the Jews that Jesus was the promised Anointed One of God was to prove that he was the fulfilment of Old Testament prophecy. And in his eagerness to do that, he finds prophecies in the Old Testament where no prophecies were ever meant. When we read a passage like this, we must remember that, though it seems strange and unconvincing to us, it would appeal to those Jews for whom Matthew was writing.

The Second Sunday of Christmas
The Goal of History *and* The Word Became Flesh

Ephesians 1:3–14

It is from verse 9 onwards that Paul really gets to grips with his subject. He says, as the Authorized Version has it, that God has made known to us 'the mystery of his will'. The New Testament uses the word *mystery* in a special sense. It is not something mysterious in the sense that it is hard to understand. It is something which has long been kept secret and has now been revealed, but is still incomprehensible to the person who has not been initiated into its meaning. Let us take an example. Suppose someone who knew nothing whatever about Christianity was brought into a communion service. To that person, it would be a complete mystery; he or she would not understand in the least what was going on. But to anyone who knows the story and the meaning of the Last Supper, the whole service has a meaning which is quite clear. So, in the New Testament sense, a mystery is something which is hidden to non-Christians but clear to Christians.

What, for Paul, was the mystery of the will of God? It was that the gospel was open to the Gentiles too. In Jesus, God has revealed that his love and care, his grace and mercy, are meant not only for the Jews but for the whole world. Now Paul, in one sentence, introduces his great thought. Up until now, people had been living in a divided world. There was division between the animals and human beings. There was division between Jews and Gentiles, Greeks and barbarians. All over the world, there was strife and tension. Jesus came into the world to wipe out the divisions. That, for Paul, was the secret of God. It was God's purpose that all the many different strands and all the warring elements in this world should be gathered into one in Jesus Christ. Here, we have another tremendous thought. Paul says that all history has been a working out of this process. He says that all through the ages there has been an arranging and an administering of things so that this day of unity should come. The word which Paul uses for this preparation is intensely interesting. It is *oikonomia*, which literally means *household management*. The *oikonomos* was the steward who saw to it that the family affairs ran smoothly.

It is the Christian conviction that history is the working out of the will of God. That is by no means what every historian or thinker has been able to see. The historian and poet Sir George Clark, in his inaugural lecture at Oxford, said: 'There is no secret and no plan in history to be discovered. I do not believe that any future consummation could make sense of all the irrationalities of preceding ages. If it could not explain them, still less could it justify them.' In the introduction to *A History of Europe*, H. A. L. Fisher writes: 'One intellectual excitement, however, has been denied to me. Men wiser and more learned than I have discovered in history a plot, a rhythm, a predetermined pattern. These harmonies are concealed from me. I can see only one emergency following another, as wave follows upon wave, only one great fact with respect to which, since it is unique, there can be no generalizations, only one safe rule for the historian: that he should recognize in the development of human destinies the play of the contingent and the unforeseen.' The French novelist and biographer André Maurois says: 'The universe is indifferent. Who created it? Why are we here on this puny mud-heap spinning in infinite space? I have not the slightest idea, and I am quite convinced that no one has the least idea.'

It so happens that we are living in an age in which many people have lost their faith in any purpose for this world. But it is the faith of Christians that in this world God's purpose is being worked out;

and Paul's conviction is that it is God's purpose that one day all things and all people should be one family in Christ. As Paul sees it, that mystery was not even grasped until Jesus came, and now it is the great task of the Church to work out God's purpose of unity, revealed in Jesus Christ.

John 1:10–18

It is John's great thought that Jesus is none other than God's creative and life-giving and light-giving word, that Jesus is the power of God which created the world and the reason of God which sustains the world come to earth in human and bodily form.

In verse 14 we come to the sentence for the sake of which John wrote his gospel. He has thought and talked about the word of God, that powerful, creative, dynamic word which was the agent of creation, that guiding, directing, controlling word which puts order into the universe and intelligence into human beings. These were ideas which were known and familiar to both Jews and Greeks. Now he says the most startling and incredible thing that he could have said. He says quite simply: 'This word which created the world, this reason which controls the order of the world, has become a person, and with our own eyes we saw him.' The word that John uses for *seeing* this word is *theasthai*; it is used in the New Testament more than twenty times and is always used of *actual physical sight*. This is no spiritual vision seen with the eye of the soul or of the mind. John declares that the word actually came to earth in the form of a man and was seen by human eyes. He says: 'If you want to see what this creating word, this controlling reason, is like, look at Jesus of Nazareth.'

This is where John parted with all thought which had gone before him. This was the entirely new thing which John brought to the Greek world for which he was writing. Augustine afterwards said that in his pre-Christian days he had read and studied the great pagan philosophers and had read many things, but he had never read that the word became flesh.

To a Greek, this was the impossible thing. The one thing that no Greek would ever have dreamed of was that God could take a body. To a Greek, the body was an evil, a prison house in which the soul was shackled, a tomb in which the spirit was confined. Plutarch, the wise old Greek, did not even believe that God could control the happenings of this world directly; he had to do it by deputies and intermediaries, for, as Plutarch saw it, it was nothing less than blasphemy to involve God in the affairs of the world. Philo could never have said it. He said: 'The life of God has not descended to us; nor has it come as far as the necessities of the body.' The great Roman Stoic emperor, Marcus Aurelius, despised the body in comparison with the spirit. 'Therefore despise the flesh – blood and bones and a network, a twisted skein of nerves and veins and arteries . . . The composition of the whole body is under corruption.'

Here was the shatteringly new thing – that God could and would become a human person, that God could enter into this life that we live, that eternity could appear in time, that somehow the Creator could appear in creation in such a way that he could actually be seen.

So staggeringly new was this conception of God in a human form that it is not surprising that even in the Church there were some who could not believe it. What John says is that the word became *sarx*. Now *sarx* is the very word Paul uses over and over again to describe what he called *the flesh*, human nature in all its weakness and in all its liability to sin. The very thought of taking this word and applying it to God was something that their minds staggered at. So there arose in the Church a body of people called *Docetists*.

Dokein is the Greek word for *to seem to be*. These people held that Jesus in fact was only a phantom; that his human body was not a real body; that he could not really feel hunger and weariness, sorrow and pain; that he was in fact a disembodied spirit in the apparent form of a man. John dealt with these people much more directly in his First Letter. 'By this you know the Spirit of God: every spirit which confesses that Jesus Christ has come *in the flesh* is from God, and every spirit that does not confess Jesus is not from God. And this is the spirit of the antichrist' (1 John 4:2–3). It is true that this heresy was born of a kind of mistaken reverence which recoiled from saying that Jesus was really, fully and truly human. To John, it contradicted the whole Christian gospel.

It may well be that we are often so eager to conserve the fact that Jesus was fully God that we tend to forget the fact that he was fully human. *The word became flesh* – here, perhaps as nowhere else in the New Testament, we have the full humanity of Jesus gloriously proclaimed. In Jesus we see the creating word of God, the controlling reason of God, taking human nature upon himself. In Jesus we see God living life as he would have lived it if he had been a man. Supposing we said nothing else about Jesus, we could still say that he shows us how God would live this life that we have to live.

The First Sunday of Epiphany (The Baptism of Christ)
The Heart of the Gospel *and* Jesus and His Baptism

Acts 10:34–43

The tenth chapter of Acts tells a story that is one of the great turning points in the history of the Church. For the first time, a Gentile, Cornelius, a Roman centurion stationed at Caesarea, is to be admitted into its fellowship.

It is clear that we have here only the barest summary of what Peter said to Cornelius, which makes it all the more important because it gives us the very essence of the first preaching about Jesus.

(1) Jesus was sent by God and equipped by him with the Spirit and with power. Jesus, therefore, is God's gift to us. Often, we make the mistake of thinking in terms of an angry God who had to be pacified by something a gentle Jesus did. The early preachers never preached that. To them, the very coming of Jesus was due to the love of God.

(2) Jesus exercised a ministry of healing. It was his great desire to banish pain and sorrow from the world.

(3) They crucified him. Once again, for those who can read between the lines, the sheer horror in the crucifixion is stressed. That is what human sin can do.

(4) He rose again. The power which was in Jesus was not to be defeated. It could conquer the worst that people could do, and in the end it could conquer death.

(5) Christian preachers and teachers are witnesses of the resurrection. To them, Jesus is not a figure in a book or about whom they have heard. He is a living presence whom they have met.

(6) The result of all this is forgiveness of sins and a new relationship with God. Through Jesus, the friendship which should always have existed between men and women and God, but which sin interrupted, has dawned upon the world.

Matthew 3:13–17

When Jesus came to John to be baptized, John was startled and unwilling to baptize him. It was John's conviction that it was he who needed what Jesus could give, not Jesus who needed what he could give. From the very beginning of study of the gospel story, people have found the baptism of Jesus difficult to understand. In John's baptism, there was a summons to repentance and the offer of a way to the forgiveness of sins. But, if Jesus is who we believe him to be, he did not stand in need of repentance, and did not need forgiveness from God. John's baptism was for sinners conscious of their sin, and therefore it does not seem applicable to Jesus at all.

A very early writer suggested that Jesus came to be baptized only to please his mother and his brothers, and that it was in answer to their entreaties that he was almost compelled to let this thing be done. The Gospel according to the Hebrews, which is one of the gospels which failed to be included in the New Testament, has a passage like this: 'Behold the mother of the Lord and his brethren said to him, "John the Baptist baptizeth for the remission of sins; let us go and be baptized by him." But he said to them, "What sin have I committed, that I should go and be baptized by him? Except perchance this very thing that I have said is ignorance."'

From the earliest times, thinkers were puzzled by the fact that Jesus submitted to be baptized. But there were reasons, and good reasons, why he did.

(1) For thirty years, Jesus had waited in Nazareth, faithfully performing the simple duties of the home and of the carpenter's shop. All the time, he knew that a world was waiting for him. All the time, he grew increasingly conscious of his waiting task. The success of any undertaking is determined by the wisdom with which the moment to embark upon it is chosen. Jesus must have waited for the hour to strike, for the moment to come, for the summons to sound. And when John emerged, Jesus knew that the time had arrived.

(2) Why should that be so? There was one very simple and very vital reason. It is the fact that never in all history before this had any Jew submitted to being baptized. The Jews knew and used baptism, but only for converts who came into Judaism from some other faith. It was natural that sin stained, polluted converts should be baptized; but the Jews had never conceived that they, the chosen people, children of Abraham, assured of God's salvation, could ever need baptism. Baptism was for sinners, and the Jews never conceived of themselves as sinners shut out from God. Now, for the first time in their national history, they became aware of their own sin and their own urgent need of God. Never before had there been such a unique national movement of penitence and of search for God.

This was the very moment for which Jesus had been waiting. Men and women were conscious of their sin and conscious of their need of God as never before. This was his opportunity, and in his baptism he identified himself with those he came to save, in the hour of their new consciousness of their sin, and of their search for God.

The voice which Jesus heard at the baptism is of supreme importance. 'This is my Son, the Beloved,' it said, 'with whom I am well pleased.' That sentence is composed of two quotations. 'This is my Son' is a reference to Psalm 2:7. Every Jew accepted that Psalm as a description of the Messiah, the mighty King of God who was to come. 'With whom I am well pleased' is a reference to Isaiah 42:1, which is a description of the Suffering Servant, a description which culminates in Isaiah 53.

So, in the baptism there came to Jesus two certainties – the certainty that he was indeed the chosen one of God, and the certainty that the way in front of him was the way of the cross. In that moment, he knew that he was chosen to be King, but he knew also that his throne must be a cross. In that moment, he knew that he was destined to be a conqueror, but that his conquest must have as its only weapon the power of suffering love. In that moment, there was set before Jesus both his task and the only way to the fulfilling of it.

The Second Sunday of Epiphany
An Apostolic Introduction *and* The First Disciples

1 Corinthians 1:1–9

In the first nine verses of Paul's First Letter to the Corinthians, the name of Jesus Christ occurs no fewer than nine times. This was going to be a difficult letter, for it was going to deal with a difficult situation – and, in such a situation, Paul's first and repeated thought was of Jesus Christ. Sometimes in the Church, we try to deal with a difficult situation by means of a book of laws and in the spirit of human justice; sometimes in our own affairs, we try to deal with a difficult situation in our own mental and spiritual power. Paul did none of these things; to his difficult situation he took Jesus Christ, and it was in the light of the cross of Christ and the love of Christ that he sought to deal with it.

The introduction (verses 1–3) tells us about three things.

(1) It tells us something about the Church. Paul speaks of *the Church of God which is at Corinth*. It was not the church of Corinth; it was the Church of God. To Paul, wherever an individual congregation might be, it was a part of the one Church of God. He would not have spoken of the Church of Scotland or the Church of England; he would not have given the Church a local designation; still less would he have identified the congregation by the particular communion or sect to which it belonged. To him, the Church was the Church of God. If we thought of the Church in that way, we might well remember more of the reality which unites us and less of the local differences which divide us.

(2) This passage tells us something about Christians. Paul says three things.

(a) *Christians are consecrated in Jesus Christ.* The verb *to consecrate* (*hagiazo*) means to set a place apart for God, to make it holy, by the offering of a sacrifice upon it. Christians have been consecrated to God by the sacrifice of Jesus Christ. To be a Christian is to be one for whom Christ died and to know it, and to realize that that sacrifice, in a very special way, makes us belong to God.

(b) He describes the Christians as *those who have been called to be God's dedicated people.* We have translated one single Greek word by this whole phrase. The word is *hagios*, which the Authorized Version translates as *saints.* Nowadays, that does not paint the right picture for us. *Hagios* describes a thing or a person that has been devoted to the possession and the service of God. It is the word used to describe a temple or a sacrifice which has been marked out for God. Now, if people have been marked out as specially belonging to God, they must show themselves to be fit in life and in character for that service. That is how *hagios* comes to mean *holy, saintly.* But the root idea of the word is *separation.* People who are *hagios* are *different* from others because they have been separated from the ordinary run of things in order specially to belong to God. This was the adjective by which the Jews described themselves; they were the *hagios laos*, the holy people, the nation which was quite different from other peoples because they, in a special way, belonged to God and were set apart for his service. When Paul uses *hagios* to describe Christians, he means that they are different from other people because they specially belong to God and to God's service. And that difference is to be marked not by withdrawal from ordinary life, but by showing there a quality which will mark them out.

(c) Paul addresses his letter to those who have been called *in the company of those who in every place call upon the name of the Lord.* Christians are called into a community whose boundaries include all earth and all heaven. It would be greatly to our good if sometimes we lifted our eyes beyond our own little circle and thought of ourselves as part of the Church of God which is as wide as the world.

(3) This passage tells us something about Jesus Christ. Paul speaks of our Lord Jesus Christ, and then, as it were, he corrects himself and adds *their Lord and ours*. No individual, no church, has exclusive possession of Jesus Christ. He is our Lord, but he is also Lord of all. It is the amazing wonder of Christianity that all men and women possess all the love of Jesus Christ, that 'God loves each one of us as if there was only one of us to love.'

In the passage of thanksgiving (verses 4–9), three things stand out.

(1) There is the promise which came true. When Paul preached Christianity to the Corinthians, he told them that Christ could do certain things for them, and now he proudly claims that all that he pledged that Christ could do has come true. A missionary told one of the ancient Scottish kings: 'If you will accept Christ, you will find wonder upon wonder – and every one of them true.' In the last analysis, we cannot argue anyone into Christianity; we can only say: 'Try it and see what happens,' in the certainty that, if that challenge is taken up, the claims we make for it will all come true.

(2) There is the gift which has been given. Paul here uses a favourite word of his. It is *charisma*, which means a gift freely given to someone, a gift which was not deserved and which could never have been earned by that individual's own efforts.

(3) There is the ultimate end. In the Old Testament, the phrase *the day* of *the Lord* keeps recurring. It was the day when the Jews expected God to break directly into history, the day when the old world would be wiped out and the new world born, the day when everyone would be judged. The Christians took over this idea, only they took *the day of the Lord* in the sense of *the day of the Lord Jesus*, and regarded it as the day on which Jesus would come back in all his power and glory. It is Paul's belief that, when the ultimate judgement comes, those who are in Christ can meet it unafraid, because they will be clothed not in their own merits but in the merits of Christ so that no one will be able to impeach them.

John 1:29–42

Never was a passage of Scripture fuller of little revealing touches than this. We see John the Baptist pointing beyond himself. He must have known very well that to speak to his disciples about Jesus like that was to invite them to leave him and transfer their loyalty to this new and greater teacher; and yet he did it. There was no jealousy in John. He had come to attach people not to himself but to Christ. There is no harder task than to take the second place when once the first place was enjoyed. But as soon as Jesus emerged on the scene, John never had any other thought than to send people to him.

So the two disciples of John followed Jesus. It may well be that they were too shy to approach him directly and followed respectfully some distance behind. Then Jesus did something entirely characteristic. He turned and spoke to them. That is to say, he met them half-way. He made things easier for them. He opened the door that they might come in. Here we have the symbol of the divine initiative. It is always God who takes the first step. When the human mind begins to seek and the human heart begins to long, God comes to meet us far more than half-way. God does not leave us to search and search until we come to him; God comes out to meet us. As Augustine said, we could not even have begun to seek for God unless he had already found us. When we go to God, we do not go to one who hides himself and keeps us at a distance; we go to one who stands waiting for us, and who even takes the initiative by coming to meet us on the road.

Jesus began by asking these two men the most fundamental question in life. 'What are you looking for?' he asked them. It was very relevant to ask that question in Palestine in the time of Jesus. Were they legalists, looking only for subtle and recondite conversations about the little details of the law, like the scribes and

Pharisees? Were they ambitious timeservers looking for position and power, like the Sadducees? Were they nationalists looking for a political demagogue and a military commander who would smash the occupying power of Rome, like the Zealots? Were they humble men of prayer looking for God and for his will, like the Quiet in the Land? Or were they simply puzzled, bewildered, sinful men looking for light on the road of life and forgiveness from God?

It would be well if every now and again we were to ask ourselves: 'What am I looking for? What's my aim and goal? What am I really trying to get out of life?' Some are searching for *security*. They would like a position which is safe, money enough to meet the needs of life and to put some past for the time when work is done, a material security which will take away the essential worry about material things. This is not a wrong aim, but it is a low aim, and an inadequate thing to which to direct all life; for, in the last analysis, there is no safe security in the chances and the changes of this life.

Some are searching for what they would call a *career*, for power, prominence, prestige, for a place to fit the talents and the abilities they believe themselves to have, for an opportunity to do the work they believe themselves capable of doing. If this is directed by motives of personal ambition it can be a bad aim; if it is directed by motives of the service of our neighbours it can be a high aim. But it is not enough, for its horizon is limited by time and by the world. Some are searching for some kind of *peace*, for something to enable them to live at peace with themselves, and at peace with God, and at peace with others. This is the search for God; this aim only Jesus Christ can meet and supply.

The answer of John's disciples was that they wished to know where Jesus stayed. They called him *Rabbi*; that is a Hebrew word which literally means *My great one*. It was the title of respect given by students and seekers after knowledge to their teachers and to wise men. John, the evangelist, was writing for Greeks. He knew they would not recognize that Hebrew word, so he translated it for them by the Greek word *didaskalos, teacher*. It was not mere curiosity which made these two ask this question. What they meant was that they did not wish to speak to Jesus only on the road, in passing, as chance acquaintances might stop and exchange a few words. They wished to linger long with him and talk out their problems and their troubles. Those who would be Jesus' disciples can never be satisfied with a passing word. They want to meet Jesus, not as an acquaintance in passing, but as a friend in their own homes.

Jesus' answer was: 'Come and see!' The Jewish Rabbis had a way of using that phrase in their teaching. They would say: 'Do you want to know the answer to this question? Do you want to know the solution to this problem? Come and see, and we will think about it together.' When Jesus said: 'Come and see!' he was inviting them, not only to come and talk, but to come and find the things that he alone could open out to them.

The Third Sunday of Epiphany
A Divided Church *and* The Son of God Goes Forth

1 Corinthians 1:10–18

Paul begins the task of mending the situation which had arisen in the church at Corinth. He was writing from Ephesus. Christian slaves who belonged to the establishment of a lady called Chloe had had occasion to visit Corinth, and they had come back with a sorry tale of dissension and disunity. Twice, Paul addresses the Corinthians as *brothers*. As Theodore Beza, the sixteenth-century Calvinist commentator, said, 'In that word too there lies hidden an argument.' By the very use of the word, Paul does two things. First, he softens the rebuke which is given, not in any threatening way, but as from one who has no other emotion than love. Second, it should have shown them how wrong their dissensions and divisions were. They were fellow Christians, and they should have lived in mutual love.

In trying to bring them together, Paul uses two interesting phrases. He tells them *to make up their differences*. The phrase he uses is the regular one used of two hostile parties reaching agreement. He wishes them to be *knit together*, a medical word used of knitting together bones that have been fractured, or joining together a joint that has been dislocated. The disunion is unnatural and must be cured for the sake of the health and efficiency of the body of the Church. Paul identifies four parties in the church at Corinth. They have not broken away from the church; for the moment, the divisions remain within it. The word he uses to describe them is *schismata*, which is the word for *tears in a garment*. The Corinthian church is in danger of becoming as unsightly as a torn garment. It is to be noted that the great figures of the Church who are named, Paul and Cephas and Apollos, had nothing to do with these divisions. There were no dissensions between them. Without their knowledge and without their consent, their names had been appropriated by these Corinthian factions. It not infrequently happens that a person's so-called supporters are a bigger problem than those who are openly hostile. Let us look at these parties and see if we can find out what they stood for.

(1) There were those who claimed to belong to *Paul*. No doubt this was mainly a Gentile party. Paul had always preached the gospel of Christian freedom and the end of the law. It is most likely that this party was using their new-found Christianity as an excuse to do as they liked. The German theologian Rudolf Bultmann has said that the Christian indicative always brings the Christian imperative. They had forgotten that the fact, the indicative, of the good news brought the obligation, the imperative, of the Christian ethic. They had forgotten that they were saved not to be free to sin, but to be free not to sin.

(2) There was the party who claimed to belong to *Apollos*. There is a brief character sketch of Apollos in Acts 18:24. He was a Jew from Alexandria, an eloquent man and well versed in the Scriptures. Alexandria was the centre of intellectual activity. It was there that scholars had made a science of allegorizing the Scriptures and finding the most obscure meanings in the simplest passages. The Alexandrians were in fact the people who *intellectualized* Christianity. Those who claimed to belong to Apollos were, no doubt, the intellectuals who were fast turning Christianity into a philosophy rather than a religion.

(3) There were those who claimed to belong to *Cephas*. Cephas is the Jewish form of Peter's name. These were most probably Jews, and they sought to teach that Christians must still observe the Jewish law. They were legalists who exalted law, and, by so doing, belittled grace.

(4) There were those who claimed to belong to *Christ*. This may be one of two things.

(a) There was absolutely no punctuation in Greek manuscripts and no space whatever between the words. This statement may well not describe a party at all. It may be the comment of Paul himself. Perhaps we ought to punctuate like this: 'I am of Paul; I am of Apollos; I am of Cephas – but *I* belong to Christ.' It may well be that this is Paul's own comment on the whole wretched situation.

(b) If that is not so and this does describe a party, they must have been a small and rigid sect who claimed that they were the only true Christians in Corinth. Their real fault was not in saying that they belonged to Christ, but in acting as if Christ belonged to them. It may well describe a little, intolerant, self-righteous group. It is not to be thought that Paul is belittling baptism. The people he did baptize were very special converts. Stephanas was probably the first convert of all (1 Corinthians 16:15); Crispus had once been no less than the ruler of the Jewish synagogue at Corinth (Acts 18:8); Gaius had probably been Paul's host (Romans 16:23).

The point is this: baptism was *into the name of Jesus*. That phrase in Greek implies the closest possible connection. To sell a slave into a person's name was to give that slave into the undisputed possession of that person. A soldier swore loyalty into the name of Caesar; he belonged absolutely to the emperor. *Into the name of* implied utter possession. In Christianity, it implied even more – that the Christian was not only possessed by Christ but was in some strange way identified with him. Paul is not making little of baptism; he is simply glad that no act of his could be misconstrued as annexing anyone for himself and not for Christ.

It was Paul's claim that he set before men and women the cross of Christ in its simplest terms. To decorate the story of the cross with rhetoric and cleverness would have been to make people think more of the language than of the facts, more of the speaker than of the message. It was Paul's aim to set before men and women not himself but Christ in all his lonely grandeur.

Matthew 4:12–23

For Jesus, the time had come when he must go forth to his task. Let us note what he did first of all. He left Nazareth and took up residence in the town of Capernaum. There was a kind of symbolic finality in that move. In that moment, Jesus left his home, never again to return to live in it. It is as if he shut the door that lay behind him before he opened the door that stood in front of him. It was a clean surgical cut between the old and the new. One chapter was ended and another had begun. Into life, there come these moments of decision. It is always better to meet them with an even surgical cut than to waver undecided between two courses of action.

Jesus had chosen to begin his mission in Galilee; and we have seen how well prepared Galilee was to receive the seed. With Galilee, Jesus chose to launch his campaign in the synagogues. The synagogue was the most important institution in the life of any Jew. There was a difference between the synagogues and the Temple. There was only one Temple, the Temple in Jerusalem, but wherever there was the smallest colony of Jews there was a synagogue. The Temple existed solely for the offering of sacrifice; in it there was no preaching or teaching. The synagogue was essentially a teaching institution. The synagogues have been defined as 'the popular religious universities of their day'. If a man had any religious teaching or religious ideas to disseminate, the synagogue was unquestionably the place to start.

Further, the synagogue service was such that it gave the new teacher his chance. In the synagogue service, there were three parts. The first part consisted of prayers. The second part consisted of readings from the law and from the prophets, readings in which members of the congregation took part. The third part was the address. The important fact is that there was no one person to give the address.

There was no such thing as a professional ministry. The president of the synagogue presided over the arrangements for the service. Any distinguished stranger could be asked to give the address, and anyone with a message to give might volunteer to give it; and, if the ruler or president of the synagogue judged him to be a fit person to speak, he was allowed to speak. Thus, at the beginning, the door of the synagogue and the pulpit of the synagogue were open to Jesus. He began in the synagogue because it was there he would find the most sincerely religious people of his day, and the way to speak to them was open to him. After the address, there came a time for talk, and questions, and discussion. The synagogue was the ideal place in which to get a new teaching across to the people.

But not only did Jesus preach; he also healed the sick. It was little wonder that reports of what he was doing went out and people came crowding to hear him, and to see him, and to benefit from his compassion. They came from Syria. Syria was the great province of which Palestine was only a part. It stretched away to the north and the north-east with the great city of Damascus as its centre. Very naturally they came from Galilee, and the word about Jesus had spread south to Jerusalem and Judaea also, and they came from there. They came from the land across the Jordan, which was known as Peraea, and which stretched from Pella in the north to Arabia Petra in the south. They came from the Decapolis. The Decapolis was a federation of ten independent Greek cities, all of which, except Scythopolis, were on the far side of the Jordan. This list is symbolic, for in it we see not only the Jews but the Gentiles also coming to Jesus Christ for what he alone could give them. Already the ends of the earth are gathering to him.

This passage is of great importance because it gives us in brief summary the three great activities of Jesus' life.

(1) He came *proclaiming* the gospel, or, as the Authorized Version and Revised Standard Version have it, he came *preaching*. Now,

preaching is the proclamation of certainties. Therefore, *Jesus came to defeat human ignorance.* He came to tell men and women the truth about God, to tell them something that they could never have found out for themselves. He came to put an end to guessing and to groping, and to show them what God is like.

(2) He came *teaching* in the synagogues. What is the difference between *teaching* and *preaching*? Preaching is the uncompromising proclamation of certainties; teaching is the explanation of the meaning and the significance of them. Therefore, *Jesus came to defeat human misunderstandings.* There are times when we know the truth and misinterpret it. We know the truth and draw the wrong conclusions from it. Jesus came to tell men and women the meaning of true religion.

(3) He came *healing* all those who had need of healing. That is to say, *Jesus came to defeat human pain.* The important thing about Jesus is that he was not satisfied with simply telling the truth in *words*; he came to turn that truth into deeds. Florence Allshorn, the great missionary teacher, said: 'An ideal is never yours until it comes out of your fingertips.' The ideal is not yours until it is made real in action. Jesus embodied his own teaching in deeds of help and healing.

Jesus came *preaching* that he might defeat all *ignorance.* He came *teaching* that he might defeat all *misunderstandings.* He came *healing* that he might defeat all *pain.* We, too, must proclaim our certainties; we, too, must be ready to explain our faith; we, too, must turn the ideal into action and into deeds.

The Fourth Sunday of Epiphany

A Stumbling-block to the Jews and Foolishness to the Greeks *and* The New Exhilaration

1 Corinthians 1:18–31

Both to cultured Greeks and to pious Jews, the story that Christianity had to tell sounded like the sheerest folly. Paul begins by making free use of two quotations from Isaiah (29:14, 33:18) to show how mere human wisdom is bound to fail. He cites the undeniable fact that, for all its wisdom, the world had never found God and was still blindly and gropingly seeking him. That very search was designed by God to show men and women their own helplessness and so to prepare the way for the acceptance of the one who is the one true way.

What, then, was this Christian message? If we study the four great sermons in the Book of Acts (2:14–39, 3:12–26, 4:8–12, 10:36–43), we find that there are certain constant elements in the Christian preaching. (1) There is the claim that the great promised time of God has come. (2) There is a summary of the life, death and resurrection of Jesus. (3) There is a claim that all this was the fulfilment of prophecy. (4) There is the assertion that Jesus will come again. (5) There is an urgent invitation to men and women to repent and receive the promised gift of the Holy Spirit.

(1) To the *Jews*, that message was a stumbling-block. There were two reasons.

(a) To them, it was incredible that someone who had ended life upon a cross could possibly be God's chosen one. They pointed to their own law which unmistakably said: 'Anyone hung on a tree is under God's curse' (Deuteronomy 21:23). To a Jew, the fact of the crucifixion, so far from proving that Jesus was the Son of God, disproved it finally. It may seem extraordinary, but, even with Isaiah 53 before their eyes, the Jews had never dreamt of a suffering Messiah. The cross, to the Jews, was and is an insuperable barrier to belief in Jesus.

(b) The Jews sought for signs. When the golden age of God came, they looked for startling happenings. This very time during which Paul was writing produced a crop of false Messiahs, and all of them had tricked and deceived the people into accepting them by the promise of wonders. In AD 54, a man from Egypt arrived in Jerusalem, claiming to be the Prophet. He persuaded 30,000 people to follow him out to the Mount of Olives by promising that, at his word of command, the walls of Jerusalem would fall down. That was the kind of thing that the Jews were looking for. In Jesus, they saw one who was meek and lowly, one who deliberately avoided the spectacular, one who served and who ended on a cross – and it seemed to them an impossible picture of the chosen one of God.

(2) To the *Greeks*, the message was foolishness. Again, there were two reasons.

(a) In Greek thought, the first characteristic of God was *apatheia*. That word means more than *apathy*; it means *total inability to feel*. The Greeks argued that, if God can feel joy or sorrow or anger or grief, it means that some human being has for that moment influenced God and is therefore greater than God. So, they went on to argue, it follows that God must be incapable of all feeling, so that none may ever affect him.

A God who suffered was to the Greeks a contradiction in terms.

They went further. Plutarch, the great historian and philosopher, declared that it was an insult to God to involve him in human affairs. God, of necessity, was utterly detached. The very idea of *incarnation*, of God becoming a man, was revolting to the Greek mind. St Augustine, who was a very great scholar long before he became a Christian, could say that, in the Greek philosophers, he found a parallel to almost all the teaching of Christianity; but one thing, he said, he never found: 'The Word became flesh and dwelt among us.' Celsus, who attacked the Christians with such vigour towards the end of the second century AD, wrote: 'God is good and beautiful and happy and is in that which is most beautiful and best. If then "He descends to men" it involves change for him, and change from good to bad, from beautiful to ugly, from happiness to unhappiness, from what is best to what is worst. Who would choose such a change? For mortality it is only nature to alter and be changed; but for the immortal to abide the same forever. God would never accept such a change.' To any thinking Greek, the incarnation was a total impossibility. To people who thought like that, it was incredible that one who had suffered as Jesus had suffered could possibly be the Son of God.

(b) The Greeks sought wisdom. Originally, the Greek word *sophist* meant a *wise man* in the good sense; but it came to mean a man with a clever mind and cunning tongue, a mental acrobat, a man who with glittering and persuasive rhetoric could make the worse appear the better reason. It meant a man who had no real interest in solutions but who simply gloried in the stimulus of 'the mental hike'. It is impossible to exaggerate the almost fantastic mastery that the silver-tongued rhetorician held in Greece. Plutarch says: 'They made their voices sweet with musical cadences and modulations of tone and echoed resonances.' They thought not of what they were saying, but of how they were saying it. Their thought might be poisonous as long as it was enveloped in honeyed words. The Greeks were intoxicated with fine words; and, to them, a Christian preacher with a blunt message seemed a crude and uncultured figure, to be laughed at and ridiculed rather than to be listened to and respected.

It looked as if the Christian message had little chance of success against the background of Jewish or Greek life; but, as Paul said, 'What looks like God's foolishness is wiser than human wisdom; and what looks like God's weakness is stronger than human strength.'

John 2:1–11

We should note three general things about this wonderful deed which Jesus did.

(1) We note *when* it happened. It happened at a wedding feast. Jesus was perfectly at home at such an occasion. He was no severe, austere killjoy. He loved to share in the happy rejoicing of a wedding feast. There are certain religious people who shed a gloom wherever they go. They are suspicious of all joy and happiness. To them, religion is a thing of black clothes, the lowered voice, the expulsion of social fellowship. It was said of Alice Freeman Palmer by one of her students: 'She made me feel as if I was bathed in sunshine.' Jesus was like that. Jesus never counted it a crime to be happy. Why should his followers do so?

(2) We note *where* it happened. It happened in a humble home in a village in Galilee. This miracle was not performed against the background of some great occasion and in the presence of vast crowds. It was performed in a home. Jesus' action at Cana of Galilee shows what he thought of a home. As the Revised Standard Version has it, he 'manifested forth his glory', and that manifestation took place within a home.

There is a strange paradox in the attitude of many people to the place they call home. Many of us treat the ones we love most in a way that we would never dare to treat a chance acquaintance. So often it is strangers who see us at our best and those who live with us who see us at our worst. We ought always to remember that it was in a humble home that Jesus manifested forth his glory. To him, home was a place for which nothing but his best was good enough.

(3) We note *why* it happened. In the Middle East hospitality was always a sacred duty. It would have brought embarrassed shame to that home that day if the wine had run out. It was to save a humble Galilaean family from hurt that Jesus put forth his power. It was in sympathy, in kindness, in understanding for ordinary people that Jesus acted.

Nearly everyone can do the big thing on the big occasion; but it takes Jesus to do the big thing on a simple, homely occasion like this. There is a kind of natural human maliciousness which rather enjoys the misfortunes of others and which delights to make a good story of them in idle gossip. But Jesus, the Lord of all life, and the King of glory, used his power to save a Galilaean wedding couple from humiliation. It is just by such deeds of understanding, simple kindliness that we too can show that we are followers of Jesus Christ.

Now we must think of the deep and permanent truth which John is seeking to teach when he tells this story. John was writing out of a double background. He was a Jew and he was writing for Jews; but his great object was to write the story of Jesus in such a way that it would come home also to the Greeks.

Let us look at it first of all from the *Jewish* point of view. Beneath John's simple stories there is a deeper meaning which is open only to those who have eyes to see. In all his gospel, John never wrote an unnecessary or an insignificant detail. Everything means something, and everything points beyond.

There were six stone water pots; and at the command of Jesus, the water in them turned to wine. According to the Jews, *seven* is the number which is complete and perfect; and *six* is the number which is unfinished and imperfect. The six stone water pots stand for all the imperfections of the Jewish law. Jesus came to do away with the imperfections of the law and to put in their place the new wine of the gospel of his grace. Jesus turned the imperfection of the law into the perfection of grace.

Let us look at it now from the Greek point of view. The Greeks actually possessed stories like this. Dionysos was the Greek god of wine. Pausanias, a Greek who wrote a description of his country and of its ancient ceremonies, describes an old ceremony and belief: 'Between the market place and the Menius is an old theatre and a sanctuary of Dionysos; the image is by Praxiteles. No god is more revered by the Eleans than Dionysos is, and they say that he attends their festival of the Thyia. The place where they hold the festival called the Thyia is about a mile from the city. Three empty kettles are taken into the building and deposited there by the priests in the presence of the citizens and of any strangers who may happen to be staying in the country. On the doors of the buildings the priests, and all who choose to do so, put their seals. Next day they are free to examine the seals, and on entering the building they find the kettles full of wine.'

So the Greeks, too, had their stories like this; and it is as if John said to them: 'You have your stories and your legends about your gods. They are only stories and you know that they are not really true. But Jesus has come to do what you have always dreamed that your gods could do. He has come to make the things you longed for come true.'

To the Jews, John said: 'Jesus has come to turn the imperfection of the law into the perfection of grace.' To the Greeks, he said: 'Jesus has come really and truly to do the things you only dreamed the gods could do.' Now we can see what John is teaching us. Every story tells us not of something Jesus did once and never again, but of something which he is forever doing. John tells us not of things that Jesus once did in Palestine, but of things that he still does today. And what John wants us to see here is not that Jesus once on a day turned some water pots of water into wine; he wants us to see that whenever Jesus comes into a person's life, there comes a new quality which is like turning water into wine. Without Jesus, life is dull and stale and flat; when Jesus comes into it, life becomes vivid and sparkling and exciting. Without Jesus, life is drab and uninteresting; with him it is thrilling and exhilarating. This story is John saying to *us*: 'If you want the new exhilaration, become a follower of Jesus Christ, and there will come a change in your life which will be like water turning into wine.'

Sunday between 3 and 9 February
The Wisdom which is from God *and* The Light of the World

1 Corinthians 2:1–12

Paul is remembering the time when first he came to Corinth; He came speaking in *simplicity*. It is worth noting that Paul had come to Corinth from Athens. It was at Athens that, for the only time in his life, as far as we know, he attempted to reduce Christianity to philosophic terms. There, on Mars' Hill, he had met the philosophers and had tried to speak in their own language (Acts 17:22–31); and it was there that he had one of his very few failures. His sermon in terms of philosophy had had very little effect (Acts 17:32–4). It would almost seem that he had said to himself: 'Never again! From now on, I will tell the story of Jesus in utter simplicity. I will never again try to wrap it up in human categories. I will know nothing but Jesus Christ, and him upon his cross.'

He came with results and not with words alone. The result of Paul's preaching was that things happened. He says that his preaching was unanswerably demonstrated to be true by the Spirit and by power. The word he uses is the word for the most stringent possible proof, the kind against which there can be no argument. What was it? It was the proof of changed lives. Something with the power to re-create had entered into the polluted society of Corinth. No one can argue against the proof of a changed life. It is our weakness that too often we have tried to talk people into Christianity instead of, in our own lives, showing them Christ. 'A saint', as someone said, 'is someone in whom Christ lives again.'

Verses 6–9 introduce us to a distinction between different kinds of Christian instruction and different stages of the Christian life. In the early Church, there was a quite clear distinction between two kinds of instruction. (1) There was what was called *kerygma*. *Kerygma* means *a herald's announcement from a king*, and this was the plain announcement of the basic facts of Christianity, the announcement of the facts of the life, death and resurrection of Jesus and his coming again. (2) There was what was called *didache*. *Didache* means *teaching*, and this was the explanation of the meaning of the facts which had already been announced. Obviously, it is a second stage for those who have already received *kerygma*.

That is what Paul is getting at here. So far, he has been talking about Jesus Christ and about Christ crucified. That was the basic announcement of Christianity; but, he goes on to say, we do not stop there. Christian instruction goes on to teach not only the facts but also the meaning of the facts. Paul says that this is done among those who are *teleioi*. The Authorized Version translates that word as *perfect*. That is certainly one of its meanings; but it is not appropriate here. *Teleios* has a physical sense; it describes an animal or a person who has reached the height of physical development. It also has a mental sense. Pythagoras divided his disciples into those who were babes and those who were *teleioi*. That is to say, it describes a person who is a mature student. That is the translation given in the Revised Standard Version, and that is the sense in which Paul uses it here. He says: 'Out in the streets, and to those who have just newly come into the Church, we talk about the basic elements of Christianity; but, when people are a little more mature, we give them deeper teaching about what these basic facts mean.' It is not that Paul is hinting at a kind of caste or class distinction between Christians; it is a difference of the stages at which they are. The tragedy so often is that people are content to remain at the elementary stage when they should be going on strenuously to think things out for themselves.

Paul uses a word here which has a technical sense. The Authorized Version has it: 'We speak the wisdom of God *in a mystery.*' The Greek word *musterion* means something the meaning of which is hidden from those who have not been initiated, but is crystal clear to those who have. It would describe a ceremony carried out in some society whose meaning was quite clear to the members of the society but unintelligible to the outsider. What Paul is saying is: 'We go on to explain things which only those who have already given their hearts to Christ can understand.'

He insists that this special teaching is not the product of intellectual activity; it is the gift of God, and it came into the world with Jesus Christ. All our discoveries are not so much what our minds have found out as what God has told us. This by no means frees us from the responsibility of human effort. Only students who work can make themselves fit to receive the real riches of the mind of a great teacher. It is the same with us and God. The more we strive to understand, the more God can tell us; and there is no limit to this process, because the riches of God are infinite and cannot be measured.

Matthew 5:13–20

When Jesus said that Christians must be the light of the world, what did he mean?

(1) A light is first and foremost something which is meant to be seen. The houses in Palestine were very dark, with only one little circular window perhaps not more than eighteen inches across. The lamp was like a sauce-boat filled with oil with the wick floating in it. It was not so easy to rekindle a lamp in the days before matches existed. Normally the lamp stood on the lamp stand, which would be no more than a roughly shaped branch of wood; but when people went out, for safety's sake, they took the lamp

from its stand and put it under an earthen bushel measure, so that it might burn without risk until they came back. The primary duty of the light of the lamp was to be seen.

So, Christianity is something which is meant to be seen. As someone has well said, 'There can be no such thing as secret discipleship, for either the secrecy destroys the discipleship, or the discipleship destroys the secrecy.' Our Christianity should be perfectly visible to everyone. Further, this Christianity should be visible not only within the Church. A Christianity whose effects stop at the church door is not much use to anyone. It should be even more visible in the ordinary activities of the world. Our Christianity should be visible in the way we treat a shop assistant across the counter, in the way we order a meal in a restaurant, in the way we treat our employees or serve our employer, in the way we play a game or drive or park a car, in the daily language we use, in the daily literature we read. As Christians, we should be just as much a Christian in the factory, the workshop, the shipyard, the mine, the schoolroom, the surgery, the kitchen, the golf course and the playing field as we are in church. Jesus did not say: 'You are the light of the *Church*'; he said: 'You are the light of the *world*' – and in our lives in the world our Christianity should be evident to all.

(2) A light is a guide. On the estuary of any river, we may see the line of lights which marks the channel for the ships to sail in safety. We know how difficult even the city streets are when there are no lights. A light is something to make clear the way. So, Christians must make the way clear to others. That is to say, Christians must of necessity be examples. One of the things which this world needs more than anything else is people who are prepared to be channels for goodness. Suppose there is a group of people, and suppose it is suggested that some questionable thing should be done. Unless someone makes a protest, the thing will be done. But if someone rises and says: 'I will not be a party to that,' another and another and another will rise to say: 'Neither will I.' But, had they not been

given the lead, they would have remained silent. There are many people in this world who do not have the moral strength and courage to take a stand by themselves, but if someone gives them a lead, they will follow; if they have someone strong enough to lean on, they will do the right thing. It is the Christian's duty to take the stand which the weaker brother or sister will support, to give the lead which those with less courage will follow. The world needs its guiding lights; there are people waiting and longing for a lead to take the stand and to do the thing which they do not dare by themselves.

(3) A light can often be a *warning light*. A light is often the warning which tells us to halt when there is danger ahead. It is sometimes the duty of Christians to bring to others the necessary warning. That is often difficult, and it is often hard to do it in a way which will not do more harm than good; but one of the most poignant tragedies in life is for someone, especially a young person, to come and say to us: 'I would never have been in the situation in which I now find myself, if you had only spoken in time.' It was said of Florence Allshorn, the famous teacher and principal, that if she ever had occasion to rebuke her students, she did it 'with her arm round about them'. If our warnings are given not in anger, not in irritation, not in criticism, not in condemnation, not in the desire to hurt, but in love, they will be effective.

The light which can be seen, the light which warns, the light which guides – these are the lights which Christians must be.

Sunday between 10 and 16 February
The Supreme Importance of God *and* The Surgical Cure

1 Corinthians 3:1–9

Paul has just been talking about the difference between the person who is spiritual (*pneumatikos*), and who therefore can understand spiritual truths, and the person who is *psuchikos*, whose interests and aims do not go beyond physical life and who is therefore unable to grasp spiritual truth. He now accuses the Corinthians of being still at the physical stage. But he uses two new words to describe them.

In verse 1, he calls them *sarkinoi*. This word comes from *sarx*, which means *flesh* – a word that is so common in Paul. Now, all Greek adjectives ending in *-inos* mean *made of something or other*. So, Paul begins by saying that the Corinthians are made of flesh. That was not in itself a rebuke; human beings by their very nature are made of flesh, *but* they must not stay that way. The trouble was that the Corinthians were not only *sarkinoi*, they were *sarkikoi*, which means not only *made of flesh* but *dominated by the flesh*. To Paul, the *flesh* is much more than merely a physical thing. It means *human nature apart from God*, that part of men and women, both mental and physical, which provides a point of entry for sin. So, the fault that Paul finds with the Corinthians is not that they are made of flesh – all human beings are – but that they have allowed this lower side of their nature to dominate all their outlook and all their actions.

What is it about their life and conduct that makes Paul level such a rebuke at them? It is their partisan attitude, their strife and their factions. This is extremely significant because it means that *you can tell what a person's relationship with God is by looking at the way that person relates to others.* If someone is at variance with others and is a quarrelsome, argumentative, troublemaking type, that person may be a diligent church-attender, even a church office-bearer, but not a child of God. But if someone is at one with others, and has relationships that are marked by love and unity and concord, then that person is on the way to being one of God's children. If we love God, we will also love our neighbours. It was this truth that the nineteenth-century poet Leigh Hunt took from an old eastern tale and enshrined in his poem 'Abou Ben Adhem':

Abou Ben Adhem (may his tribe increase!)
Awoke one night from a deep dream of peace,
And saw, within the moonlight in his room,
Making it rich, and like a lily in bloom,
An angel writing in a book of gold:
Exceeding peace had made Ben Adhem bold,
And to the presence in the room he said,
'What writest thou?' – The vision raised its head,
And with a look made of all sweet accord,
Answered, 'The names of those who love the Lord.'
'And is mine one?' said Abou. 'Nay, not so,'
Replied the angel. Abou spoke more low,
But cheerly still; and said, 'I pray thee then,
Write me as one that loves his fellow men.'
The angel wrote, and vanished. The next night
It came again with a great wakening light,
And showed the names whom love of God had blest,
And lo! Ben Adhem's name led all the rest.

Paul goes on to show the essential folly of this partisan attitude with its glorification of human leaders. In a garden, one person may plant a seed and another may water it; but neither can claim to have made the seed grow. That claim belongs to God and to God alone. The one who plants and the one who waters are on the same level. Neither can claim any precedence over the other; they are only servants working together for the one Master – God. God uses human instruments to bring to men and women the message of his truth and love; but it is he alone who wakes human hearts to new life. As he alone created the heart, so he alone can re-create it.

Matthew 5:21–37

In verses 29–30 Jesus makes a great demand, and it is literally a surgical demand. He insists that anything which is a cause of, or a seduction to, sin should be completely cut out of life. The word he uses for a *stumbling-block* is interesting. It is the word *skandalon*. *Skandalon* is a form of the word *skandalēthron*, which means the *bait-stick* in a trap. It was the stick or arm on which the bait was fixed and which operated the trap to catch the animal lured to its own destruction. So the word came to mean *anything which causes a person's destruction.*

Behind it there are two pictures. First, there is the picture of a hidden stone in a path against which someone may stumble, or of a cord stretched across a path, deliberately put there to make them trip. Second, there is the picture of a pit dug in the ground and deceptively covered over with a thin layer of branches or of turf, and so arranged that, when unwary travellers set foot on it, they are immediately thrown into the pit. The *skandalon*, the *stumbling-block*, is something which trips people up, something which sends them crashing to destruction, something which lures them to their own ruin. Of course, the words of Jesus are not to be taken with a crude literalism. What they mean is that anything which helps to seduce us to sin is to be ruthlessly rooted out of life. If there is a habit which can be seduction to evil, if there is an association which can be the cause of wrongdoing, if there is a pleasure which could turn out to be our ruin, then that thing must be surgically excised from our life.

Coming as it does immediately after the passage which deals with forbidden thoughts and desires, this passage compels us to ask: how shall we free ourselves from these unclean desires and corrupting thoughts? It is the fact of experience that thoughts and pictures come unbidden into our minds, and it is the hardest thing on earth to shut the door to them. There is one way in which these forbidden thoughts and desires cannot be dealt with – and that is to sit down and to say, I will not think of these things. The more we say, I will not think of such and such a thing, the more our thoughts are in fact concentrated on it.

The outstanding example in history of the wrong way to deal with such thoughts and desires was that of the hermits and the monks in the desert in the time of the early Church. They were individuals who wished to free themselves from all earthly things, and especially of the desires of the body. To do so, they went away into the Egyptian desert with the idea of living alone and thinking of nothing but God. The most famous of them all was Saint Anthony. He lived the hermit's life; he fasted; he did without sleep; he tortured his body. For thirty-five years he lived in the desert, and these thirty-five years were a non-stop battle, without respite, with his temptations. The story is told in his biography. 'First of all the devil tried to lead him away from discipline, whispering to him the remembrance of his wealth, cares for his sister, claims of kindred, love of money, love of glory, the various pleasures of the table, and the other relaxations of life, and, at last, the difficulty of virtue and the labour of it . . . The one would suggest foul thoughts, and the other counter them with prayers; the one fire him with lust, the other, as one who seemed to blush, fortify his body with prayers, faith and fasting. The devil one night even took upon him the shape of a woman, and imitated all her acts simply to beguile Anthony.' So for thirty-five years the struggle went on.

The plain fact is that, if ever anyone was asking for trouble, Anthony and his friends were. It is the inevitable law of human nature that the more we say we will not think of something, the more that something will present itself to our thoughts. There are only two ways to defeat the forbidden thoughts.

The first way is by Christian action. The best way to defeat such thoughts is to do something, to fill life so full with Christian labour and Christian service that there is no time for these thoughts to enter in; to think so much of others that in the end we entirely forget ourselves; to rid ourselves of a diseased and morbid introspection by concentrating not on ourselves but on other people. The real cure for evil thoughts is good action.

The second way is to fill the mind with good thoughts. There is a famous scene in J. M. Barrie's *Peter Pan*. Peter is in the children's bedroom; they have seen him fly; and they wish to fly too. They have tried it from the floor and they have tried it from the beds and the result is failure. 'How do you do it?' John asked. And Peter answered: 'You just think lovely, wonderful thoughts and they lift you up in the air.' The only way to defeat evil thoughts is to begin to think of something else. If people are harassed by thoughts of the forbidden and unclean things, they will certainly never defeat the evil things by withdrawing from life and saying, I will not think of these things. They can do so only by plunging into Christian action and Christian thought. They will never do it by trying to save their own lives; they can do it only by flinging their lives away for others.

Sunday between 17 and 23 February

Wisdom and Foolishness *and*
The Meaning of Christian Love

1 Corinthians 3:10–11, 16–23

To Paul, the Church was the very temple of God because it was the society in which the Spirit of God dwelt. As the third-century theologian Origen said: 'We are most of all God's temple when we prepare ourselves to receive the Holy Spirit.' But, if people introduce dissension and division into the fellowship of the Church, they destroy the temple of God in a double sense.

(1) They make it impossible for the Spirit to operate. As soon as bitterness enters a church, love goes from it. The truth can neither be spoken nor heard rightly in that atmosphere. 'Where love is, God is,' but, where hatred and strife are, God stands at the door and knocks and receives no entry. The very badge of the Church is love for the community. Anyone who destroys that love destroys the Church and thereby destroys the temple of God.

(2) They split up the Church and reduce it to a series of disconnected ruins. No building can stand firm and foursquare if sections of it are removed. The Church's greatest weakness is still its divisions. They, too, destroy it. Paul goes on once again to pin down the root cause of this dissension and consequent destruction of the Church. It is the worship of intellectual, worldly wisdom. He shows the condemnation of that wisdom by two Old Testament quotations – Job 5:13 and Psalm 94:11. It is by this very worldly wisdom that the Corinthians assess the worth of different teachers and leaders. It is this pride in the human mind which makes them

evaluate and criticize the way in which the message is delivered, the correctness of the rhetoric, the weight of the oratory and the subtleties of the arguments, rather than think only of the content of the message itself. The trouble about this intellectual pride is that it is always two things.

(1) It is always *argumentative*. It cannot keep silent and admire; it must talk and criticize. It cannot bear to have its opinions contradicted; it must prove that it and it alone is right. It is never humble enough to learn; it must always be laying down the law.

(2) Intellectual pride is characteristically *exclusive*. Its tendency is to look down on others rather than to sit down beside them. Its outlook is that all who do not agree with it are wrong. Long ago, the Lord Protector of England, Oliver Cromwell, wrote to the Scots: 'I beseech you by the bowels of Christ, think it possible that you may be mistaken.' That is precisely what intellectual pride cannot think. It tends to cut people off from one another rather than unite them. Paul urges anyone who would be wise to become a fool. This is simply a vivid way of urging people to be humble enough to learn. No one can teach those who think that they know it all already. Plato said: 'He is the wisest man who knows himself to be very ill-equipped for the study of wisdom.' The Roman teacher Quintilian said of certain students: 'They would doubtless have become excellent scholars if they had not been so fully persuaded of their own scholarship.' The old proverb laid it down: 'He who knows not, and knows not that he knows not, is a fool; avoid him. He who knows not, and knows that he knows not, is a wise man; teach him.'

The only way to become wise is to realize that we are fools; the only way to knowledge is to confess our ignorance. In verse 22, as so often happens in his letters, the march of Paul's prose suddenly takes wings and becomes a lyric of passion and poetry. The Corinthians are doing what is to Paul an inexplicable thing. They are seeking to give themselves over into the hands of another person. Paul tells them that, in point of fact, it is not they who belong to that person but the other way round. This identification with some party is the acceptance of slavery by those who should be rulers. In fact, they are already rulers over all things, because they belong to Christ and Christ belongs to God. Those who give their strength and their hearts to some little splinter of a party have surrendered everything to a petty thing, when they could have entered into possession of a fellowship and a love as wide as the universe. They have confined into narrow limits lives which should be limitless in their outlook.

Matthew 5:38–48

C. G. Montefiore, the Jewish scholar, called this 'the central and most famous section' of the Sermon on the Mount, and there is no other passage of the New Testament which contains such a concentrated expression of the Christian ethic of personal relations. To the ordinary person, this passage describes essential Christianity in action, and even the person who never darkens the door of the church knows that Jesus said this, and very often condemns the professing Christian for falling so far short of its demands. We must first try to find out what Jesus was really saying and what he was demanding of his followers. If we are to try to live this out, we must obviously first of all be quite clear as to what it is asking. What does Jesus mean by *loving our enemies*? Greek is a language which is rich in synonyms; its words often have shades of meaning which English does not possess. In Greek, there are four different words for *love*.

(1) There is the noun *storgē* with its accompanying verb *stergein*. These words are the characteristic words of *family love*. They are the words which describe the love of a parent for a child and a child for a parent. 'Sweet is a father to his children,' said Philemon, 'if he has *love* [*storgē*].' These words describe family affection.

(2) There is the noun *erōs* and the accompanying verb *eran*. These words describe the love between the sexes; there is always passion there; and there is always sexual love. Sophocles described *erōs* as 'the terrible longing'. In these words, there is nothing essentially bad; they simply describe the passion of human love; but as time went on, they began to be tinged with the idea of lust rather than love, and they never occur in the New Testament at all.

(3) There is *philia* with its accompanying verb *philein*. These are the warmest and the best Greek words for love. They describe real love, real affection. *Ho philountes*, the present participle, is the word which describes a person's closest and nearest and truest friends. *Philein* can mean to *caress* or to *kiss*. It is the word of warm, tender affection, the highest kind of love.

(4) There is *agapē* with its accompanying verb *agapan*. These words indicate *unconquerable benevolence, invincible goodwill. (Agapē* is the word which is used here.) If we regard people with *agapē*, it means that no matter what they do to us, no matter how they treat us, no matter if they insult us or injure us or grieve us, we will never allow any bitterness against them to invade our hearts, but will regard them with that unconquerable benevolence and goodwill which will seek nothing but their highest good. From this, certain things emerge.

(1) Jesus never asked us to love our enemies in the same way as we love our nearest and dearest. The very word is different; to love our enemies in the same way as we love our nearest and dearest would be neither possible nor right. This is a different kind of love.

(2) Wherein does the main difference lie? In the case of our nearest and dearest, we cannot help loving them; we speak of *falling in love*; it is something which comes to us quite unsought; it is something which is born of the emotions of the heart. But in the case of our enemies, love is not only something of the *heart*; it is also something of the *will*. It is not something which we cannot

help; it is something which we have to will ourselves into doing. It is in fact a victory over that which comes instinctively to us by our very nature. *Agapē* does not mean a feeling of the heart, which we cannot help, and which comes unbidden and unsought; it means a determination of the mind, whereby we achieve this unconquerable goodwill even to those who hurt and injure us. We can only have *agapē* when Jesus Christ enables us to conquer our natural tendency to anger and to bitterness, and to achieve this invincible goodwill to all people.

(3) It is then quite obvious that the last thing *agapē*, Christian love, means is that we allow people to do absolutely as they like, and that we leave them quite unchecked. If we regard people with invincible goodwill, it will often mean that we must punish them, that we must restrain them, that we must discipline them, that we must protect them against themselves. But it will also mean that we do not punish them to satisfy our desire for revenge, but in order to make them better people. It will always mean that all Christian discipline and all Christian punishment must be aimed not at vengeance but at cure. Punishment will never be merely retributive; it will always be remedial.

(4) It must be noted that Jesus laid this love down as a basis for *personal relationships*. People use this passage as a basis for pacifism and as a text on which to speak about international relationships. Of course, it includes that, but first and foremost it deals with our personal relationships with our family and the people we meet with every day in life. It is very much easier to go about declaring that there should be no such thing as war between nation and nation, than to live a life in which we personally never allow any such thing as bitterness to invade our relationships with those we meet with every day. First and foremost, this commandment of Jesus deals with personal relationships. It is a commandment of which we should say first and foremost: 'This means me.'

(5) We must note that this commandment is possible only for a Christian. Only the grace of Jesus Christ can enable us to have this unconquerable benevolence and this invincible goodwill in our personal relationships with other people. It is only when Christ lives in our hearts that bitterness will die and this love will spring to life. It is often said that this world would be perfect if only people would live according to the principles of the Sermon on the Mount; but the plain fact is that no one can even begin to live according to these principles without the help of Jesus Christ. We need Christ to enable us to obey Christ's command.

(6) Last – and it may be most important of all – we must note that this commandment does not only involve allowing people to do as they like to us; it also involves us doing something for them. *We are bidden to pray for them.* No one can pray for others and still hate them. When we take ourselves and those whom we are tempted to hate to God, something happens. We cannot go on hating others in the presence of God. The surest way of killing bitterness is to pray for those whom we are tempted to hate.

The Second Sunday before Lent
The Glorious Hope *and* The Forbidden Worry

Romans 8:18–25

Paul here speaks about the troubled state of this present world. He draws a great picture. He speaks with a poet's vision. He sees all nature waiting for the glory that shall be. At the moment, creation is in bondage to decay. As that great hymn 'Abide with me' has it:

Change and decay in all around I see.

The world is one where beauty fades and loveliness decays; it is a dying world; but it is waiting for its liberation from all this, and the coming of the state of glory. When Paul was painting this picture, he was working with ideas that any Jew would recognize and understand. He talks of this present age and of the glory that will be disclosed. Jewish thought divided time into two sections – this present age and the age to come. This present age was wholly bad, subject to sin and death and decay. Some day, there would come the day of the Lord. That would be a day of judgement when the world would be shaken to its foundations; but out of it there would come a new world.

The renewal of the world was one of the great Jewish thoughts. The Old Testament speaks of it without elaboration and without detail. 'For I am about to create new heavens and a new earth' (Isaiah 65:17). But, in the days between the Testaments, when the Jews were oppressed and enslaved and persecuted, they dreamed their dreams of that new earth and that renewed world.

The vine shall yield its fruit 10,000 fold, and on each
vine there shall be 1,000 branches; and each branch shall
produce 1,000 clusters; and each cluster produce 1,000
grapes; and each grape a cor of wine. And those who
have hungered shall rejoice; moreover, also, they shall
behold marvels every day. For winds shall go forth from
before me to bring every morning the fragrance of
aromatic fruits, and at the close of the day clouds
distilling the dews of health.
(The Apocalypse of Baruch 29:5–7)

And earth, and all the trees, and the innumerable flocks
of sheep shall give their true fruit to mankind, of wine
and of sweet honey and of white milk and corn, which
to men is the most excellent gift of all.
(Sibylline Oracles 3:620–33)

The dream of the renewed world was dear to the Jews. Paul knew
that; and here he, as it were, endows creation with consciousness.
He thinks of nature longing for the day when sin's dominion would
be broken, death and decay would be gone, and God's glory would
come. With a touch of imaginative insight, he says that the state of
nature was even worse than the human state. Human beings had
sinned deliberately; but it was involuntarily that nature was subjected
to the consequences of sin. Unwittingly, nature was involved in the
consequences of human sin. 'Cursed is the ground because of you,'
God said to Adam after his sin (Genesis 3:17). So here, with a poet's
eye, Paul sees nature waiting for liberation from the death and decay
that human sin had brought into the world. If that is true of nature,
it is even more true for us. So, Paul goes on to think of human longing. In the experience of the Holy Spirit, men and women had a
foretaste, a first instalment, of the glory that shall be; now they long
with all their hearts for the full realization of what adoption into the

family of God means. That final adoption will be the redemption of their bodies. In the state of glory, Paul did not think of people as disembodied spirits. In this world, every individual is a body and a spirit; and, in the world of glory, the total person will be saved. But the body will no longer be the victim of decay and the instrument of sin; it will be a spiritual body fit for the life of a spiritual person.

Then comes a great saying: 'We are saved by hope.' The blazing truth that lit life for Paul was that the human situation is not hopeless. Paul was no pessimist. He saw human sin and the state of the world; but he also saw God's redeeming power; and the end of it all for him was hope. Because of that, to Paul, life was not a state of permanent despair, waiting for an inevitable end in a world encompassed by sin, death and decay; life was an eager anticipation of a liberation, a renewal and a re-creation brought about by the glory and the power of God. In verse 19, he uses a wonderful word for *eager expectation*. It is *apokaradokia*, and it describes the stance of someone who scans the horizon with head thrust forward, eagerly searching the distance for the first signs of the dawn breaking – the daybreak of glory.

To Paul, life was not a weary, defeated waiting; it was a throbbing, vivid expectation. Christians are involved in the human situation. Within, they must battle with their own evil human nature; without, they must live in a world of death and decay. Nonetheless, Christians do not live only in the world; they also live in Christ. They do not see only the world; they look beyond it to God. They do not see only the consequences of human sin; they see the power of God's mercy and love. Therefore, the keynote of the Christian life is always hope and never despair. Christians wait not for death but for life.

Matthew 6:25–34

We must make sure that we understand what Jesus is forbidding and what he is demanding. The Authorized Version translates Jesus' commandment: 'Take no thought for the morrow.' Strange to say, the Authorized Version was the first translation to translate it in that way. John Wyclif's translation had it: 'Be not busy to your life.' The translations of Tyndale, Cranmer and the Geneva Version all had: 'Be not careful for your life.' They used the word *careful* in the literal sense of *full of care*. The older versions were in fact more accurate. It is not ordinary, prudent foresight that Jesus forbids; it is *worry*. Jesus is not advocating a shiftless, thriftless, reckless, thoughtless, improvident attitude to life; he is forbidding a careworn, worried fear, which takes all the joy out of life. The Greek word which is used means *to worry anxiously*. Its corresponding noun is the characteristic word for anxiety, worry and care.

The Jews themselves were very familiar with this attitude to life. It was the teaching of the great Rabbis that life ought to be met with a combination of prudence and serenity. They insisted, for instance, that every man must teach his son a trade; for, they said, not to teach him a trade was to teach him to steal. But at the same time, they said: 'He who has a loaf in his basket, and who says, "What will I eat tomorrow?" is a man of little faith.' Jesus is here teaching a lesson which the people knew well – the lesson of prudence and forethought and serenity and trust combined.

In these verses, Jesus sets out seven different arguments and defences against worry.

(1) He begins by pointing out (verse 25) that God gave us life, and if he gave us life, surely we can trust him to give us food to sustain that life. If God gave us bodies, surely we can trust him for garments to clothe these bodies. If anyone gives us a gift which is beyond price, surely we can be certain that such a giver will not

be mean, stingy, niggardly, careless and forgetful about much less costly gifts. So, the first argument is that if God gave us life, we can trust him for the things which are necessary to support life.

(2) Jesus goes on to speak about the birds (verse 26). There is no worry in their lives, no attempt to pile up goods for an unforeseen and unforeseeable future; and yet their lives go on. The point that Jesus is making is not that the birds do not work; it has been said that no one works harder than the average sparrow to make a living; the point that he is making is that they do not worry. There is not to be found in them the human weakness of straining to see a future which cannot be seen, and of seeking to find security in things stored up and accumulated against the future.

(3) In verse 27, Jesus goes on to prove that worry is in any event useless. The verse can bear two meanings. It can mean that none of us by worrying can add a cubit to our height; but a cubit is eighteen inches, and we surely would never contemplate adding eighteen inches to our height! It can mean that by worrying we cannot add the shortest space to our lives; and that meaning is more likely. It is Jesus' argument that worry is pointless anyway.

(4) Jesus goes on to speak about the flowers (verses 28–30), and he speaks about them as one who loved them. The lilies of the field were the scarlet poppies and anemones. They bloomed one day on the hillsides of Palestine; and yet in their brief life they were clothed with a beauty which surpassed the beauty of the robes of kings. When they died, they were used for nothing better than for burning. The Palestinian oven was made of clay. It was like a clay box set on bricks over the fire. When it was desired to raise the temperature of it especially quickly, some handfuls of dried grasses and wild flowers were flung *inside* the oven and set alight. The flowers had but one day of life; and then they were set alight to help a woman to heat an oven when she was baking in a hurry; and yet God clothes them with a beauty which is beyond human power to imitate. If God gives such beauty to a short-lived flower, how much

more will he care for us? Surely the generosity which is so lavish to the flower of a day will not be forgetful of human life, the crown of creation.

(5) Jesus goes on to advance a very fundamental argument against worry. Worry is essentially distrust of God. Such a distrust is beyond comprehension in anyone who has learned to call God by the name of Father. Christians cannot worry because they believe in the love of God.

(6) Jesus goes on to advance two ways in which to defeat worry. The first is to seek first, to concentrate upon, the kingdom of God. To be in the kingdom and to do the will of God is one and the same thing (see Matthew 6:10). We know how in our own lives a great love can drive out every other concern. Such a love can inspire our work, intensify our study, purify our lives, dominate our whole being. It was Jesus' conviction that worry is banished when God becomes the dominating power of our lives.

(7) Last, Jesus says that worry can be defeated when we acquire the art of living one day at a time (verse 34). The Jews had a saying: 'Do not worry over tomorrow's evils, for you know not what today will bring forth. Perhaps tomorrow you will not be alive, and you will have worried for a world which will not be yours.' If each day is lived as it comes, if each task is done as it appears, then the sum of all the days is bound to be good. It is Jesus' advice that we should handle the demands of each day as it comes, without worrying about the unknown future and the things which may never happen.

The Sunday next before Lent
The Message and the Right to Give It
and The Mount of Transfiguration

2 Peter 1:16–21

Peter comes to the message which it was his great aim to bring to his people, concerning 'the power and the coming of our Lord Jesus Christ'. As we shall see quite clearly as we go on, the great aim of this letter is to bring people back to certainty with regard to the second coming of Jesus Christ. The heretics whom Peter is attacking no longer believed in it; it was so long delayed that people had begun to think it would never happen at all.

Such, then, was Peter's message. Having stated it, he goes on to speak of his right to state it – and he does something which is, at least at first sight, surprising. His right to speak is that he was with Jesus on the Mount of Transfiguration and that there he saw the glory and the honour which were given to him and heard the voice of God speak to him. That is to say, Peter uses the transfiguration story not as a foretaste of the resurrection of Jesus, as it is commonly viewed, but as a foretaste of the triumphant glory of the second coming. The transfiguration story is told in Matthew 17:1–8, Mark 9:2–8 and Luke 9:28–36. Was Peter right in seeing in it a foretaste of the second coming rather than a prefiguring of the resurrection?

There is one particularly significant thing about the transfiguration story. In all three gospels, it immediately follows the prophecy of Jesus that said that there were some standing there who would not pass from the world until they had seen the Son of Man coming in his kingdom (Matthew 16:28; Mark 9:1; Luke 9:27). That would certainly seem to indicate that the transfiguration and the second coming were in some way linked together. Whatever we may say, this much is certain: that Peter's great aim in this letter is to bring his people back to a living belief in the second coming of Christ, and he bases his right to do so on what he saw on the Mount of Transfiguration.

In verse 16, there is a very interesting word. Peter says: 'We were made *eyewitnesses* of his majesty.' The word he uses for *eyewitness* is *epoptēs*. In the Greek usage of Peter's day, this was a technical word. The practices of the mystery religions took the form of passion plays, in which the story of a god who lived, suffered, died and rose again was played out. It was only after a long course of instruction and preparation that the worshipper was finally allowed to be present at the passion play, and to be offered the experience of becoming one with the dying and rising God. When he reached this stage, he was an initiate, and the technical word to describe him was *epoptēs*; he was a privileged eyewitness of the experiences of God. So Peter says that Christians are eyewitnesses of the sufferings of Christ. With the eye of faith, they see the cross; in the experience of faith, they die with Christ to sin and rise to righteousness. Their faith has made them one with Jesus Christ in his death and in his risen life and power.

Matthew 17:1–9

The great moment of Caesarea Philippi recorded in chapter 16 was followed by the great hour on the Mount of Transfiguration. Let us first look at the scene where this time of glory came to Jesus and his three chosen disciples. There is a tradition which connects the transfiguration with Mount Tabor, but that is unlikely. The top of Mount Tabor was an armed fortress and a great castle; it seems almost impossible that the transfiguration could have happened on a mountain which was a fortress. Much more likely, the scene of the transfiguration was Mount Hermon. Hermon was fourteen miles from Caesarea Philippi. Hermon is 9,400 feet high, 11,000 feet above the level of the Jordan valley – so high that it can actually be seen from the Dead Sea, at the other end of Palestine, more than 100 miles away.

It was somewhere on the slopes of the beautiful and stately Mount Hermon that the transfiguration happened. It must have happened in the night. Luke tells us that the disciples were weighed down with sleep (Luke 9:32). It was the next day when Jesus and his disciples came back to the plain to find the father of the epileptic boy waiting for them (Luke 9:37). It was some time in the sunset, or the late evening, or the night, that this amazing vision took place. Why did Jesus go there? Why did he make this expedition to these lonely mountain slopes? Luke gives us the clue. He tells us that Jesus was praying (Luke 9:29). We must put ourselves, as far as we can, in Jesus' place. By this time, he was on the way to the cross. Of that he was quite sure; again and again he told his disciples that it was so. At Caesarea Philippi Jesus was facing one problem and dealing with one question. He was seeking to find out if there was anyone who had recognized him for who and what he was. That question was triumphantly answered, for Peter had grasped the great fact that Jesus could only be described as the Son of God. But there was an even greater question than that which Jesus had to solve before he set out on the last journey.

He had to make quite sure, sure beyond all doubt, that he was doing what God wished him to do. He had to make certain that it was indeed God's will that he should go to the cross. Jesus went up Mount Hermon to ask God: 'Am I doing your will in setting my face to go to Jerusalem?' Jesus went up Mount Hermon to listen for the voice of God. He would take no step without consulting God. How then could he take the biggest step of all without consulting him? Of everything, Jesus asked one question and only one question: 'Is it God's will for me?' And that is the question he was asking in the loneliness of the slopes of Hermon. It is one of the supreme differences between Jesus and us that Jesus always asked: 'What does *God* wish me to do?' We nearly always ask: 'What do *I* wish to do?' We often say that the unique characteristic of Jesus was that he was *sinless*. What do we mean by that? We mean precisely this, that Jesus had no will but the will of God. In Horatius Bonar's great words, the hymn of the Christian must always be:

Thy way, not mine, O Lord,
However dark it be!
Lead me by thine own hand;
Choose out the path for me.
I dare not choose my lot,
I would not if I might:
Choose thou for me, my God,
So shall I walk aright.
Not mine, not mine the choice
In things or great or small;
Be thou my Guide, my Strength,
My Wisdom and my All.

When Jesus had a problem, he did not seek to solve it only by the power of his own thought; he did not take it to others for human advice; he took it to the lonely place and to God.

The First Sunday of Lent
Ruin and Rescue *and* The Temptations of Christ

Romans 5:12–19

If we were to put the thought of this passage into one sentence, it would be this: 'By the sin of Adam, all human beings became sinners and were alienated from God; by the righteousness of Jesus Christ, all human beings became righteous and are restored to a right relationship with God.' Paul, in fact, said this very much more clearly in 1 Corinthians 15:21: 'For since death came through a human being, the resurrection of the dead has also come through a human being; for as all die in Adam, so all will be made alive in Christ.' There are two basic Jewish ideas in the light of which this passage must be read.

(1) There is the idea of *solidarity*. Jews never really thought of themselves as individuals but always as part of a clan, a family or a nation, apart from which the individual had no real existence. In the Old Testament, one vivid instance of this idea of solidarity is related in Joshua 7. At the siege of Jericho, Achan kept to himself certain spoils in direct defiance of the commandment of God that everything should be destroyed. The next stage in the campaign was the siege of Ai, which should have fallen without trouble. The assaults against it, however, failed disastrously. Why? Because Achan had sinned, and, as a result, the whole nation was branded as having sinned and was punished by God. Achan's sin was not one man's sin but the nation's. The nation was not a collection of individuals; it was a mass of people in solidarity. That is how Paul sees Adam. Adam was not an individual. He was one of all humanity; and, because of this, his sin was the sin of all.

Paul says that all sinned in Adam. If we are ever to understand Paul's thought here, we must be quite sure what he means, and we must be equally sure that he was serious. All through the history of Christian thinking, there have been efforts to interpret in different ways this conception of the connection between Adam's sin and that of all humanity.

(a) The passage has been taken to mean that 'each individual is his or her own Adam'. This really means that, just as Adam sinned, all have sinned, but that there is no real connection between the sin of Adam and the sin of humanity, other than that it could be said that Adam's sin is typical of the sin of all human beings.

(b) There is what has been called the legal interpretation. This would hold that Adam was *the representative* of the human race, and the human race shares in the deed of its representative. But representatives must be *chosen* by the people they represent; and in no sense can we say that of Adam.

(c) There is the interpretation that what we inherit from Adam is *the tendency* to sin. That is true enough, but that is not what Paul meant. It would not, in fact, suit his argument at all.

(d) The passage ought to be given what is called the realistic interpretation, namely that, because of the solidarity of the human race, all humanity actually sinned in Adam. This idea was not strange to a Jew; it was the actual belief of the Jewish thinkers. The writer of 2 Esdras is quite clear about it. 'For the first Adam, burdened with an evil heart, transgressed and was overcome, as were all who were descended from him' (3:21).

(2) The second basic idea is intimately connected with this in Paul's argument. *Death is the direct consequence of sin.* It was the Jewish belief that, if Adam had not sinned, human beings would have been immortal. The Book of Wisdom has it: 'God created us for incorruption, and made us in the image of his own eternity, but through the devil's envy death entered the world' (2:23). In Jewish thought, sin and death are integrally connected. This is what Paul

is getting at in the involved and difficult line of thought in verses 12–14. We may trace his thought there in a series of ideas.

(a) Adam sinned because he broke a direct commandment of God not to eat of the fruit of the forbidden tree – and, because he sinned, he died, although he was meant to be immortal.

(b) The law did not come until the time of Moses. Now, if there is no law, there can be no breaking of the law; that is to say, there can be no sin. Therefore, the men and women who lived between Adam and Moses did in fact commit sinful actions, but they could not be counted sinners, for the law did not yet exist.

(c) In spite of the fact that sin could not be counted against them, they still died. Death reigned over them, although they could not be accused of breaking a non-existent law.

(d) So, why did they die? It was because they had sinned in Adam. Their involvement in his sin caused their deaths, although there was no law for them to break. That, in fact, is Paul's proof that all humanity did sin in Adam.

So, we have extracted the essence of one side of Paul's thought. Because of this idea of the complete solidarity of humanity, all men and women literally sinned in Adam; and, because it is the consequence of sin, death reigned over them all.

But this very same conception, which can be used to produce so desperate a view of the human situation, can be used in reverse to fill it with a blaze of glory. Into this situation comes Jesus. To God, Jesus offered perfect goodness. And, just as all human beings were involved in Adam's sin, all are involved in Jesus' perfect goodness; and, just as Adam's sin was the cause of death, so Jesus' perfect goodness conquers death and gives to men and women life eternal. Paul's triumphant argument is that, as all humanity was in solidarity with Adam and was therefore condemned to death, so human beings are in solidarity with Christ and are therefore acquitted and given the gift of life. Even though the law has come and made sin

84

much more terrible, the grace of Christ overcomes the condemnation which the law must bring.

Matthew 4:1–11

Jesus went into the wilderness to be alone. His task had come to him; God had spoken to him; he must think how he was to attempt the task which God had given him to do; he had to get things straightened out before he started; and he had to be alone.

There are certain things we must note

(1) All three gospel writers seem to stress the immediacy with which the temptations followed the baptism of Jesus. As Mark has it: 'The Spirit *immediately* drove him out into the wilderness' (Mark 1:12).

It is one of the truths of life that after every great moment there comes a moment of reaction – and again and again it is in the reaction that the danger lies. That is what happened to Elijah. With magnificent courage, Elijah in all his loneliness faced and defeated the prophets of Baal on Mount Carmel (1 Kings 18:17–40). That was Elijah's greatest moment of courage and of witness. But the slaughter of the prophets of Baal provoked the wicked Jezebel to wrath, and she threatened Elijah's life. 'Then he was afraid; he got up and fled for his life, and came to Beer-sheba' (1 Kings 19:3). The man who had stood fearlessly against all comers is now fleeing for his life with terror at his heels. The moment of reaction had come.

It seems to be the law of life that just after our resistance power has been at its highest, it nosedives until it is at its lowest. The tempter carefully, subtly and skilfully chose his time to attack Jesus – but Jesus conquered him. We will do well to be specially on our guard whenever life has brought us to the heights, for it is just then that we are in gravest danger of the depths.

(2) We must not regard this experience of Jesus as an outward experience. It was a struggle that went on in his own heart and mind and soul. The proof is that there is no possible mountain from which all the kingdoms of the earth could be seen. This is an inner struggle.

It is through our inmost thoughts and desires that the tempter comes to us. His attack is launched in our own minds. It is true that that attack can be so real that we almost see the devil. To this day you can see the ink stain on the wall of Martin Luther's room in the Castle of Wartburg in Germany; Luther caused that ink stain by throwing his ink pot at the devil as he tempted him. But the very power of the devil lies in the fact that he breaches our defences and attacks us from within. He finds his allies and his weapons in our own inmost thoughts and desires.

(3) We must not think that in one campaign Jesus conquered the tempter forever and that the tempter never came to him again. The tempter spoke again to Jesus at Caesarea Philippi when Peter tried to dissuade him from taking the way to the cross, and when he had to say to Peter the very same words he had said to the tempter in the wilderness, 'Begone Satan' (cf. Matthew 16:23). At the end of the day, Jesus could say to his disciples: 'You are those who have stood by me in my trials' (Luke 22:28). And never in all history was there such a fight with temptation as Jesus waged in Gethsemane when the tempter sought to deflect him from the cross (Luke 22:42–4).

Eternal vigilance is the price of freedom. In the Christian warfare, there is no release. Sometimes people grow worried because they think that they should reach a stage when they are beyond temptation, a stage at which the power of the tempter is forever broken. Jesus never reached that stage. From the beginning to the end of the day, he had to fight his own battle against temptation; that is why he can help us to fight ours.

(4) One thing stands out about this story – the temptations are such as could only come to a person who had very special powers and who knew that he had them. The temptations which came to Jesus could only have come to one who knew that there were amazing things which he could do. We must always remember that again and again we are tempted *through our gifts*. The person who is gifted with charm will be tempted to use that charm 'to get away with anything'. Those who are gifted with the power of words will be tempted to use their command of words to produce glib excuses to justify their own conduct. The person with a vivid and sensitive imagination will undergo agonies of temptation that a more stolid person will never experience. Those with great gifts of mind will be tempted to use these gifts for themselves and not for others, to control and not to serve others. It is the grim fact of temptation that it is just where we are strongest that we must be forever on the watch.

(5) No one can ever read this story without remembering that its source must have been Jesus himself. In the wilderness, he was alone. No one was with him when this struggle was being fought out. And we know about it only because Jesus himself must have told his disciples about it. It is Jesus telling us his own spiritual autobiography.

We must always approach this story with a unique and special reverence, for in it Jesus is laying bare his inmost heart and soul. He is telling us what he went through. It is the most sacred of all stories, for in it Jesus is saying to us that he can help others who are tempted because he himself was tempted. He draws the veil from his own struggles to help us in our struggle.

The Second Sunday of Lent
The Father of the Faithful *and* The Man Who Came by Night

Romans 4:1–5, 13–17

Paul here speaks of Abraham for three reasons.

(1) The Jews regarded Abraham as the great founder of the race and the pattern of all that an individual should be. Very naturally, they ask: 'If all that you say is true, what was the special thing that was given to Abraham when God picked him out to be the ancestor of his special people? What makes him different from other people?' That is the question which Paul is going on to answer.

(2) Paul has been seeking to prove that what makes us right with God is not the performance of the works that the law lays down, but the simple trust of complete submission which takes God at his word and believes that he still loves us even when we have done nothing to deserve that love.

(3) Paul begins to speak about Abraham because he was a wise teacher who knew the human mind and the way it works. He has been talking about *faith*. Now, faith is an abstract idea. Many people find abstract ideas very hard to grasp. The wise teacher knows that every idea must be fleshed out, for the only way in which those who find such things difficult can grasp an abstract idea is to see it in action, embodied in a person. So Paul, in effect, says: 'I have been talking about faith. If you want to see what faith is, look at Abraham.'

To Abraham, God made a very great and wonderful promise. He promised that he would become a great nation, and that in him all families of the earth would be blessed (Genesis 12:2–3). In truth, the earth would be given to him as his inheritance. Now, that promise came to Abraham because of the faith that he showed towards God. It did not come because he piled up merit by doing works of the law. It was the outgoing of God's generous grace in answer to Abraham's absolute faith. The promise, as Paul saw it, was dependent on two things and two things only – the free grace of God and the perfect faith of Abraham. The Jews were still asking: 'How can anyone enter into the right relationship with God in order to inherit this great promise also?' Their answer was: 'This can be done by acquiring merit in the sight of God through doing works which the law prescribes.' People must do it by their own efforts. Paul saw with absolute clearness that this Jewish attitude *had completely destroyed the promise*. No one can fully keep the law; therefore, if the promise depends on keeping the law, it can never be fulfilled.

When Paul began to speak about Abraham, he was on ground that every Jew knew and understood. In their thoughts, Abraham held a unique position. He was the founder of the nation. He was the man to whom God had first spoken. He was the man who, in a unique way, had been chosen by God and who had heard and obeyed him. To Paul, the essence of his greatness was this. God had come to Abraham and told him to leave home and friends and relatives and livelihood, and had said to him: 'If you make this great venture of faith, you will become the father of a great nation.' And so Abraham had taken God at his word. He had not argued; he had not hesitated; he went out not knowing where he was to go (Hebrews 11:8). It was not the fact that Abraham had meticulously performed the demands of the law that put him into his special relationship with God, it was his complete trust in God and his complete willingness to abandon his life to him. That for Paul was faith, and it was Abraham's faith which made God regard him as a good man.

A few, but only a few, of the more advanced Rabbis believed that. There was a Rabbinic commentary which said: 'Abraham, our father, inherited this world and the world to come solely by the merit of faith whereby he believed in the Lord; for it is said: "And he believed in the Lord, and he accounted it to him for righteousness." '

But the great majority of the Rabbis held that, because he was the only righteous man of his generation, *therefore* he was chosen to be the ancestor of God's special people. The immediate answer is: 'But how could Abraham keep the law when he lived hundreds of years before it was given?' The Rabbis advanced the odd theory that he kept it by *intuition* or *anticipation*. 'He kept the law of the Most High,' says Sirach (Ecclesiasticus) (44:20–1), 'and entered into a covenant with him . . . Therefore the Lord assured him with an oath that the nations would be blessed through his offspring.'

The Rabbis were so in love with their theory of works that they insisted that it was because of his works that Abraham was chosen, although it meant that they had to argue that he knew the law by anticipation, since it had not yet come.

Paul's argument was – and he was unanswerably right – that Abraham entered into a right relationship with God, not because he did all kinds of legal works, but because he cast himself, just as he was, on God's promise. In the words of the hymn-writer F. W. Faber:

If our love were but more simple,
We should take him at his word;
And our lives would be all sunshine,
In the sweetness of our Lord.

It is the supreme discovery of the Christian life that we do not need to torture ourselves with a losing battle to earn God's love but rather need to accept in perfect trust the love which God offers to us. True, after that, we are bound under the life-long obligation to show ourselves worthy of that love. But we are no longer in the position of criminals seeking to obey an impossible law; we are, through love, able to offer all that we are to one who loved us when we did not deserve it.

John 3:1–17

When Nicodemus came to Jesus, he said that no one could help being impressed with the signs and wonders that he did. Jesus' answer was that it was not the signs and the wonders that were really important; the important thing was such a change in a person's inner life that it could only be described as a new birth.

When Jesus said that it was necessary to be *born anew*, Nicodemus misunderstood him, and the misunderstanding came from the fact that the word which the Revised Standard Version translates *anew*, the Greek word *anēthen*, has three different meanings. (1) It can mean *from the beginning, completely radically*. (2) It can mean *again*, in the sense of *for the second time*. (3) It can mean *from above*, and, therefore, *from God* (as in the New Revised Standard Version). It is not possible for us to get all these meanings into any English word; and yet all three of them are in the phrase *born anew*. To be born anew is to undergo such a radical change that it is like a new birth; it is to have something happen to the soul which can only be described as being born all over again; and the whole process is not a human achievement, because it comes from the grace and power of God.

When we read the story, it looks at first sight as if Nicodemus took the word *anew* with a crude literalism. How can anyone, he said, enter again into his mother's womb and be born a second time when he is already an old man? But there is more to Nicodemus' answer than that. In his heart, there was a great unsatisfied longing. It is as if he said with infinite, wistful yearning: 'You talk about being born anew; you talk about this radical, fundamental change which is so necessary. I know that it is *necessary*; but in my experience it is *impossible*. There is nothing I would like more; but you might as well tell me, a fully grown man, to enter into my mother's womb and be born all over again.' It is not the *desirability* of this change that Nicodemus questioned; that he knew only too well; it is the *possibility*. Nicodemus is up against the eternal problem, the problem of someone who wants to be changed and who cannot change himself.

This phrase *born anew*, this idea of *rebirth*, runs all through the New Testament. Peter talks about being *born anew* not of perishable seed, but of imperishable (1 Peter 1:23). James speaks of God giving us birth by the word of truth (James 1:18). The Letter to Titus speaks of *the water of rebirth* (Titus 3:5). Sometimes this same idea is spoken of as a death followed by a resurrection or a re-creation. Paul speaks of the Christian as dying with Christ and then rising to life anew (Romans 6:1–11). If any are in Christ, it is as if they had been *created* all over again (2 Corinthians 5:17). In Christ, there is a new creation (Galatians 6:15). The person who is at the first beginnings of the Christian faith is a child (Hebrews 5:12–14). All over the New Testament, this idea of *rebirth* and *re-creation* occurs.

What, then, does this rebirth mean for us? In the New Testament, and especially in the Fourth Gospel, there are four closely inter-related ideas. There is the idea of rebirth; there is the idea of the kingdom of heaven, into which people cannot enter unless they are reborn; there is the idea of being children of God; and there is the idea of eternal life. These great related conceptions – entry into the kingdom of heaven, becoming children of God and eternal life – are all dependent on and are the products of perfect obedience to the will of God. It is just here that the idea of being *reborn* comes in. It is what links all these three conceptions together. It is quite clear that, as we are and in our own strength, we are quite unable to render to God this perfect obedience; it is only when God's grace enters into us and takes possession of us and changes us that we can give to him the reverence and the devotion we ought to give. It is through Jesus Christ that we are reborn; it is when he enters into possession of our hearts and lives that the change comes. When that happens, we are born of *water and the Spirit*.

There are two thoughts there. *Water* is the symbol of cleansing. When Jesus takes possession of our lives, when we love him with all our heart, the sins of the past are forgiven and forgotten. *The Spirit* is the symbol of *power*. When Jesus takes possession of our lives, it is not only that the past is forgotten and forgiven; if that were all, we might well proceed to make the same mess of life all over again; but into life there enters a new power which enables us to be what by ourselves we could never be and to do what by ourselves we could never do. Water and the Spirit stand for the cleansing and the strengthening power of Christ, which wipes out the past and gives victory in the future.

Finally, in this passage, John lays down a great law. That which is born of the flesh is flesh, and that which is born of the Spirit is spirit. Human beings by themselves are flesh, and their power is limited to what the flesh can do. By themselves, they cannot be other than defeated and frustrated; that we know only too well; it is the universal fact of human experience. But the very essence of the Spirit is power and life which are beyond human power and human life; and when the Spirit takes possession of us, the defeated life of human nature becomes the victorious life of God.

To be born again is to be changed in such a way that it can be described only as rebirth and re-creation. The change comes when we love Jesus and allow him into our hearts. Then we are forgiven for the past and armed by the Spirit for the future; then we can truly accept the will of God. And then we become citizens of the kingdom; then we become children of God; then we enter into eternal life, which is the very life of God.

The Third Sunday of Lent
The Final Proof of Love *and* The Living Water

Romans 5:1–11

The fact that Jesus Christ died for us is the final proof of God's love. It would be difficult enough to get someone to die for a just person; it might be possible to persuade someone to die for some great and good principle; any one of us might have the greater love that would make us lay down our life for a friend. But the wonder of Jesus Christ is that he died for us when we are sinners and in a state of hostility to God. Love can go no further than that.

Rita Snowdon relates an incident from the life of T. E. Lawrence, better known as Lawrence of Arabia. In 1915, he was journeying across the desert with some Arabs. Things were desperate. Food was almost gone, and water was at its last drop. Their hoods were over their heads to shelter them from the wind, which was like a flame and full of the stinging sand of the sandstorm. Suddenly, someone said: 'Look, Jasmin's camel has no rider. His rifle is strapped to the saddle, but Jasmin is not there.' A second said: 'Someone has shot him on the march.' A third said: 'He is not strong in the head, perhaps he is lost in a mirage; he is not strong in the body, perhaps he has fainted and fallen off his camel.' Then the first said: 'What does it matter? Jasmin was not worth anything.' And the Arabs hunched themselves up on their camels and rode on. But Lawrence turned and rode back the way he had come. Alone, in the blazing heat, at the risk of his life, he went back. After an hour and a half's ride, he saw something against the sand. It was Jasmin, blind and mad with heat and thirst, being murdered by the desert. Lawrence lifted him up on his camel, gave him some of the last drops of precious water, and slowly plodded back to his company. When he came up to them, the Arabs looked in amazement. 'Here is Jasmin,' they said, 'Jasmin, not worth anything, saved at his own risk by Lawrence, our lord.' That is a parable. It was not good people Christ died to save but sinners, not God's friends but those who were hostile to him.

Then Paul goes a step further. Through Jesus, our *status* with God was changed. Sinners though we were, we were put into a right relationship with God. *But that is not enough.* Not only our *status* must be changed but also our *state*. The saved sinner cannot go on being a sinner, but must become good. Christ's death changed our *status*; his risen life changes our *state*. He is not dead but alive; he is with us always to help us and guide us, to fill us with his strength in order to overcome temptation, to clothe our lives with something of his radiance. Jesus begins by putting sinners into a right relationship with God even when they are still sinners; he goes on, by his grace, to enable them to quit their sin and become good. There are technical names for these things. The change of our *status* is *justification*; that is where the whole saving process begins. The change of our *state* is *sanctification*; that is where the saving process goes on, and never ends, until we see him face to face and are like him.

There is one thing to note here of quite extraordinary importance. Paul is quite clear that the whole saving process, the coming of Christ and the death of Christ, is the proof of *God's* love. Sometimes it is stated as if on the one side there was a gentle and loving Christ, and on the other an angry and vengeful God; and as if Christ had done something which changed God's attitude to men and women. Nothing could be further from the truth. The whole matter springs from the love of God. Jesus did not come to change God's attitude; he came to show what it is and always was. He came to prove beyond question that God is love.

John 4:5-42

We have to note that this conversation with the Samaritan woman follows exactly the same pattern as the conversation with Nicodemus. Just as Nicodemus did, the woman took the words of Jesus quite literally when she was meant to understand them spiritually. It was *living* water of which Jesus spoke. In ordinary language, to a Jew, *living* water was *running* water. It was the water of the running stream as against the water of the stagnant cistern or pool. This well was not a springing well, but a well into which the water percolated from the subsoil. To a Jew, *running, living* water from the stream was always better. So the woman is saying: 'You are offering me pure stream water. Where are you going to get it?'

She goes on to speak of 'our father Jacob'. The Jews would, of course, have strenuously denied that Jacob was the father of the Samaritans, but it was part of the Samaritan claim that they were descended from Joseph, the son of Jacob, by way of Ephraim and Manasseh. The woman is in effect saying to Jesus: 'This is blasphemous talk. Jacob, our great ancestor, when he came here, had to dig this well to gain water for his family and his cattle. Are you claiming to be able to get fresh, running stream water? If you are, you are claiming to be wiser and more powerful than Jacob. That is a claim that no one has any right to make.'

The Jews had another way of using the word *water*. They often spoke of the *thirst* of the soul for God; and they often spoke of quenching that thirst with *living water*. Jesus was not using terms that were bound to be misunderstood; he was using terms that anyone with spiritual insight should have understood. In the Book of Revelation, that promise is: 'To the thirsty I will give water as a gift from the spring of the water of life' (Revelation 21:6). The Lamb is to lead them to springs of living waters (Revelation 7:17). The promise was that the chosen people would draw water with joy from the wells of salvation (Isaiah 12:3). The psalmist spoke of his soul being thirsty for the living God (Psalm 42:1). God's promise was: 'I will pour water on the thirsty land' (Isaiah 44:3). The summons was that everyone who was thirsty should come to the waters and freely drink (Isaiah 55:1). Ezekiel had had his vision of the river of life (Ezekiel 47:1–12). In the new world, there would be a cleansing fountain opened (Zechariah 13:1). The waters would go forth from Jerusalem (Zechariah 14:8).

Sometimes the Rabbis identified this living water with the wisdom of the law; sometimes they identified it with nothing less than the Holy Spirit of God. All Jewish pictorial religious language was full of this idea of the thirst of the soul which could be quenched only with the living water which was the gift of God. But the woman chose to understand this with an almost crude literalism. She was blind because she would not see.

Jesus went on to make a still more startling statement that he could give her living water which would banish her thirst forever. The point is that again the woman took this literally; but in point of fact it was nothing less than a messianic claim. In the prophetic vision of the age to come, the age of God, the promise was: 'They shall not hunger or thirst' (Isaiah 49:10). It was with God and none other that the living fountain of the all quenching water existed. 'With you is the fountain of life,' the psalmist had cried (Psalm 36:9). It is from the very throne of God that the river of life is to flow (Revelation 22:1). It is in the messianic age that the parched ground is to become a pool and the thirsty ground springs of water (Isaiah 35:7). When Jesus spoke about bringing to men and women the water which quenches thirst forever, he was doing no less than stating that he was the Anointed One of God who was to bring in the new age.

Again the woman did not see it. And I think that this time she spoke with a jest, as if humouring one who was a little mad. 'Give me this water,' she said, 'so that I will never be thirsty again and

97

will not have to walk to the well day after day.' She was jesting with a kind of humouring contempt about eternal things.

At the heart of all this, there is the fundamental truth that in the human heart there is a thirst for something that only Jesus Christ can satisfy. In each of us, there is a nameless unsatisfied longing, a vague discontent, something lacking, a frustration. William Wordsworth, in the 'Ode on the Intimations of Immortality', speaks of

> Those obstinate questionings
> Of sense and outward things,
> Fallings from us, vanishings;
> Blank misgivings of a creature
> Moving about in worlds not realized.

Augustine talks about 'our hearts being restless till they find rest in thee'.

Part of the human situation is that we cannot find happiness out of the things that the human situation has to offer. As Robert Browning expressed it in 'Bishop Blougram's Apology':

> Just when we're safest, there's a sunset touch,
> A fancy from a flower-bell, someone's death,
> A chorus ending from Euripides –
> And that's enough for fifty hopes and fears
> As old and new at once as Nature's self
> To rap and knock and enter in our soul.

We are never safe from the longing for eternity which God has put into the human soul. There is a thirst which only Jesus Christ can satisfy.

The Fourth Sunday of Lent
The Children of Light *and* Light for Blind Eyes

Ephesians 5:8–14

Paul saw the non-Christian life as life in the dark, and the Christian life as life in the light. So vividly does he wish to put this that he does not say that those who are not Christians are children of the dark and the Christians children of the light; he says the non-Christians *are* dark and the Christians *are* light. He has certain things to say about the light which Jesus Christ brings to us.

(1) The light produces good fruit. It produces benevolence, righteousness and truth. Benevolence (*agathôsunê*) is a certain generosity of spirit. The Greeks themselves defined righteousness (*dikaiosunê*) as 'giving to men and to God that which is their due'. Truth (*alêtheia*) is not in New Testament thought simply an intellectual thing to be grasped with the mind; it is moral truth, not only something to be *known* but something to be *done*. The light which Christ brings makes us useful citizens of this world; it makes us men and women who never fail in duty, human or divine; it makes us strong to do what we know is true.

(2) The light enables us to discriminate between what is well-pleasing and what is not pleasing to God. It is in the light of Christ that all motives and all actions must be tested. In the bazaars of the Middle East, the shops are often simply little covered enclosures with no windows. Someone might want to buy a piece of silk or an article of beaten brass. Before buying it, the buyer takes it out to the street and holds it up to the sun, so that the light might reveal any flaws which happen to be in it. It is the Christian's duty to

expose every action, every decision and every motive to the light of Christ.

(3) The light exposes whatever is evil. The best way to rid the world of any evil is to drag it into the light. As long as something is being done in secret, it goes on; but when it is taken into the light of day, it dies a natural death. The surest way to cleanse the depths of our own hearts and the practices of any society in which we happen to be involved is to expose them to the light of Christ.

(4) Finally, Paul says: 'Everything which is illuminated becomes light.' What he seems to mean is that light has in itself a cleansing quality. In our own time, we know that many diseases have been conquered simply by letting the sunlight in. The light of Christ is like that. We must never think of the light of Christ as only condemnatory; it is a healing thing too.

Paul concludes this passage with a quotation in poetry. In James Moffatt's translation, it runs: 'Wake up, O sleeper, and rise from the dead; so Christ will shine upon you.'

Paul introduces the quotation as if everybody knew it, but no one now knows where it came from. There are certain interesting suggestions. Almost certainly, being in the form of poetry, it is a fragment of an early Christian hymn. It may well have been part of a baptismal hymn. In the early Church, nearly all baptisms were of adults, confessing their faith as they came out of the old religion into Christianity. Perhaps these were the lines which were sung as they rose out of the water, to symbolize the passage from the dark sleep of the past life to the awakened life of the Christian way.

Alternatively, it has been suggested that these lines are part of a hymn, which was supposed to give the summons of the archangel when the last trumpet sounded over the earth. Then would come the great awakening when men and women rose from the sleep of death to receive the eternal life of Christ. These things are speculations; but it seems certain that, when we read these lines, we are reading a fragment of one of the first hymns the Christian Church ever sang.

John 9:1–41

In this passage, there are two great eternal principles.

(1) Jesus does not try to follow up or to explain the connection of sin and suffering. He says that this man's affliction came to him to give an opportunity of showing what God can do. There are two senses in which that is true.

(a) For John, the miracles are always a sign of the glory and the power of God. The writers of the other gospels had a different point of view, and regarded them as a demonstration of the compassion of Jesus. When Jesus looked on the hungry crowd he had *compassion* on them, because they were as sheep not having a shepherd (Mark 6:34). When the leper came with his desperate request for cleansing, Jesus was *moved with pity* (Mark 1:41). It is often urged that in this the Fourth Gospel is quite different from the others. Surely there is no real contradiction here. It is simply two ways of looking at the same thing. At its heart is the supreme truth that the glory of God lies in his compassion, and that he never so fully reveals his glory as when he reveals his pity.

(b) But there is another sense in which the man's suffering shows what God can do. Affliction, sorrow, pain, disappointment and loss are always opportunities for displaying God's grace. First, it enables the sufferer to show God in action. When trouble and disaster fall upon someone who does not know God, that person may well collapse; but when they fall on someone who walks with God, they bring out the strength and the beauty, and the endurance and the nobility, which are within a person's heart when God is there. Any kind of suffering is an opportunity to demonstrate the glory of God in our own lives. Second, by helping those who are in trouble or in pain, we can demonstrate to others the glory of God. The American missionary Frank Laubach has the great thought that when Christ, who is the Way, enters into us, 'we become part of the Way. God's highway runs straight through us.' When we spend ourselves to help those in trouble, in distress, in pain, in sorrow, in affliction, God is using us as the highway by which he sends his help into the lives of his people. To help another person in need is to manifest the glory of God, for it is to show what God is like.

(2) Jesus goes on to say that he and all his followers must do God's work while there is time to do it. God gave the day for work and the night for rest; the day comes to an end, and the time for work is also ended. For Jesus, it was true that he had to press on with God's work in the day, for the night of the cross lay close ahead. But it is true for everyone. We are given only so much time. Whatever we are to do must be done within it. We should never put things off until another time, for another time may never come. Christians have a duty to fill the time they have – and no one knows how much that will be – with the service of God and of others. There is no more poignant sorrow than the tragic discovery that it is too late to do something which we might have done. But there is another opportunity we may miss. Jesus said: 'So long as I am in the world, I am the light of the world.' When Jesus said that, he did not mean that the time of his life and work were limited but that our opportunity of laying hold on him is limited. There comes to each one of us a chance to accept Christ as our Saviour, our Master and our Lord; and if that opportunity is not seized it may well never come back. God is always saying to us: '*Now* is the time.' It is not that the power of Jesus grows less, or that his light grows dim; it is that if we put off the great decision we become increasingly less able to take it as the years go on. Work must be done, decisions must be taken, while it is day, before the night falls.

John finishes this story with two of his favourite thoughts.

(1) Jesus came into this world for judgement. Whenever people are confronted with Jesus, they at once pass a judgement on them-

selves. If they see in Jesus nothing to desire, nothing to admire, nothing to love, then they have condemned themselves. If they see in Jesus something to wonder at, something to respond to, something to reach out to, then they are on the way to God. Those who are conscious of their own blindness, and who long to see better and to know more, are men and women whose eyes can be opened and who can be led more and more deeply into the truth. Those people who think they know it all, those who do not realize that they cannot see, are men and women who are truly blind and beyond hope and help. Only those who realize their own weakness can become strong. Only those who realize their own blindness can learn to see. Only those who realize their own sin can be forgiven.

(2) The more knowledge people have, the more they are to be condemned if they do not recognize the good when they see it. If the Pharisees had been brought up in ignorance, they could not have been condemned. Their condemnation lay in the fact that they knew so much and claimed to see so well, and yet failed to recognize God's Son when he came. The law that responsibility is the other side of privilege is written into life.

The Fifth Sunday of Lent
Two Principles of Life *and*
The Resurrection and the Life

Romans 8:6–11

Paul is drawing a contrast between two kinds of life.

(1) There is the life which is dominated by sinful human nature; whose focus and centre is self; whose only law is its own desires; which takes what it likes where it likes. In different people, that life will be differently described. It may be passion-controlled, or lust-controlled, or pride-controlled, or ambition-controlled. Its characteristic is its absorption in the things that human nature without Christ sets its heart upon.

(2) There is the life that is dominated by the Spirit of God. As men and women live in the air, they live in Christ, never separated from him. As they breathe in the air and the air fills them, so Christ fills them. They have no mind of their own; Christ is their mind. They have no desires of their own; the will of Christ is their only law. They are Spirit-controlled, Christ-controlled, God-focused.

These two lives are going in diametrically opposite directions. The life that is dominated by the desires and activities of sinful human nature is on the way to death. In the most literal sense, there is no future in it – because it is getting further and further away from God. To allow the things of the world completely to dominate life is self-extinction; it is spiritual suicide. By living it, people are making themselves totally unfit ever to stand in the presence of God. They are hostile to him, resentful of his law and his control. God is not their friend but their enemy, and no one ever won the last battle against him.

The Spirit-controlled life, the Christ-centred life, the God-focused life is daily coming nearer heaven even when it is still on earth. It is a life which is such a steady progress to God that the final transition of death is only a natural and inevitable stage on the way. It is like Enoch, who walked with God and God took him (cf. Genesis 5:24). As the child said: 'Enoch was a man who went for walks with God – and one day he didn't come back.'

No sooner has Paul said this than an inevitable objection strikes him. Someone may object: 'You say that those who are Spirit-controlled are on the way to life; but in point of fact everyone must die. Just what do you mean?' Paul's answer is this. All die because they are involved in the human situation. Sin came into this world, and with sin came death, the consequence of sin. Inevitably, therefore, all people die; but those who are Spirit-controlled and whose hearts are Christ-occupied die only to rise again. Paul's basic thought is that every Christian is indissolubly one with Christ. Now, Christ died and rose again; and those who are one with Christ are one with death's conqueror and share in that victory. Spirit-controlled, Christ-possessed men and women are on the way to life; death is only an inevitable interlude that has to be passed through on the way.

John 11:1–45

When Martha met Jesus, her heart spoke through her lips. Here is one of the most human speeches in all the Bible, for Martha spoke, half with a reproach that she could not keep back, and half with a faith that nothing could shake. 'If you had been here,' she said, 'my brother would not have died.' Through the words, we read her mind. Martha would have liked to say: 'When you got our message, why didn't you come at once? And now you have left it too late.' No sooner are the words out than there follow the words of faith, faith which defied the facts and defied experience: 'Even yet,' she said with a kind of desperate hope, 'even yet, I know that God will give you whatever you ask.' Jesus said: 'Your brother will rise again.' Martha answered: 'I know quite well that he will rise in the general resurrection on the last day.'

When Martha declared her belief in the orthodox Jewish belief in the life to come, Jesus suddenly said something which brought to that belief a new vividness and a new meaning. 'I am the resurrection and the life,' he said. 'He who believes in me will live even if he has died; and everyone who lives and believes in me shall never die.' What exactly did he mean? One thing is clear – Jesus was not thinking in terms of physical life; for, speaking physically, it is not true that those who believe in him will never die. Christians experience physical death just like other people. We must look for a more than physical meaning.

(1) Jesus was thinking of the death of sin. He was saying: 'Even if people are dead in sin, even if, through their sins, they have lost all that makes life worth calling life, I can make them alive again.' In point of historical fact, that is abundantly true. We have and example in the Japanese criminal Tokichi Ishii. Ishii had an almost unparalleled criminal record. He had murdered men, women and children in the most brutal way. Anyone who stood in his way was pitilessly eliminated. Now he was in prison awaiting death. While in prison, he was visited by two Canadian women who tried to talk to him through the bars, but he only glowered at them like a caged and savage animal. In the end they abandoned the attempt; but they gave him a Bible, hoping that it might succeed where they had failed. He began to read it, and, having started, could not stop. He read on until he came to the story of the crucifixion. He came to the words: 'Father, forgive them, for they know not what they do,' and these words broke him. 'I stopped,' he said. 'I was stabbed to the heart, as if pierced by a five-inch nail. Shall I call it the love of Christ? Shall I call it his compassion? I do not know what to

call it. I only know that I believed, and my hardness of heart was changed.' Later, when the condemned man went to the gallows, he was no longer the hardened, surly brute he had once been, but a smiling, radiant man. The murderer had been born again; Christ had brought Tokichi Ishii to life.

It does not need to be so dramatic as that. People can become so selfish that they are dead to the needs of others. They can become so insensitive that they are dead to the feelings of others. They can become so involved in the petty dishonesties and the petty disloyalties of life that they are dead to honour. People can become so hopeless that they are filled with an inertia, which is spiritual death. Jesus Christ can resurrect them. The witness of history is that he has resurrected millions and millions of people like them, and his touch has not lost its ancient power.

(2) Jesus was also thinking of the life to come. He brought into life the certainty that death is not the end. The last words of Edward the Confessor were: 'Weep not, I shall not die; and as I leave the land of the dying I trust to see the blessings of the Lord in the land of the living.' We call this world *the land of the living*; but it would in fact be more correct to call it *the land of the dying*. Through Jesus Christ, we know that we are journeying not to the sunset but to the sunrise; we know that death is a gate on the skyline. In the most real sense, we are not on our way to death but on our way to life.

How does this happen? It happens when we believe in Jesus Christ. What does that mean? To believe in Jesus means to accept everything that Jesus said as absolutely true, and to stake our lives upon that in perfect trust. When we do that, we enter into two new relationships.

(1) We enter into a new relationship with God. When we believe that God is as Jesus told us that he is, then we become absolutely sure of his love; we become absolutely sure that he is above all a redeeming God. The fear of death vanishes, for death means going to the great lover of human souls.

(2) We enter into a new relationship with life. When we accept Jesus' way, when we take his commands as our laws, and when we realize that he is there to help us to live as he has commanded, life becomes a new thing. It is clad with a new loveliness, a new charm, a new strength. And when we accept Christ's way as our way, life becomes so lovely a thing that we cannot conceive of it ending incomplete. When we believe in Jesus, when we accept what he says about God and about life and stake everything on it, in truth we are resurrected, for we are freed from the fear which is characteristic of the godless life; we are freed from the frustration which is characteristic of the sin-ridden life; we are freed from the futility of the Christless life. Life is raised from sin's death and becomes so rich that it cannot die but must find in death only the transition to a higher life.

Palm Sunday
Humiliation and Exaltation *and*
The Triumph of the End

Philippians 2:5–11

In many ways, this is the greatest and most moving passage Paul
ever wrote about Jesus. It states a favourite thought of his. The essence of it is in the simple statement Paul made to the Corinthians
that, although Jesus was rich, yet for our sakes he became poor
(2 Corinthians 8:9). Here, that simple idea is stated with a fullness
which is without parallel. Paul is pleading with the Philippians to
live in harmony, to lay aside their discords, to shed their personal
ambitions and their pride and their desire for prominence and
prestige, and to have in their hearts that humble, selfless desire to
serve, which was the essence of the life of Christ. His final and
unanswerable appeal is to point to the example of Jesus Christ.

It is always to be remembered that, when Paul thought and
spoke about Jesus, his interest and his intention were never primar-
ily intellectual and speculative; they were always practical. To him,
theology and action were always bound together. Any system of
thought must become a way of life. In many ways, this passage is
one which extends to the very limits of theological thinking in the
New Testament; but its aim was to persuade the Philippians to live
a life in which disunity, discord and personal ambition had no place.
So, Paul says of Jesus that he humbled himself and became obedient to the point of death, even death on a cross. The great characteristics of Jesus' life were humility, obedience and self-renunciation. He wanted not to dominate men and women but only to serve
them; he wanted not his own way but only God's way; he wanted
not to exalt himself but only to renounce all his glory for the sake

of the world. Again and again, the New Testament is sure that only those who humble themselves will be exalted (Matthew 23:12; Luke 14:11, 18:14). If humility, obedience and self-renunciation were the supreme characteristics of the life of Jesus, they must also be the hallmarks of Christians. Selfishness, self-seeking and self-display destroy our likeness to Christ and our fellowship with each other.

But the self-renunciation of Jesus Christ brought him the greater glory. It made certain that one day, sooner or later, every living creature in all the universe – in heaven, in earth and even in hell – would worship him. It is to be carefully noted where that worship comes from. *It comes from love.* Jesus won the hearts of men and women, not by forcing them through his power, but by showing them a love they could not resist. At the sight of this person who set aside his glory for all people and loved them to the extent of dying for them on a cross, human hearts are melted and human resistance is broken down. When people worship Jesus Christ, they fall at his feet in wondering love. They do not say: 'I cannot resist a might like that' but, as Isaac Watts expressed it in the hymn 'When I survey the wondrous cross', 'Love so amazing, so divine, demands my life, my soul, my all.' Worship is founded not on fear but on love.

Further, Paul says that, as a consequence of his sacrificial love, God gave Jesus the name which is above every name. One of the common biblical ideas is the giving of a new name to mark a new stage in a person's life. Abram became Abraham when he received the promise of God (Genesis 17:5). Jacob became Israel when God entered into the new relationship with him (Genesis 32:28). The promise of the risen Christ to both Pergamos and to Philadelphia is the promise of a new name (Revelation 2:17, 3:12).

What then is the new name given to Jesus Christ? We cannot be quite certain what exactly was in Paul's mind, but most likely the new name is *Lord*. The great title by which Jesus came to be known in the early Church was *kurios*, *Lord*, which has an illuminating history. (1) It began by meaning *master* or *owner*. (2) It became the official title of the Roman emperors. (3) It became the title of the Greek and Roman gods. (4) It was the word by which the Hebrew *Yahweh* was translated in the Greek version of the Hebrew Scriptures. So, when Jesus was called *kurios*, *Lord*, it meant that he was the Master and the Owner of all life; he was the King of kings; he was the Lord in a way in which the gods of the old religions and the idols could never be; he was nothing less than divine.

Verse 11 is one of the most important verses in the New Testament. In it, we read that the aim of God is a day when every tongue will confess that *Jesus Christ is Lord*. These four words were the first creed that the Christian Church ever had. To be a Christian was to confess that Jesus Christ is Lord (cf. Romans 10:9). This was a simple creed, yet all-embracing. Perhaps we would do well to go back to it. Later, people tried to define more closely what it meant, and argued and quarrelled about it, calling each other heretics and fools. But it is still true that anyone who can say 'For me, Jesus Christ is Lord' is a Christian. If we can say that, we mean that for us Jesus Christ is unique and that we are prepared to give him an obedience we are prepared to give no one else. We may not be able to put into words who and what we believe Jesus to be; but, as long as there is in our hearts this wondering love and in our lives this unquestioning obedience, we are indeed Christians, because Christianity consists less in the mind's understanding than it does in the heart's love.

Matthew 27:11–54

As we read the story of the crucifixion, everything seems to have been happening very quickly; but in reality the hours were slipping past. It is Mark who is most precise in his note of time. He tells us that Jesus was crucified at the third hour, that is at 9 am (Mark 15:25), and that he died at the ninth hour, that is at 3 pm (Mark 15:34). That is to say, Jesus hung on the cross for six hours. For him the agony was mercifully brief, for it often happened that criminals hung upon their crosses for days before death came to them.

In verse 46, we have what must be the most staggering sentence in the gospel record, the cry of Jesus: 'My God, my God, why have you forsaken me?' That is a saying before which we must bow in reverence, and yet at the same time we must try to understand. There have been many attempts to penetrate behind its mystery; we can look at only three.

(1) It is strange how Psalm 22 runs through the whole crucifixion narrative; and this saying is actually the first verse of that Psalm. Later on, it says: 'All who see me mock at me; they make mouths at me, they shake their heads; "Commit your cause to the Lord; let him deliver – let him rescue the one in whom he delights!"' (Psalm 22: 7–8). Still further on, we read: 'They divide my clothes among themselves, and for my clothing they cast lots' (Psalm 22:18). Psalm 22 is interwoven with the whole crucifixion story. It has been suggested that Jesus was, in fact, repeating that Psalm to himself; and, though it begins in complete dejection, it ends in soaring triumph – 'From you comes my praise in the great congregation . . . For dominion belongs to the Lord, and he rules over the nations' (Psalm 22:25–8). So it is suggested that Jesus was repeating Psalm 22 on the cross, as a picture of his own situation, and as a song of his trust and confidence, in the full knowledge that it began in the depths, but that it finished on the heights.

It is an attractive suggestion; but on a cross a man does not repeat poetry to himself, even the poetry of a psalm; and besides that, the whole atmosphere is one of unrelieved tragedy.

(2) It is suggested that in that moment the weight of the world's sin fell upon the heart and the being of Jesus; that that was the moment when he who knew no sin was made sin for us

(2 Corinthians 5:21); and that the penalty which he bore for us was the inevitable separation from God which sin brings. No one may say that that is not true; but, if it is, it is a mystery which we can only state and at which we can only wonder.

(3) It may be that there is something – if we may put it so – more human here. It seems to me that Jesus would not be Jesus unless he had plumbed the uttermost depths of human experience. In human experience, as life goes on and as bitter tragedy enters into it, there come times when we feel that God has forgotten us; when we are immersed in a situation beyond our understanding and feel bereft even of God. It seems to me that that is what happened to Jesus here. In the garden Jesus knew only that he had to go on, because to go on was God's will, and he must accept what even he could not fully understand. Here we see Jesus plumbing the uttermost depths of the human situation, so that there might be no place that we might go where he has not been before.

Those who listened did not understand. Some thought he was calling on Elijah; they must have been Jews. One of the great gods of the pagans was the sun – Helios. A cry to the sun god would have begun 'Helie!' and it has been suggested that the soldiers may have thought that Jesus was crying to the greatest of the pagan gods. In any event, his cry was to the watchers a mystery.

But here is the point. It would have been a terrible thing if Jesus had died with a cry like that upon his lips – but he did not. The narrative goes on to tell us that, when he shouted with a great shout, he gave up his spirit. That great shout left its mark upon people's minds. It is in every one of the gospels (Matthew 27:50; Mark 15:37; Luke 23:46). But there is one gospel which goes further. John tells us that Jesus died with a shout: 'It is finished' (John 19:30). *It is finished* is in English three words; but in Greek it is one – *Tetelestai* – as it would also be in Aramaic. And *tetelestai* is the victor's shout; it is the cry of all those who have completed their task; it is the cry of those who have won through the struggle; it is the cry of those who have come out of the dark into the glory of the light, and who have grasped the crown. So, Jesus died a victor with a shout of triumph on his lips.

Here is the precious thing. Jesus passed through the uttermost abyss, and then the light broke. If we too cling to God, even when there seems to be no God, desperately and invincibly clutching the remnants of our faith, quite certainly the dawn will break and we will win through. True victory comes to those who refuse to believe that God has forgotten them, even when every fibre of their being feels that they have been forsaken. Victory comes to those who will never let go of their faith, even when they feel that its last grounds are gone. Victory comes to those who have been beaten to the depths and still hold on to God, for that is what Jesus did.

Easter Day
The Heart of the Gospel *and* The Great Discovery

Acts 10:34–43

It is clear that we have here only the barest summary of what Peter said to Cornelius, which makes it all the more important because it gives us the very essence of the first preaching about Jesus.

(1) Jesus was sent by God and equipped by him with the spirit and with power. Jesus, therefore, is God's gift to us. Often, we make the mistake of thinking in terms of an angry God who had to be pacified by something a gentle Jesus did. The early preachers never preached that. To them, the very coming of Jesus was due to the love of God.

(2) Jesus exercised a ministry of healing. It was his great desire to banish pain and sorrow from the world.

(3) They crucified him. Once again, for those who can read between the lines, the sheer horror in the crucifixion is stressed. That is what human sin can do.

(4) He rose again. The power which was in Jesus was not to be defeated. It could conquer the worst that people could do, and in the end it could conquer death.

(5) Christian preachers and teachers are witnesses of the resurrection. To them, Jesus is not a figure in a book or about whom they have heard. He is a living presence whom they have met.

(6) The result of all this is forgiveness of sins and a new relationship with God. through Jesus, the friendship which should always have existed between men and women and God, but which sin interrupted, has dawned upon the world.

John 20:1–18

When Mary arrived at the tomb she was amazed and shocked. Tombs in ancient times were not commonly closed by doors. In front of the opening was a groove in the ground; and in the groove ran a stone, circular like a cartwheel; and the stone was wheeled into position to close the opening. Further, Matthew tells us that the authorities had actually sealed the stone to make sure that no one would move it (Matthew 27:66). Mary was astonished to find it removed. Two things may have entered her mind. She may have thought that the Jews had taken away Jesus' body; that, not satisfied with killing him on a cross, they were inflicting further indignities on him. But there were ghoulish creatures who made it their business to rob tombs; and Mary may have thought that this had happened here.

It was a situation Mary felt that she could not face herself; so she returned to the city to seek out Peter and John. Mary is the supreme instance of one who went on loving and believing even when she could not understand; and that is the love and the belief which in the end finds glory.

One of the illuminating things in this story is that Peter was still the acknowledged leader of the apostolic band. It was to him that Mary went. In spite of his denial of Jesus – and a story like that would not be long in being broadcast – Peter was still the leader. We often talk of Peter's weakness and instability, but there must have been something outstanding about a man who could face his fellow men after that disastrous crash into cowardice; there must have been something about a man whom others were prepared to accept as leader even after that. His moment's weakness must never blind us to the moral strength and stature of Peter, and to the fact that he was a born leader.

So, then, it was to Peter and John that Mary went; and they immediately set out for the tomb. They went at a run; and John, who must have been a younger man than Peter since he lived on until the end of the century, outstripped Peter in this breathless race. When they came to the tomb, John looked in but went no further. Peter with typical impulsiveness not only looked in, but went in. For the moment, Peter was only amazed at the empty tomb; but things began to happen in John's mind. If someone had removed Jesus' body, if tomb-robbers had been at work, why should they leave the grave-clothes?

Then something else struck him – the grave-clothes were not dishevelled and disarranged. They were lying there *still in their folds* – that is what the Greek means – the clothes for the body where the body had been; the napkin where the head had lain. The whole point of the description is that the grave-clothes did not look as if they had been put off or taken off; they were lying there in their regular folds as if the body of Jesus had simply evaporated out of them. The sight suddenly penetrated to John's mind; he realized what had happened – and he believed. It was not what he had read in Scripture which convinced him that Jesus had risen; it was what he saw with his own eyes.

The part that love plays in this story is extraordinary. It was Mary, who loved Jesus so much, who was first at the tomb. It was John, the disciple whom Jesus loved and who loved Jesus, who was first to believe in the resurrection. That must always be John's great glory. He was the first man to understand and to believe. Love gave him eyes to read the signs and a mind to understand.

Here we have the great law of life. In any kind of work, it is true that we cannot really interpret the thought of others, unless between us and them there is a bond of sympathy. It is at once clear, for instance, when the conductor of an orchestra is in sympathy with the music of the composer whose work is being played. Love is the great interpreter. Love can grasp the truth when intellect is left groping and uncertain. Love can realize the meaning of a thing when research is blind.

Once a young artist brought a picture of Jesus to the nine-teenth-century French painter and illustrator, Gustave Doré, for his verdict. Doré was slow to give it; but at last he did so in one sentence. 'You don't love him, or you would paint him better.' We can neither understand Jesus nor help others to understand him, unless we take our hearts to him as well as our minds.

The Second Sunday of Easter
The Great Inheritance *and*
The Doubter Convinced

1 Peter 1:3–9

This passage begins with the idea of *rebirth*; Christians are men and women who have been reborn; they have been given new birth by God to a new kind of life. Whatever else this means, it means that, when people become Christians, there comes into their lives a change so radical that the only thing that can be said is that life has begun all over again for them. This idea of rebirth runs all through the New Testament. Let us try to collect what it says about it.

(1) Christian rebirth happens by the will and by the act of God (John 1:13; James 1:18). It is not something which we achieve any more than we achieve our physical birth.

(2) Another way to put that is to say that this rebirth is the work of the Spirit (John 3:1–15). It happens to people, not by their own effort, but when they give themselves up to be possessed and re-created by the Spirit within them.

(3) It happens by the word of truth (James 1:18; 1 Peter 1:23). In the beginning, it was the word of God which created heaven and earth and all that is in them. God spoke and the chaos became a world, and the world was equipped with and for life. It is the creative word of God in Jesus Christ which brings about this rebirth in our lives.

(4) The result of this rebirth is that those who are reborn become the first fruits of a new creation (James 1:18). It lifts them out of this world of space and time, of change and decay, of sin and defeat, and brings them here and now into touch with eternity and eternal life.

(5) When we are reborn, it is to a living hope (1 Peter1:3). Paul describes the world without Christ as being without hope (Ephesians 2:12). Sophocles wrote: 'Not to be born at all – that is by far the best fortune; the second best is as soon as one is born with all speed to return thither whence one has come.' To the Gentiles, the world was a place where all things faded and decayed; it might be pleasant enough in itself, but it was leading out into nothing but an endless dark. To the ancient world, the Christian characteristic was hope. That hope came from two things. (a) Christians felt that they had been born not of perishable but of imperishable seed (1 Peter 1:23). They had something of the very seed of God in them and, therefore, had in them a life which neither time nor eternity could destroy. (b) It came from the resurrection of Jesus Christ (1 Peter 1:3). Christians had always beside them – even more, were one with – this Jesus Christ who had conquered even death, and therefore there was nothing of which they needed to be afraid.

(6) The rebirth of Christians is a rebirth to righteousness (1 John 2:29, 3:9, 5:18). In this rebirth, they are cleansed from themselves, the sins which shackle them and the habits which bind them; and they are given a power which enables them to walk in righteousness. That is not to say that those who are reborn will never sin, but it is to say that every time they fall, they will be given the power and the grace to rise again.

(7) The rebirth of Christians is a rebirth to love (1 John 4:7). Because the life of God is in them, they are cleansed from the essential unforgiving bitterness of the self-centred life, and there is in them something of the forgiving and sacrificial love of God.

(8) Finally, the rebirth of Christians is rebirth to victory (1 John 5:4). Life ceases to be defeat and begins to be victory, over self and sin and circumstances. Because the life of God is in them, Christians have learned the secret of victorious living.

Further, Christians have entered into a great *inheritance* (*klēronomia*). Here is a word with a history; for it is the word which is regularly used in the Greek Old Testament for the inheritance of Canaan, the Promised Land. Again and again, the Old Testament speaks of the land which God had given his people *for an inheritance to possess* (cf. Deuteronomy15:4, 19:10). To us, *inheritance* tends to mean something which we shall possess in the future; but as the Bible uses the word, it means a secure possession. To the Jews, the great settled possession was the Promised Land.

But the Christian inheritance is even greater. Peter uses three words with three pictures behind them to describe it. It is *imperishable (aphthartos)*. The word does mean *imperishable*, but it can also mean *unravaged by any invading army*. Time after time, Palestine had been ravaged by the armies of other nations; it had been fought over and destroyed. But Christians possess a peace and a joy, which no invading army can ravage and destroy. It is *undefilable*. The word is *amiantos*; and the verb from which this adjective comes means to *pollute* with an impurity that is unholy.

Time after time, Palestine had been rendered impure by false worship of false gods (Jeremiah 2:7, 2:23, 3:2; Ezekiel 20:43). The defiling things had often left their touch and their mark even on the Promised Land; but Christians have a purity which the sin of the world cannot infect. It is *unfading (amarantos)*. In the promised land, as in any land, even the loveliest flower fades and the loveliest blossom dies. But Christians are lifted into a world where there is no change and decay, and where their peace and joy are untouched by the chances and the changes of life.

What, then, is this wonderful inheritance which reborn Christians possess? There may be many secondary answers to that question, but there is only one primary answer – the inheritance of Christians is God himself. The psalmist said: 'The Lord is my chosen portion . . . I have a goodly heritage' (Psalm 16:5–6). God is his portion forever (Psalm 73:23–6). 'The Lord', said the prophet, 'is my portion . . . therefore I will hope in him' (Lamentations 3:24).

It is because Christians possess God and are possessed by God that they have the inheritance which is imperishable and undefilable and which can never fade away.

John 20:19–31

To Thomas, the cross was only what he had expected. When Jesus had proposed going to Bethany, after the news of Lazarus' illness had come, Thomas' reaction had been: 'Let us also go, that we may die with him' (John 11:16). Thomas never lacked courage, but he was the natural pessimist. There can never be any doubt that he loved Jesus. He loved him enough to be willing to go to Jerusalem and die with him when the other disciples were hesitant and afraid. What he had expected had happened, and when it came, for all that he had expected it, he was broken-hearted, so broken-hearted that he could not meet the eyes of others, but must be alone with his grief.

King George V used to say that one of his rules of life was: 'If I have to suffer, let me be like a well-bred animal, and let me go and suffer alone.' Thomas had to face his suffering and his sorrow alone. So it happened that, when Jesus came back again, Thomas was not there; and the news that he had come back seemed to him far too good to be true, and he refused to believe it. Belligerent in his pessimism, he said that he would never believe that Jesus had risen from the dead until he had seen and handled the print of the nails in his hands and thrust his hand into the wound the spear had made in Jesus' side. (There is no mention of any wound-print in Jesus' feet because in crucifixion the feet were usually not nailed, but only loosely bound to the cross.)

Another week elapsed and Jesus came back again; and this time Thomas was there. And Jesus knew Thomas' heart. He repeated

Thomas' own words, and invited him to make the test that he had demanded. And Thomas' heart ran out in love and devotion, and all he could say was: 'My Lord and my God!' Jesus said to him: 'Thomas, you needed the eyes of sight to make you believe; but the days will come when people will see with the eye of faith and believe.'

The character of Thomas stands out clearly before us.

(1) He made one mistake. He withdrew from the Christian fellowship. He sought loneliness rather than togetherness. And because he was not there with his fellow Christians, he missed the first coming of Jesus. We miss a great deal when we separate ourselves from the Christian fellowship and try to be alone. Things can happen to us within the fellowship of Christ's Church which will not happen when we are alone. When sorrow comes and sadness envelops us, we often tend to shut ourselves up and refuse to meet people. That is the very time when, in spite of our sorrow, we should seek the fellowship of Christ's people, for it is there that we are likeliest of all to meet him face to face.

(2) But Thomas had two great virtues. He absolutely refused to say that he understood what he did not understand, or that he believed what he did not believe. There is an uncompromising honesty about him. He would never still his doubts by pretending that they did not exist. He was not the kind of man who would rattle off a creed without understanding what it was all about. Thomas had to be sure – and he was quite right. In *In Memoriam*, Tennyson wrote:

There lives more faith in honest doubt,
Believe me, than in half the creeds.

There is more ultimate faith in people who insist on being sure than in those who glibly repeat things which they have never thought out, and which they may not really believe. It is doubt like that which in the end arrives at certainty.

(3) Thomas' other great virtue was that when he was sure, he went the whole way. 'My Lord and my God!' said he. There was no half-way house about Thomas. He was not airing his doubts just for the sake of mental acrobatics; he doubted in order to become sure; and when he did, his surrender to certainty was complete. And when people fight their way through their doubts to the conviction that Jesus Christ is Lord, they have attained to a certainty that those who unthinkingly accept things can never reach.

The Third Sunday of Easter
Jesus Christ Redeemer and Lord *and*
The Sunset Road that Turned to Dawn

1 Peter 1:17–23

This passage has great things to say about Jesus Christ as Redeemer and Lord.

(1) Jesus Christ is the liberator, through whom men and women are delivered from the bondage of sin and death; he is the lamb without blemish and without spot (verse 19). When Peter spoke like that about Jesus, his mind was going back to two Old Testament pictures – to Isaiah 53, with its picture of the Suffering Servant, through whose suffering the people were saved and healed, and above all to the picture of the Passover lamb (Exodus 12:5). On the memorable night when they left the slavery of Egypt, the children of Israel were told to take a lamb and kill it and mark their door-posts with its blood; and, when the angel of death went through the land slaying the first-born sons of the Egyptians, he passed over every house marked in that way. In that picture of the Passover lamb, there are the twin thoughts of freedom from slavery and deliverance from death. No matter how we interpret it, it cost the life and death of Jesus Christ to free us from our bondage to sin and to death.

(2) Jesus Christ is the eternal purpose of God. It was before the creation of the world that he was predestined for the work which was given to him to do (verse 20). Here is a great thought. Sometimes we tend to think of God as first Creator and then Redeemer, as having created the world and then, when things went wrong, finding a way to rescue it through Jesus Christ. But here we have the vision of a God who was Redeemer *before* he was Creator.

His redeeming purpose was not an emergency measure to which he was compelled when things went wrong. It goes back before creation.

(3) Peter has a connection of thought which is universal in the New Testament. Jesus Christ is not only the lamb who was slain; he is the resurrected and triumphant one to whom God gave glory. The New Testament thinkers seldom separate the cross and the resurrection; they seldom think of the *sacrifice* of Christ without thinking of his *triumph*. The Methodist, Edward Rogers, in *That they might have Life*, tells us that on one occasion he went carefully through the whole story of the passion and the resurrection in order to find a way to represent it dramatically, and goes on: 'I began to feel that there was something subtly and tragically wrong in any emphasis on the agony of the Cross which dimmed the brightness of the Resurrection, any suggestion that it was endured pain rather than overcoming love which secured man's salvation.' He asks where the eyes of Christians turn at the beginning of Lent. What above all else do we see? 'Is it the darkness that covered the earth at noon, swirling round the pain and anguish of the Cross? Or is it the dazzling, mysterious early-morning brightness that shone from an empty tomb?' He continues: 'There are forms of most earnest and devoted evangelical preaching and theological writing which convey the impression that somehow the Crucifixion has overshadowed the Resurrection and that the whole purpose of God in Christ was completed on Calvary. The truth, which is obscured only at grave spiritual peril, is that the Crucifixion cannot be interpreted and understood save in the light of the Resurrection.'

Through his death, Jesus freed men and women from their bondage to slavery and death, but through his resurrection he gives them a life which is as glorious and indestructible as his own. Through this triumphant resurrection, we have faith and hope in God (verse 21).

In this passage, we see Jesus the great liberator at the cost of Calvary; we see Jesus the eternal redeeming purpose of God; we see Jesus the triumphant victor over death and the glorious Lord of life, the giver of life which death cannot touch and the bringer of hope which nothing can take away.

Luke 24:13–35

This is one of the immortal short stories of the world.

(1) It tells of two people who were walking towards the sunset. It has been suggested that that is the very reason why they did not recognize Jesus. Emmaus was west of Jerusalem. The sun was sinking, and the setting sun so dazzled them that they did not know their Lord. However that may be, it is true that the Christian is someone who walks not towards the sunset but towards the sunrise. Long ago it was said to the children of Israel that they journeyed in the wilderness towards the sunrising (Numbers 21:11). The Christian goes onwards, not to a night which falls, but to a dawn which breaks – and that is what, in their sorrow and their disappointment, the two on the Emmaus road had not realized.

(2) It tells us of the ability of Jesus to make sense of things. The whole situation seemed to have no explanation. For these followers of Jesus all their hopes and dreams were shattered. There is all the poignant, wistful, bewildered regret in the world in their sorrowing words, 'We were hoping that he was the one who was going to rescue Israel.' They are the words of people whose hopes are dead and buried. Then Jesus came and talked with them, and the meaning of life became clear and the darkness became light. A storyteller makes one of his characters say to the one with whom he has fallen in love, 'I never knew what life meant until I saw it in your eyes.' It is only in Jesus that, even in the bewildering times, we learn what life means.

(3) It tells us of the courtesy of Jesus. He made as if he would have gone on. He would not force himself upon them; he awaited their invitation to come in. God gave us the greatest and the most perilous gift in the world, the gift of free will; we can use it to invite Christ to enter our lives or to allow him to pass on.

(4) It tells how he was known to them in the breaking of bread. This always sounds a little as if it meant the sacrament; but it does not. It was at an ordinary meal in an ordinary house, when an ordinary loaf was being divided, that Jesus was recognized. It has been beautifully suggested that perhaps these people had been present at the feeding of the 5,000, and, as he broke the bread in their cottage home, they recognized his hands again. It is not only at the communion table we can be with Christ; we can be with him at the dinner table too. He is not only the host in his Church; he is the guest in every home. The Christian lives always and everywhere in a Christ-filled world.

(5) It tells of two people who, when they received such great joy, hastened to share it. It was a seven-mile journey back to Jerusalem, but they could not keep the good news to themselves. The Christian message is never fully ours until we have shared it with someone else.

(6) It tells how, when they reached Jerusalem, they found others who had already shared their experience. It is the glory of any Christian to live in a fellowship of people who have all had the same experience. It has been said that true friendship begins only when people share a common memory and can say to each other, 'Do you remember?' Each of us is one of a great fellowship of people who share a common experience and a common memory of their Lord.

(7) It tells that Jesus appeared to Peter. That must remain one of the great untold stories of the world. But surely it is a lovely thing that Jesus should make one of his first appearances to the man who had denied him. It is the glory of Jesus that he can restore the penitent sinner's self-respect.

The Fourth Sunday of Easter
Two Precious Names for God *and*
The Shepherd and His Sheep

1 Peter 2:19–25

In the last verse of this passage, we come upon two of the great names for God – the Shepherd and Bishop of our souls, as the Authorized Version has it.

(1) God is *the Shepherd of our souls*. The Greek is *poimēn*, and *shepherd* is one of the oldest descriptions of God. The psalmist has it in the best-loved of all the Psalms: 'The Lord is my shepherd' (Psalm 23:1). Isaiah has it: 'He will feed his flock like a shepherd; he will gather the lambs in his arms, and carry them in his bosom, and gently lead the mother sheep' (Isaiah 40:11).

The great king whom God was going to send to Israel would be the shepherd of his people. Ezekiel hears the promise of God: 'I will set up over them one shepherd, my servant David, and he shall feed them: he shall feed them and be their shepherd' (Ezekiel 34:23, 37:24).

This was the title which Jesus took to himself when he called himself the good shepherd and when he said that the good shepherd lays down his life for the sheep (John 10:1–18). To Jesus, the men and women who did not know God and who were waiting for what he could give them were like sheep without a shepherd (Mark 6:34). The great privilege given to the servant and the minister of Christ is to shepherd the flock of God (John 21:16; 1 Peter 5:2).

It may be difficult for those of us who live in an industrial civilization to grasp the greatness of this picture; but, in the Middle East the picture would be very vivid, particularly in Judaea, where there was a narrow central plateau which held danger on either side.

It was on this narrow tableland that the sheep grazed. Grass was sparse; there were no protecting walls; and the sheep wandered. The shepherd, therefore, had to be ceaselessly and sleeplessly on the watch in case any harm should come to his flock.

In *The Historical Geography of the Holy Land*, George Adam Smith describes the shepherd of Judaea. 'With us, sheep are often left to themselves; but I do not remember ever to have seen in the East a flock of sheep without a shepherd. In such a landscape as Judaea, where a day's pasture is thinly scattered over an unfenced tract of country, covered with delusive paths, still frequented by wild beasts, and rolling off into the desert, the man and his character are indispensable. On some high moor, across which at night the hyenas howl, when you meet him, sleepless, far-sighted, weather-beaten, armed, leaning upon his staff, and looking out over his scattered sheep, every one of them on his heart, you understand why the shepherd of Judaea sprang to the front in his people's history; why they gave his name to their king, and made him the symbol of providence; why Christ took him as the type of self-sacrifice.'

This word *shepherd* tells us most vividly of the ceaseless vigilance and the self-sacrificing love of God for us who are his flock. 'We are his people, and the sheep of his pasture' (Psalm 100:3).

(2) The Authorized Version speaks of God as the Shepherd and *Bishop* of our souls, but nowadays *Bishop* is an inadequate and misleading translation of the Greek (*episkopos*). *Episkopos* is a word with a great history. In Homer's *Iliad*, Hector, the great champion of the Trojans, is called the *episkopos* who, during his lifetime, guarded the city of Troy and kept safe its noble wives and infants. *Episkopos* is used of the gods who are the guardians of the treaties which people make and of the agreements to which they come, and who are the protectors of house and home. Justice, for instance, is the *episkopos*, who sees to it that individuals shall pay the price for the wrong that they have done.

In Plato's *Laws*, the Guardians of the state are those whose duty it is to oversee the games, the feeding and the education of the children that 'they may be sound of hand and foot, and may in no wise, if possible, get their natures warped by their habits'. The people whom Plato calls market-stewards are the *episkopoi* who 'supervise personal conduct, keeping an eye on intemperate and outrageous behaviour, so as to punish him who needs punishment'.

In Athenian law and administration, the *episkopoi* were governors and administrators and inspectors sent out to subject states to see that law and order and loyalty were observed. In Rhodes, the main magistrates were five *episkopoi* who presided over the good government and the law and order of the state.

Episkopos is, therefore, a many-sided but always a noble word. It means the protector of public safety; the guardian of honour and honesty; the overseer of right education and of public morals; the administrator of public law and order. So, to call God the *episkopos* of our souls is to call him our Guardian, our Protector, our Guide, and our Director. God is the Shepherd and the Guardian of our souls. In his love he cares for us; in his power he protects us; and in his wisdom he guides us in the right way.

John 10:1–10

There is no better-loved picture of Jesus than the good shepherd. The picture of the shepherd is woven into the language and imagery of the Bible. In the Old Testament, God is often pictured as the shepherd, and the people as his flock. 'The Lord is my shepherd, I shall not want' (Psalm 23:1). 'We your people, the flock of your pasture, will give thanks to you for ever' (Psalm 79:13). 'Give ear, O Shepherd of Israel, you who lead Joseph like a flock' (Psalm 80:1).

This picture passes over into the New Testament. Jesus is the good shepherd. He is the shepherd who will risk his life to seek and to save the one straying sheep (Matthew 18:12; Luke 15:4). He has pity upon the people because they are as sheep without a shepherd (Matthew 9:36; Mark 6:34). His disciples are his little flock (Luke 12:32). He is the shepherd of human souls (1 Peter 2:25), and the great shepherd of the sheep (Hebrews 13:20).

The relationship between sheep and shepherd is quite different in Palestine. In Britain, the sheep are largely kept for killing, but in Palestine largely for their wool. It thus happens that in Palestine the sheep are often with the shepherd for years, and often they have names by which the shepherd calls them. It is strictly true that in this part of the world the sheep know and understand the shepherd's voice, and that they will never answer to the voice of a stranger.

W. M. Thomson in *The Land and the Book* has the same story to tell. 'The shepherd calls sharply from time to time, to remind them of his presence. They know his voice, and follow on; but, if a stranger call, they stop short, lift up their heads in alarm, and if it is repeated, they turn and flee, because they know not the voice of a stranger. I have made the experiment repeatedly.' That is exactly John's picture.

The Jews did not understand the meaning of the story of the good shepherd. So Jesus, plainly and without concealment, applied it to himself.

He began by saying: 'I am the door.' In this parable, Jesus spoke about two kinds of sheepfolds. In the villages and towns themselves, there were communal sheepfolds where all the village flocks were sheltered when they returned home at night. These folds were protected by a strong door of which only the guardian of the door held the key. It was to that kind of fold Jesus referred in verses 2 and 3. But when the sheep were out on the hills in the warm season and did not return at night to the village at all, they were collected into sheepfolds on the hillside. These hillside sheepfolds were just open spaces enclosed by a wall. In them, there was an opening by which the sheep came in and went out; but there was no door of any kind. What happened was that at night the shepherd himself lay down across the opening, and no sheep could get out or in except over his body. In the most literal sense, the shepherd was the door.

That is what Jesus was thinking of when he said: 'I am the door.' Through him, and through him alone, we find access to God. 'Through him', said Paul, we 'have access to . . . the Father' (Ephesians 2:18). The writer to the Hebrews calls him 'the new and living way' (Hebrews 10:20). Jesus opens the way to God. Until Jesus came, people could think of God only as, at best, a stranger and as, at worst, an enemy. But Jesus came to show people what God is like, and to open the way to him. He is the door through whom alone entrance to God becomes possible.

To describe something of what that entrance to God means, Jesus uses a well-known Hebrew phrase. He says that through him *we can go in and come out.* To be able to come and go unmolested was the Jewish way of describing a life that is absolutely secure and safe. When people can go in and out without fear, it means that their country is at peace, that the forces of law and order are supreme, and that they enjoy perfect security. The leader of the nation is to be one who can bring them out and lead them in (Numbers 27:17). A child is one who is not yet able by himself to go out and to come in (1 Kings 3:7). The psalmist is certain that God will keep him in his going out and in his coming in (Psalm 121:8). Once anyone discovers, through Jesus Christ, what God is like, a new sense of safety and of security enters into life. If life is known to be in the hands of a God like that, the worries and the fears are gone.

Jesus said that those who came before him were thieves and rob-bers. He was of course not referring to the great succession of the prophets and the heroes, but to those adventurers who were continually arising in Palestine and promising that, if people would follow them, they would bring in the golden age. All these claimants were insurrectionists. They believed that people would have to wade through blood to the golden age. There have been, and still are, those who believe that the golden age must be brought in with violence, class warfare, bitterness and destruction. It is the message of Jesus that the only way that leads to God in heaven and to the golden age on earth is the way of love.

Jesus claims that he came that men and women might have life and might have it more abundantly. The Greek phrase used for *having it more abundantly* means to have *a superabundance of a thing*. To be a follower of Jesus, to know who he is and what he means, is to have a superabundance of life. When we try to live our own lives, life is a dull, dispirited thing. When we walk with Jesus, there comes a new vitality, a superabundance of life. It is only when we live with Christ that life becomes really worth living and we begin to live in the real sense of the word.

The Fifth Sunday of Easter
The Glory and Function of the Church
and The Vision of God

1 Peter 2:2–10

In this passage, we read of the things to which Christians are witnesses.

(1) God has called Christians out of darkness into his glorious light. *Christians are called out of darkness into light.* When we come to know Jesus Christ, we come to know *God.* We no longer need to guess and to feel our way. 'Whoever has seen me', said Jesus, 'has seen the Father' (John 14:9). In Jesus is the light of the knowledge of God. When we come to know Jesus, we come to know *goodness.* In Christ, we have a standard by which all actions and motives may be tested. When we come to know Jesus Christ, we come to know the *way.* Life is no longer a trackless road without a star to guide. In Christ, the way becomes clear. When we come to know Jesus Christ, we come to know *power.* It would be little use to know God without the power to serve him. It would be little use to know goodness and yet be helpless to attain it. It would be little use to see the right way and be quite unable to take it. In Jesus Christ, there is both the vision *and* the power.

(2) God has made those who were not a people into the people of God. Here, Peter is quoting from Hosea 1:6, 1:9–10, 2:1, 2:23. This means that *Christians are called out of insignificance into significance.* It continually happens in this world that greatness lies not in the self but in what an individual has been given to do. The greatness for Christians lies in the fact that God has chosen them to be his people and to do his work in the world. Christians can never be ordinary, for they are people of God.

(3) *Christians are called out of no mercy into mercy.* The characteristic of non-Christian religion is the fear of God. Christians have discovered the love of God and know that they need no longer fear him, because all is well with their souls.

In verse 9, Peter uses a whole series of phrases which are a summary of the functions of the Church. He calls Christians 'a chosen race, a royal priesthood, a people dedicated to God, a nation for him specially to possess'. Peter is steeped in the Old Testament, and these phrases are all great descriptions of the people of Israel.

They come from two main sources. In Isaiah 43:21, Isaiah hears God say: 'The people whom I formed for myself.' But even more in Exodus 19:5–6 the voice of God is heard: 'Now therefore, if you will obey my voice and keep my covenant, you shall be my treasured possession out of all the peoples. Indeed, the whole earth is mine, but you shall be for me a priestly kingdom and a holy nation.' The great promises which God made to his people Israel are being fulfilled to the Church, the new Israel. Every one of these titles is full of meaning.

(1) Christians are *a chosen people.* Here, we are back to the covenant idea. Exodus 19:5–6 is from the passage which describes how God entered into his covenant with Israel. In the covenant, he offered a special relationship with himself to Israel, but it depended on the people of Israel accepting the conditions of the covenant and keeping the law. That relationship would hold only 'if you will obey my voice and keep my covenant' (Exodus 19:5).

From this, we learn that Christians are chosen for three things. (a) They are chosen for *privilege.* In Jesus Christ, a new and intimate fellowship with God is offered to them.

God has become their friend, and they have become God's friends. (b) They are chosen for *obedience.* Privilege brings with it responsibility. Christians are chosen in order that they may become the obedient children of God. They are chosen not to do as they like but to do as God likes. (c) They are chosen for *service.* Their honour is that they are the servants of God. Their privilege is that they will be used for the purposes of God. But they can be so used only when they bring to God the obedience he desires. Chosen for privilege, chosen for obedience, chosen for service – these three great facts go hand in hand.

(2) Christians are *a royal priesthood*. We have already seen that this means that all Christians have the right of access to God, and that they must offer their work, their worship and themselves to God.

(3) Christians are what the Revised Standard Version calls *a holy nation*. The basic meaning of *hagios* (holy) is *different*. Christians have been chosen in order that they may be different from other people. That difference lies in the fact that they are dedicated to God's will and to God's service. Other people may follow the standards of the world, but for Christians the only standards are God's. People need not even start on the Christian way unless they realize that it will compel them to be different from others.

(4) Christians are *a people for God specially to possess*. It frequently happens that the value of a thing lies in the fact that someone has possessed it. A very ordinary thing acquires a new value if it has been possessed by some famous person. In any museum, we find quite ordinary things – clothes, a walking-stick, a pen, books, pieces of furniture – which are of value only because they were once possessed by some great person. It is the same with Christians. Christians may be very ordinary people, but they acquire a new value because they belong to God.

John 14:1–14

To the Greeks, God was characteristically *The Invisible*; the Jews would count it as an article of faith that no one had seen God at any time. To people who thought like that, Jesus said: 'If you had known me, you would have known my Father too.' It may well be that to the ancient world this was the most staggering thing Jesus ever said. Then Philip asked what he must have believed to be the impossible. Maybe he was thinking back to that tremendous day when God revealed his glory to Moses (Exodus 33:12–23). But even in that great day, God had said to Moses: 'You shall see my back; but my face shall not be seen.' In the time of Jesus, people were oppressed and fascinated by what is called the transcendence of God and by the thought of the difference and the distance between God and human beings. They would never have dared to think that they could see God. Then Jesus says with utter simplicity: 'He who has seen me has seen the Father.' To see Jesus is to see what God is like. It has been said that Luke in his gospel 'domesticated God', meaning that Luke shows us God in Jesus taking a share in the most intimate and homely things. When we see Jesus, we can say: 'This is God living our life.' God entered into an ordinary home and into an ordinary family. God was not ashamed to be associated with work. God knows what it is to be tempted. In Jesus, we see God loving. In Jesus, we see God upon a cross. 'He who has seen me has seen the Father.' Jesus is the revelation of God, and that revelation leaves human minds staggered and amazed.

Jesus goes on to say something else. One thing no Jew would ever lose grip of was the sheer loneliness of God. The Jews were unswerving monotheists – they believed in the one true God. The danger of the Christian faith is that we may set up Jesus as a kind of secondary God. But Jesus himself insists that the things he said and the things he did came not from his own initiative or his own power or his own knowledge but from God. His words were God's voice speaking to us. His deeds were God's power flowing through him to us. He was the channel by which God came to us.

Let us take two simple and imperfect analogies, from the relationship between student and teacher. Teachers have the responsibility of transmitting something of the glory of their subjects to those who listen to them; and those who teach about Jesus Christ can, if they are sufficiently saintly, transmit the vision and the presence of God to their students. That is, in an infinitely greater way, what Jesus did. He transmitted the glory and the love of God to men and women.

Here is the other analogy. Great teachers stamp their students with something of themselves. Sometimes if a divinity student has been trained by a great preacher whom he or she loves, we will see in the student something of the teacher and hear something of the teacher's voice. Jesus did something like that, only immeasurably more so. He brought God's accent, God's message, God's mind and God's heart to men and women.

We *must* every now and then remember that all is of God. It was not a self-chosen expedition to the world which Jesus made. He did not do it to soften a hard heart in God. He came because God sent him, because God so loved the world. At the back of Jesus, and in him, there is God. Jesus went on to make a claim and to offer a test, based on two things: his *words* and his *works*.

(1) He claimed to be tested by what *he said*. It is as if Jesus said: 'When you listen to me, can you not realize at once that what I am saying is God's own truth?' The words of any genius are always self-evidencing. When we read great poetry, we cannot for the most part say why it is great and grips our hearts. We may analyse the vowel sounds and so on, but in the end there is something which defies analysis, but nevertheless is easily and immediately recognizable. It is so with the words of Jesus. When we hear them, we cannot help saying: 'If only the world would live on these principles, how different it would be! If only *I* would live on these principles, how different I would be!'

(2) He claimed to be tested by his *deeds*. He said to Philip: 'If you cannot believe in me because of what I say, surely you will allow what I can do to convince you.' That was the same answer as Jesus sent back to John when he sent his messengers to ask whether Jesus was the Messiah, or if they must look for another. 'Go back,' he

said, 'and tell John what is happening – and that will convince him' (Matthew 11:1– 6). Jesus' proof is that no one else ever succeeded in making bad people good.

Jesus said in effect to Philip: 'Listen to me! Look at me! And believe!' Still the way to Christian belief is not to argue about Jesus but to listen to him and to look at him. If we do that, the sheer personal impact will compel us to believe.

The Sixth Sunday of Easter
The Example of the Work of Christ *and* The Promised Helper

1 Peter 3:13–22

The point that Peter is making here is that, even if Christians are compelled to suffer unjustly for their faith, they are only walking the way that their Lord and Saviour has already walked. Suffering Christians must always remember that they have a suffering Lord. Peter has the greatest and the deepest things to say here about the work of Christ.

(1) He lays it down that the work of Christ was *unique* and need never be repeated. Christ died *once and for all* for sins. The New Testament says this same thing often. When Christ died, he died once and for all (Romans 6:10). The priestly sacrifices in the Temple have to be repeated daily, but Christ made the perfect sacrifice once and for all when he offered himself up (Hebrews 7:27). We are sanctified through the offering of the body of Christ once and for all (Hebrews 10:10). The New Testament is completely sure that on the cross something happened which never needs to happen again and that in that happening sin is finally defeated. On the cross, God dealt with human sin in a way which is adequate for all sin, for all people, for all time.

(2) He lays it down that that sacrifice was *for sin*. Christ died once and for all *for sins*. This, again, is frequently said in the New Testament. Christ died for our sins according to the Scriptures (1 Corinthians 15:3). Christ gave himself for our sins (Galatians 1:4). He is the atoning sacrifice for our sins (1 John 2:2).

Peter is laying it down that the death of Christ is the sacrifice which atones for the sin of all. We may put it this way. Sin is that

which interrupts the relationship which should exist between God
and all humanity. The object of sacrifice is to restore that lost relationship. The death of Christ upon the cross, however we explain
it, restores the lost relationship between God and human beings.
As Charles Wesley put it in verse, in the hymn 'And Can it Be?':

No condemnation now I dread:
Jesus, and all in him, is mine!
Alive in him, my living Head,
And clothed in righteousness divine,
Bold I approach the eternal throne,
And claim the crown, through Christ my own.

It may be that we will never agree in our theories of what exactly
happened on the cross – for, indeed, as Charles Wesley said in that
same hymn: ''Tis mystery all!' But on one thing we can agree –
through what happened there, we may enter into a new relationship with God.

(3) He lays it down that that sacrifice was *vicarious*, that is, it was
on behalf of others. Christ died once and for all for sins, *the just for
the unjust*. That the just should suffer for the unjust is an extraordinary thing. At first sight, it looks like injustice. As the Baptist writer
Edwin H. Robertson put it: 'Only forgiveness without reason can
match sin without excuse.' The suffering of Christ was for us; and
the mystery is that he who deserved no suffering bore that suffering
for us who deserved to suffer. He sacrificed himself to restore our
lost relationship with God.

(4) He lays it down that the work of Christ was *to bring us to God*.
Christ died once and for all for sins, the just for the unjust, *that he
might bring us to God*. The word for *to bring* has two vivid strands to
its background.

(a) It has a Jewish background. It is used in the Old Testament of
bringing to God those who are to be priests. It is God's instruction:

'You shall bring Aaron and his sons to the entrance of the tent of meeting' (Exodus 29:4). The point is this – as the Jews saw it, only the priests had the right of close access to God. In the Temple, the ordinary worshippers might come so far; they could pass through the Court of the Gentiles, the Court of the Women, the Court of the Israelites – but there they must stop. Into the Court of the Priests, into the nearer presence of God, they could not go; and, of the priests, only the high priest could enter into the Holy of Holies. But Jesus Christ brings *us* to God; he opens the way for *all* men and women to come into his nearer presence.

(b) It has a Greek background. In the New Testament, the corresponding noun means the right of *access*, the result of bringing in. Through Christ, we have *access* to grace (Romans 5:2). Through him, we have *access* to God the Father (Ephesians 2:18). Through him, we have boldness and *access* and confidence to come to God (Ephesians 3:12). In Greek, this had a specialized meaning. At the court of kings, there was an official called the *introducer*, the *giver of access*, and it was his function to decide who should be admitted to the king's presence and who should be kept out. He, as it were, held the keys of access. It is Jesus Christ, through what he did, who gives us access to God.

(5) Peter sees the work of Christ in terms of *complete triumph*. He says that, after his resurrection, Jesus went into heaven and is at the right hand of God, angels and authorities and powers having been made subject to him (3:22). The meaning is that there is nothing in earth and heaven outside the empire of Christ. To all people, he brought the new relationship between human beings and God; in his death, he even brought the good news to the dead; in his resurrection, he conquered death; even the angelic and the demonic powers are subject to him; and he shares the very power and throne of God. Christ the sufferer has become Christ the victor; Christ the crucified has become Christ the crowned.

John 14:15–21

To John, there is only one test of love, and that is obedience. It was by his obedience that Jesus showed his love of God; and it is by our obedience that we must show our love of Jesus. The New Testament scholar C. K. Barrett says: 'John never allowed love to devolve into a sentiment or emotion. Its expression is always moral and is revealed in obedience.' We know all too well how there are those who protest their love in words but who, at the same time, bring pain and heartbreak to those whom they claim to love. There are children and young people who say that they love their parents, and who yet cause them grief and anxiety. There are husbands who say they love their wives and wives who say they love their husbands, and who yet, by their inconsiderateness and their irritability and their thoughtless unkindness, bring pain to one another. To Jesus, real love is not an easy thing. It is shown only in true obedience.

But Jesus does not leave us to struggle with the Christian life alone. He would send us another *Helper*. The Greek word is *paraklētos*, which is really untranslatable. The Authorized Version renders it *Comforter*, which, although hallowed by time and usage, is not a good translation. Moffatt translates it as *Helper*. It is only when we examine this word *paraklētos* in detail that we catch something of the riches of the doctrine of the Holy Spirit. It really means *someone who is called in*; but it is the reason *why* the person is called in which gives the word its distinctive associations. The Greeks used the word in a wide variety of ways. A *paraklētos* might be a person *called in* to give witness in a law court in someone's favour, or an advocate *called in* to plead the cause of someone under a charge which would issue in a serious penalty; an expert *called in* to give advice in some difficult situation, or a person *called in* when, for example, a company of soldiers were depressed and dispirited to put new courage into their minds and hearts. Always a *paraklētos* is *someone called to help* in time of trouble or need. *Comforter* was once a perfectly good translation. It actually goes back to John Wyclif, the first person to use it in his translation made in the fourteenth century. But in his day it meant much more than it means now. The word comes from the Latin *fortis*, which means *brave*; and a comforter was someone who enabled some dispirited creature to be brave. Nowadays *comfort* has to do almost solely with sorrow; and a comforter is someone who sympathizes with us when we are sad. Beyond a doubt the Holy Spirit does that, but to limit his work to that function is sadly to belittle him. We often talk of being able *to cope* with things. That is precisely the work of the Holy Spirit. He takes away our inadequacies and enables us to cope with life. The Holy Spirit substitutes victorious for defeated living.

So what Jesus is saying is: 'I am setting you a hard task, and I am sending you out on a very difficult engagement. But I am going to send you someone, the *paraklētos*, who will guide you as to what to do and enable you to do it.' Jesus went on to say that the world cannot recognize the Spirit. By the world is meant that section of the human race that lives as if there was no God. The point of Jesus' saying is: we can see only what we are fitted to see. An astronomer will see far more in the sky than an ordinary person. A botanist will see far more in a hedgerow than someone who knows no botany. Someone who knows about art will see far more in a picture than someone who is quite ignorant of art. Someone who understands a little about music will get far more out of a symphony than someone who understands nothing. Always what we see and experience depends on what we bring to the sight and the experience. A person who has eliminated God never listens for him; and we cannot receive the Holy Spirit unless we wait in expectation and in prayer for him to come to us.

The Holy Spirit gatecrashes no one's heart; he waits to be received. So when we think of the wonderful things which the Holy Spirit can do, surely we will set apart some time amid the bustle and the rush of life to wait in silence for his coming.

The Seventh Sunday of Easter
The Blessedness of Suffering for Christ *and* Jesus' Prayer for His Disciples

1 Peter 4:12–14; 5:6–11

In verse 14 Peter says the greatest thing of all. If someone suffers for Christ, *the presence of the glory* rests upon that person. This is a very strange phrase. We think it can mean only one thing. The Jews believed in what was called the *Shekinah*, the luminous glow of the very presence of God. This idea constantly recurs in the Old Testament. 'In the morning,' said Moses, 'you shall see the *glory* of the Lord' (Exodus 16:7). 'The *glory* of the Lord settled on Mount Sinai, and the cloud covered it for six days' when the law was being delivered to Moses (Exodus 24:16). In the tabernacle, God was to meet with Israel and it was to be sanctified with his *glory* (Exodus 29:43). When the tabernacle was completed, 'then the cloud covered the tent of meeting, and the *glory* of the Lord filled the tabernacle' (Exodus 40:34). When the ark of the covenant was brought into Solomon's temple, 'a cloud filled the house of the Lord, so that the priests could not stand to minister because of the cloud; for the *glory* of the Lord filled the house of the Lord' (1 Kings 8:10–11). Repeatedly this idea of the *Shekinah*, the luminous glory of God, occurs in the Old Testament. It is Peter's conviction that something of that glow of glory rests on those who suffer for Christ.

Then in chapter 5 Peter speaks of the law of Christian suffering. He says that, after Christians have gone through suffering, God will restore, establish, strengthen and settle them. Every one of the words which Peter uses has behind it a vivid picture. Each tells us something about what suffering is designed by God to do for us.

(a) Through suffering, God will *restore* us. The word for *restore* is difficult in this case to translate. It is the word commonly used for setting a fracture, the word used in Mark 1:19 for mending nets. It means to supply that which is missing, to mend that which is broken. So suffering, if accepted in humility and trust and love, can repair weaknesses of character and add the greatness which has not yet been achieved. It is said that the composer Sir Edward Elgar once listened to a young girl singing a solo from one of his own works. She had a voice of exceptional purity and clarity and range, and an almost perfect technique. When she had finished, Sir Edward said softly: 'She will be really great when something happens to break her heart.' The writer J. M. Barrie tells how his mother lost her favourite son, and then says: 'That is where my mother got her soft eyes, and that is why other mothers ran to her when they had lost a child.' Suffering had done something for her that an easy way could never have done. Suffering is meant by God to add an intensity to life.

(b) Through suffering, God will *establish* us. The word is *stērixein*, which means to make as solid as granite. Suffering of body and sorrow of heart do one of two things to us. They either make us collapse or they leave us with a solidity of character which we could never have gained anywhere else. If we meet them with continuing trust in Christ, we emerge like hardened steel that has been toughened in the fire.

(c) Through suffering, God will *strengthen* us. The Greek is *sthenoun*, which means *to fill with strength*. Here is the same sense again. A life with no effort and no discipline almost inevitably becomes a flabby life. We never really know what our faith means to us until it has been tried in the furnace of affliction. There is something doubly precious about a faith which has come victoriously through pain and sorrow and disappointment. The wind will extinguish a weak flame, but it will fan a strong flame into a still greater blaze. So it is with faith.

(d) Through suffering, God will *settle* us. The Greek is *themelioun*, which means *to lay the foundations*. When we have to meet sorrow and suffering, we are driven down to the very bedrock of faith. It is then that we discover the things which cannot be shaken. It is in time of trial that we discover the great truths on which real life is founded.

Suffering is very far from doing these precious things for everyone. It may well drive some people to bitterness and despair, and may well take away such faith as they have. But, if it is accepted in the trusting certainty that a father's hand will never cause his child a needless tear, then out of suffering come things which the easy way may never bring.

John 17:1–11

There is throughout this whole passage, and indeed throughout this whole chapter, a ringing confidence about the future in the voice of Jesus. He was with his disciples, the men God had given him; he thanked God for them; and he never doubted that they would carry on the work he had given them to do. Let us remember who and what they were. A great commentator said: 'Eleven Galilaean peasants after three years' labour! But it is enough for Jesus, for in these eleven he beholds the pledge of the continuance of God's work upon earth.' When Jesus left this world, he did not seem to have great grounds for hope. He seemed to have achieved so little and to have won so few, and it was the great and the orthodox and the religious of the day who had turned against him. But Jesus had that confidence which springs from God. He was not afraid of small beginnings. He was not pessimistic about the future. He seemed to say: 'I have won only eleven very ordinary men; but give me these eleven ordinary men and I will change the world.'

Jesus had two things – belief in God and belief in humanity. It is one of the most uplifting things in the world to think that Jesus put his trust in people like ourselves. We too must never be daunted by human weakness or by the small beginning. We too must go forward with confident belief in God and in one another. Then we will never be pessimists, because with these two beliefs the possibilities of life are infinite.

This passage tells us something about the disciple of Jesus.

(1) The disciple is given to Jesus by God. What does that mean? It means that the Spirit of God moves our hearts to respond to the appeal of Jesus.

(2) Through the disciple, glory has come to Jesus. The patient who has been cured brings honour to a doctor; the former pupil who becomes a scholar brings honour to the teacher; the successful athlete brings honour to the trainer. The men and women whom Jesus has redeemed bring honour to him. The bad person made good is the honour of Jesus.

(3) Disciples are those who are commissioned to a task. As God sent out Jesus, so Jesus sends out his disciples. Here is the explanation of a puzzling thing in this passage. Jesus begins by saying that he does not pray for the world; and yet he came because God so loved the world. But, as we have seen, in John's gospel *the world* stands for 'human society organizing itself without God'. What Jesus does for the world is to send out his disciples into it, in order to lead it back to God and to make it aware of God. He prays for his disciples in order that they may be such as to win the world for him.

The great interest of this passage is that it tells us of the things for which Jesus prayed for his disciples.

(1) The first essential is to note that Jesus did not pray that his disciples should be taken out of this world. He never prayed that they might find escape; he prayed that they might find victory. The kind of Christianity which buries itself in a monastery or a convent would not have seemed Christianity to Jesus at all. The kind of Christianity which finds its essence in prayer and meditation and in a life withdrawn from the world would have seemed to him a

sadly truncated version of the faith he died to bring. He insisted that it was in the rough and tumble of life that a people must live out their Christianity.

Of course there is need of prayer and meditation and quiet times, when we shut the door upon the world to be alone with God, but all these things are not the end that we seek in life, but means to that end; and the end is to demonstrate the Christian life in the ordinary work of the world. Christianity was never meant to withdraw people from life, but to equip them better for it. It does not offer us release from problems, but a way to solve them. It does not offer us an easy peace, but a triumphant warfare. It does not offer us a life in which troubles are escaped and evaded, but a life in which troubles are faced and conquered. However much it may be true that Christians are not of the world, it remains true that it is within the world that their Christianity must be lived out. We must never desire to abandon the world, but always desire to win it.

(2) Jesus prayed for the unity of his disciples. Where there are divisions, where there is exclusiveness, where there is competition between the churches, the cause of Christianity is harmed and the prayer of Jesus frustrated. The gospel cannot truly be preached in any congregation which is not one united band of brothers and sisters. The world cannot be evangelized by competing churches. Jesus prayed that his disciples might be as fully one as he and the Father are one; and there is no prayer of his which has been so hindered from being answered by individual Christians and by the churches than this.

We must always remember that God has chosen us and dedicated us for his special service. That special service is that we should love and obey him and should bring others to do the same. And God has not left us to carry out that great task in our own strength, but out of his grace he fits us for our task, if we place our lives in his hands.

Pentecost
The First Christian Preaching *and*
The Commission of Christ

Acts 2:1–21

There were three great Jewish festivals to which every male Jew living within twenty miles of Jerusalem was legally bound to come – the Passover, Pentecost and the Feast of tabernacles. Pentecost means 'the Fiftieth', and another name for Pentecost was 'the Feast of Weeks'. It was so called because it fell on the fiftieth day, a week of weeks, after the Passover. The Passover was celebrated in the middle of April; therefore Pentecost fell at the beginning of June. By that time, travelling conditions were at their best. at least as many came to the Feast of Pentecost as came to the Passover. That explains the list of countries mentioned in this chapter; never was there a more international crowd in Jerusalem than at the time of Pentecost.

The feast itself was significant in two ways. (1) It had a *historical* significance. It commemorated the giving of the law to Moses on Mount Sinai. (2) It had an *agricultural* significance. At the Passover, part of the first crop of barley was offered to God; and at Pentecost two loaves were offered in gratitude for the safe gathering in of the harvest. It had one other unique characteristic. The law laid it down that on that day people should not do their everyday work (Leviticus 23:21; Numbers 28:26). So it was a holiday for everyone, and the crowds on the streets would be greater than ever.

What happened at Pentecost we really do not know, except that the disciples had an experience of the power of the spirit flooding their beings such as they had never had before. We must remember that, for this part of Acts, Luke was not an eyewitness. He tells the story as if the disciples had suddenly acquired the gift of speaking in *foreign* languages. For two reasons, that is not likely.

(1) There was in the early Church a phenomenon which has never completely disappeared. It was called *speaking with tongues* (cf. Acts 10:46, 19:6). The main passage which describes it is 1 Corinthians 14. What happened was that someone, in an ecstasy, began to pour out a flood of unintelligible sounds in no known language. That was supposed to be directly inspired by the spirit of God and was a gift greatly coveted. Paul did not approve of it, because he preferred that a message should be given in a language that could be understood. In fact, he said that a stranger coming in might well think that the members of the congregation were mad (1 Corinthians 14:23). That precisely fits Acts 2:13. People speaking in tongues might well appear to be drunk to someone who had never witnessed the phenomenon.

(2) To speak in foreign languages was unnecessary. The crowd was made up of Jews (verse 5) and converts (verse 10) – Gentiles who had accepted the Jewish religion and the Jewish way of life. For a crowd like that, at most two languages were necessary. Almost all Jews spoke Aramaic; and, even if they were Jews of the dispersion from a foreign land, they would speak the language which almost everyone in the world spoke at that time – Greek.

It seems most likely that Luke, a Gentile, had confused speaking with tongues with speaking in *foreign* languages. What happened was that, for the first time in their lives, this mixed crowd was hearing the word of God in a way that struck straight home to their hearts and that they could understand. The power of the Spirit was such that it had given the disciples a message that could reach every heart.

Acts 2:14–42 is one of the most interesting passages in the New Testament, because it is an account of the first Christian sermon ever preached.

The first section, verses 14–21, brings us face to face with one of the basic ideas of both the Old and the New Testaments – that of *the day of the Lord*. Much in both the Old and the New Testaments is not fully intelligible unless we know the basic principles underlying that belief.

The Jews never lost the conviction that they were God's chosen people. They interpreted that status to mean that they were chosen for special privilege among the nations. They were always a small nation. History had been for them one long disaster. It was clear to them that by human means they would never reach the status they deserved as the chosen people. so, bit by bit, they reached the conclusion that what they could not achieve for themselves God must do; and they began to look forward to a day when God would intervene directly in history and raise them to the honour they dreamed of. The day of that intervention was *the day of the Lord*.

They divided all time into two ages. There was *the present age*, which was utterly evil and doomed to destruction; and there was *the age to come*, which would be the golden age of God. Between the two, there was to be *the day of the Lord*, which was to be the terrible first signs of the new age, often described in the same way as labour pains before a birth. It would come suddenly like a thief in the night; it would be a day when the world would be shaken to its very foundations; it would be a day of judgement and of terror. All over the prophetic books of the Old Testament and in much of the New Testament are descriptions of that day. Typical passages are Isaiah 2:12, 13:6ff.; Amos 5:18; Zephaniah 1:7; Joel 2; 1 Thessalonians 5:2ff.; 2 Peter 3:10.

Here, Peter is saying to the Jews: 'For generations, you have dreamed of the day of God, the day when God would break into history. Now, in Jesus, that day has come.' Behind all the old imagery stands the great truth that, in Jesus, God arrived in person on the scene of human history.

John 20:19–23

It is most likely that the disciples continued to meet in the upper room where the Last Supper had been held. But they met in something very like terror. They knew the intense bitterness of the Jews who had brought about the death of Jesus, and they were afraid that their turn would come next. So they were meeting in terror, listening fearfully for every step on the stair and for every knock at the door, lest the representatives of the Sanhedrin should come to arrest them too. As they sat there, Jesus was suddenly in their midst. He gave them the normal everyday middle-eastern greeting: 'Peace be to you.' It means far more than: 'May you be saved from trouble.' It means: 'May God give you every good thing.'

Then Jesus gave the disciples the commission which the Church must never forget.

(1) He said that as God had sent him forth, so he sent them forth. Here is what the New Testament scholar B. F. Westcott called 'The Charter of the Church'. It means three things.

(a) It means that Jesus Christ needs the Church, which is exactly what Paul meant when he called the Church 'the body of Christ' (Ephesians 1:23; 1 Corinthians 12:12). Jesus had come with a message for all people, and now he was going back to his Father. His message could never be taken to all men and women, unless the Church took it. The Church was to be a mouth to speak for Jesus, feet to run upon his errands, hands to do his work. Therefore, the first thing this means is that *Jesus is dependent on his Church.*

(b) It means that the Church needs Jesus. People who are to be sent out need someone to send them; they need a message to take; they need a power and an authority to back the message; they need someone to whom they may turn when they are in doubt and in difficulty. Without Jesus, the Church has no message; without him it has no power; without him it has no one to turn to when up against it; without him it has nothing to enlighten its mind, to strengthen its arm and to encourage its heart. This means that *the Church is dependent on Jesus.*

(c) There remains still another thing. The sending out of the Church by Jesus is parallel to the sending out of Jesus by God. But no one can read the story of the Fourth Gospel without seeing that the relationship between Jesus and God was continually dependent on Jesus' perfect obedience and perfect love. Jesus could be God's messenger only because he rendered to God that perfect obedience and love. It follows that the Church is fit to be the messenger and the instrument of Christ only when it perfectly loves him and perfectly obeys him. The Church must never be out to propagate *its own* message; it must be out to propagate the message of Christ. It must never be out to follow policies of human devising; it must be out to follow the will of Christ. The Church fails whenever it tries to solve some problem in its own wisdom and strength, and leaves out of account the will and guidance of Jesus Christ.

(2) Jesus breathed on his disciples and gave them the Holy Spirit. There is no doubt that, when John spoke in this way, he was thinking back to the old story of the creation. There the writer says: 'Then the Lord God formed man from the dust of the ground, and breathed into his nostrils the breath of life; and the man became a living being' (Genesis 2:7). This was the same picture as Ezekiel saw in the valley of dead, dry bones, when he heard God say to the wind: 'Come from the four winds, O breath, and breathe upon these slain, that they may live' (Ezekiel 37:9). The coming of the Holy Spirit is like the wakening of life from the dead. When he comes upon the Church, it is re-created for its task.

(3) Jesus said to the disciples: 'If you remit the sins of anyone, they are remitted; if you retain them, they are retained.' This is a saying whose true meaning we must be careful to understand. One thing is certain – no one can forgive anyone else's sins. But another thing is equally certain – it is the great privilege of the

Church to convey the message of God's forgiveness to men and women. Suppose someone brings us a message from another, our assessment of the value of that message will depend on how well the bringer of the message knows the sender. If someone proposes to interpret another's thought to us, we know that the value of that person's interpretation depends on the closeness they have to the other.

The apostles had the best of all rights to bring Jesus' message to all people, because they knew him best. If they knew that people were really penitent, they could with absolute certainty proclaim to them the forgiveness of Christ. But equally, if they knew that there was no penitence in their hearts or that they were trading on the love and the mercy of God, they could tell them that until their hearts were altered there was no forgiveness for them. This sentence does not mean that the power to forgive sins was ever entrusted to any individual or group; it means that the power to proclaim that forgiveness was so entrusted, along with the power to warn that forgiveness is not open to the impenitent. This sentence lays down the duty of the Church to convey forgiveness to the penitent in heart and to warn the impenitent that they are forfeiting the mercy of God.

Trinity Sunday
A Final Blessing *and* The Glory of the Final Promise

2 Corinthians 13:11–13

News came to Paul, from various sources, of trouble at Corinth. In answer to all this information, Paul wrote 1 Corinthians and despatched it to Corinth, apparently by the hand of Timothy (1 Corinthians 4:17). The result of the letter was that things became worse than ever; and, although we have no direct record of it, we can deduce that Paul paid a personal visit to Corinth.

The visit did no good at all. Matters were only exacerbated, and the result was an exceedingly severe letter. We learn about that letter from certain passages in 2 Corinthians. In 2:4, Paul writes: 'I wrote to you out of much distress and anguish of heart and with many tears.' In 7:8, he writes: 'For even if I made you sorry with my letter, I do not regret it (though I did regret it, for I see that I grieved you with that letter, though only briefly).' It was a letter which was the product of anguish of mind, a letter so severe that Paul was almost sorry that he ever sent it.

Scholars call this 'the Severe Letter'. Most scholars believe that chapters 10–13 are the severe letter. They are the most heartbroken cry Paul ever wrote. They show that he has been hurt and insulted as he never was before or afterwards by any church. His appearance, his speech, his apostleship and his honesty have all been under attack.

But Paul finishes this last chapter of what is a severe letter with *a blessing*. After the severity, the struggle and the debate, there comes the serenity of the benediction. One of the best ways of making peace with our enemies is to pray for them, for it is impossible to

157

hate people and pray for them at the same time. And so we leave the troubled story of Paul and the church of Corinth with the benediction ringing in our ears. The way has been hard, but the last word is peace.

Matthew 28:16–20

Here we come to the end of the gospel story; here we listen to the last words of Jesus to his disciples; and in this last meeting Jesus did three things.

(1) *He assured them of his power.* Surely nothing was outside the power of him who had died and conquered death. Now they were the servants of a Master whose authority upon earth and in heaven was beyond all question.

(2) *He gave them a commission.* He sent them out to make all the world his disciples. It may well be that the instruction to baptize is something which is a development of the actual words of Jesus. That may be argued about; the salient fact remains that the commission of Jesus is to win all men and women for himself.

(3) *He promised them a presence.* It must have been a staggering thing for eleven humble Galilaeans to be sent forth to the conquest of the world. Even as they heard it, their hearts must have failed them. But no sooner was the command given than the promise followed. They were sent out – as we are – on the greatest task in history, but with them there was the greatest presence in the world. As James Montgomery's hymn has it:

> Though few and small and weak your bands,
> Strong in your Captain's strength,
> Go to the conquest of all lands;
> All must be his at length.

The Sunday between 29 May and 4 June
Good News of Which to be Proud *and* The Only True Foundation

Romans 1:16, 17; 3:22b–28

In this passage, we meet three great Pauline watchwords, the three foundation pillars of his thought and belief.

(1) There is the conception of *salvation*. At this time in history, salvation was the one thing for which people were searching. It was precisely that salvation, that power, that escape, that Christianity came to offer.

(a) It was *salvation from physical illness* (Matthew 9:21; Luke 8:36). It was not a completely other-worldly thing. It aimed at rescuing an individual in body and in soul.

(b) It was *salvation from danger* (Matthew 8:25, 14:30). It was not that it gave people a life free from perils and dangers, but it gave them a security of soul no matter what was happening. As Robert Browning had it in 'Paracelsus':

> If I stoop,
> Into a dark tremendous sea of cloud,
> It is but for a time; I press God's lamp
> Close to my breast; its splendour, soon or late,
> Will pierce the gloom: I shall emerge one day.

The Christian salvation makes us safe in a way that is independent of any outward circumstance.

(c) It was *salvation from life's infection*. It is from a corrupt and perverse generation that we are saved (Acts 2:40). Those who have this Christian salvation have a kind of divine antiseptic which keeps them from infection by the evil of the world.

(d) It was *salvation from lostness* (Matthew 18:11; Luke 19:10). It was to seek and to save the lost that Jesus came. The unsaved man or woman is on the wrong road, a road that leads to death. The saved man or woman has been put on the right way.

(e) It was *salvation from sin* (Matthew 1:21). Men and women are like slaves in bondage to a master from whom they cannot escape. The Christian salvation liberates them from the tyranny of sin.

(f) It was *salvation from the wrath of God* (Romans 5:9). There is in this world an inexorable moral law and in the Christian faith an inevitable element of judgement. Without the salvation which Jesus Christ brings, we can only stand condemned.

(g) It was *a salvation which is eschatological*. That is to say, it is a salvation which finds its full meaning and blessedness in the final triumph of Jesus Christ (Romans 13:11; 1 Corinthians 5:5; 2 Timothy 4:18; 1 Peter 1:5).

The Christian faith came to a desperate world offering a salvation which would keep men and women safe in time and in eternity.

(2) There is the conception of *faith*. In the thought of Paul, this is a rich word.

(a) At its simplest, it means *loyalty*. When Paul wrote to the Thessalonians, he wanted to know about their *faith*. That is, he wanted to know how their loyalty was standing the test. In 2 Thessalonians 1:4, *faith* and *steadfastness* are combined. Faith is the enduring devotion and loyalty which marks the real follower of Jesus Christ.

(b) *Faith* means *belief*. It means the conviction that something is true. In 1 Corinthians 15:17, Paul tells the Corinthians that, if Jesus did not rise from the dead, then their faith is vain – all that they have believed is wrecked. Faith is the assent that the Christian message is true.

(c) *Faith* sometimes means *the Christian religion* (*the Faith*). In 2 Corinthians 13:5, Paul tells his opponents to examine themselves to see if they are *holding to their faith*, that is, to see if they are still within the Christian religion.

(d) *Faith* is sometimes practically equivalent to *indestructible hope*. 'We walk', writes Paul, 'by *faith*, not by *sight*' (2 Corinthians 5:7).

(e) But, in its most characteristic Pauline use, *faith* means *total acceptance* and *absolute trust*. It means 'betting your life that there is a God'. It means being utterly sure that what Jesus said is true, and staking all time and eternity on that assurance. 'I believe in God', said the writer Robert Louis Stevenson, 'and if I woke up in hell I would still believe in him.'

Faith begins with *receptivity*. It begins when we are at least willing to listen to the message of the truth. It goes on to *mental assent*. We first hear and then agree that this is true. But mental assent need not result in action. Many people know very well that something is true, but do not change their actions to meet that knowledge. The final stage is when this mental assent becomes *total surrender*. In fully fledged faith, we hear the Christian message, agree that it is true, and then cast ourselves upon it in a life of total submission.

(3) There is the conception of *justification*. Now, in all the New Testament, there are no more difficult words to understand than 'justification', 'justify', 'justice' and 'just'.

We must be quite clear that the word *justify* has a different meaning from its ordinary English meaning. If we justify ourselves, we produce reasons to prove that we were right; if someone justifies us, that person produces reasons to prove that we acted in the right way. But in Greek the word means to *treat*, or *account* or *reckon* a person as something. If God justifies sinners, it does not mean that he finds reasons to prove that they were right – far from it. It does not even mean, at this point, that he makes the sinners good. It means that *God treats sinners as if they had not been sinners at all.* Instead of treating them as criminals to be obliterated, God treats them as children to be loved. It means that God treats us not as his enemies but as his friends, not as bad people deserve but as good people deserve, not as law-breakers to be punished but as men and women to be loved. That is the very essence of the gospel.

That means that *to be justified* is to enter into a new relationship with God, a relationship of love and confidence and friendship, instead of one of distance and enmity and fear. We no longer go to a God radiating just but terrible punishment. We go to a God radiating forgiving and redeeming love. Justification is the right relationship between God and human beings.

To Paul, the whole work of Jesus was that he had enabled men and women to enter into this new and precious relationship with God. Fear was gone and love had come. The God previously thought of as an enemy had become a friend.

Matthew 7:21–29

Jesus was in a double sense an expert. He was an expert in Scripture. The writer of Proverbs gave him the hint for his picture: 'When the tempest passes, the wicked are no more, but the righteous are established for ever' (Proverbs 10:25). Here is the germ of the picture which Jesus drew of the two houses and the two builders. But Jesus was also an expert in life. He was the craftsman who knew all about the building of houses, and when he spoke about the foundations of a house he knew what he was talking about. This is no illustration formed by a scholar in his study; this is the illustration of a practical man.

Nor is this a far-fetched illustration; it is a story of the kind of thing which could well happen. In Palestine, the builder must think ahead. There were many gullies which in summer were pleasant sandy hollows, but in winter became raging torrents of rushing water. A man might be looking for a house; he might find a pleasantly sheltered sandy hollow; and he might think this a very suitable place. But, if he was a short-sighted man, he might well have built his house in the dried-up bed of a river, and when the winter came, his house would disintegrate. Even on an ordinary site, it was tempting to begin building on the smoothed-over sand and not to bother digging down to the shelf of rock below; but that way disaster lay ahead.

Only a house whose foundations are firm can withstand the storm; and only a life whose foundations are sure can stand the test. Jesus demanded two things.

(1) He demanded that men and women should *listen*. One of the great difficulties which face us today is the simple fact that people often do not know what Jesus said or what the Church teaches. In fact, the matter is worse. They often have a quite mistaken notion of what Jesus said and of what the Church teaches. It is never a matter for pride or self-congratulation to condemn either a person, or an institution, unheard – and that today is precisely what so many do. The first step to the Christian life is simply to give Jesus Christ a chance to be heard.

(2) He demanded that men and women should *do*. Knowledge only becomes relevant when it is translated into action. It would be perfectly possible to pass an examination in Christian ethics with the highest distinction, and yet not to be a Christian. Knowledge must become action; theory must become practice; theology must become life. There is little point in consulting a doctor about our health unless we are prepared to act upon the things we are told. There is little point in going to an expert unless we are prepared to act upon the advice given to us. And yet there are thousands of people who listen to the teaching of Jesus Christ every Sunday, and

who have a very good knowledge of what Jesus taught, and who yet make little or no deliberate attempt to put it into practice. If we are to be in any sense followers of Jesus, we must *hear* and *do*.

Is there any word in which *hearing* and *doing* are summed up? There is such a word, and that word is *obedience*. Jesus demands our implicit obedience. To learn to obey is the most important thing in life.

Some time ago, there was a report of the case of a sailor in the Royal Navy who was very severely punished for a breach of discipline. So severe was the punishment that in certain civilian quarters it was thought to be far too severe. A newspaper asked its readers to express their opinions about the severity of the punishment. One who answered was a man who himself had served for years in the Royal Navy. In his view, the punishment was not too severe. He held that discipline was absolutely essential, for the purpose of discipline was to condition those in service automatically and unquestioningly to obey orders, and on such obedience their lives might well depend. He cited a case from his own experience. He was in a launch which was towing a much heavier vessel in a rough sea. The vessel was attached to the launch by a wire cable. Suddenly in the midst of the wind and the spray there came a single, insistent word of command from the officer in charge of the launch. 'Down!' he shouted. On the spot, the crew of the launch flung themselves down. Just at that moment, the wire towing-cable snapped, and the broken parts of it whipped about like a maddened steel snake. If any man had been struck by it, he would have been instantly killed. But the whole crew automatically obeyed, and no one was injured. If anyone had stopped to argue or to ask why, he would have been a dead man. Obedience saved lives.

It is such obedience that Jesus demands. It is Jesus' claim that obedience to him is the only sure foundation for life; and it is his promise that the life which is founded on obedience to him is safe, no matter what storms may come.

The Sunday between 5 and 11 June

Believing in the God Who Makes the Impossible Possible *and* The Imperfect Faith and the Perfect Power

Romans 4:13–25

Paul saw things in terms of black and white. He saw two mutually exclusive ways of trying to get into a right relationship with God. On the one hand, there was dependence on human effort; on the other, dependence on divine grace. On the one hand, there was the constant losing battle to obey an impossible law; on the other, there was the faith which simply takes God at his word. On each side, there were three things to be noted.

(1) On the one side, there is God's *promise*. There are two Greek words which mean *promise*. *Huposchesis* means a promise which is entered into upon conditions. 'I promise to do this if you promise to do that.' *Epaggelia* means a promise made out of the goodness of someone's heart quite unconditionally. It is *epaggelia* that Paul uses of the promise of God. It is as if he is saying: 'God is like a human father; he promises to love his children no matter what they do.' True, he will love some of us with a love that makes him glad, and he will love some of us with a love that makes him sad; but in either case it is a love which will never let us go. It is dependent not on our merit but only on God's own generous heart.

(2) There is *faith*. Faith is the certainty that God is indeed like that. It is staking everything on his love.

(3) There is *grace*. A gift of grace is always something which is unearned and undeserved. The truth is that we can never earn the love of God. We must always find that glory not in what we can do for God but in what God has done for us.

(1) On the other side, there is *law*. The trouble about law has always been that it can diagnose the fault but cannot bring about a cure. Law shows people where they are going wrong, but does not help them to avoid going wrong. There is, in fact, as Paul will later stress, a kind of terrible paradox in law. It is human nature that, when a thing is forbidden, it has a tendency to become desirable. 'Stolen fruits are sweetest.' Law, therefore, can actually move people to desire the very thing which it forbids. The essential complement of law is judgement, and, as long as men and women live in a religion whose dominant thought is law, they cannot see themselves as anything other than condemned criminals awaiting God's justice.

(2) There is *transgression*. Whenever law is introduced, transgression follows. No one can break a law which does not exist; and we cannot be condemned for breaking a law of whose existence we were ignorant. If we introduce law and stop there, if we make religion solely a matter of obeying law, life consists of one long series of transgressions waiting to be punished.

(3) There is *wrath*. Think of *law*, think of *transgression*, and inevitably the next thought is *wrath*. Think of God in terms of law, and the only way to think of him is in terms of outraged justice. Think of human beings in terms of law, and the only way to think of them is as destined for the condemnation of God. So, Paul sets before the Romans two ways. The one is a way in which men and women seek a right relationship with God through their own efforts. It is doomed to failure. The other is a way in which men and women enter by faith into a relationship with God, which by God's grace already exists for them to come into in trust.

In verses 18–25 Paul's thoughts turn to an outstanding example of Abraham's willingness to take God at his word. The promise that all families of the earth would be blessed in his descendants was given to Abraham when he was an old man. His wife, Sarah, had always been childless; and now (Genesis 17:17), there came the promise that a son would be born to them. It seemed, on the face of it, beyond all belief and beyond all hope of fulfilment. Yet, once again, Abraham took God at his word, and once again it was this faith that was 'accounted to him as righteousness'.

It was this willingness to take God at his word which put Abraham into a right relationship with him. Now, the Jewish Rabbis had a saying to which Paul here refers. They said: 'What is written of Abraham is written also of his children.' They meant that any promise that God made to Abraham also extends to his children. Therefore, if Abraham's willingness to take God at his word brought him into a right relationship with God, so it will be the same for us. It is not works of the law, it is this trusting faith which establishes the relationship between God and his people which ought to exist.

The essence of Abraham's faith in this case was that he believed that God could make the impossible possible. As long as we believe that everything depends on our efforts, we are bound to be pessimists, for experience has taught the grim lesson that our own efforts can achieve very little. When we realize that it is not our own efforts but God's grace and power which matter, then we become optimists, because we are bound to believe that with God nothing is impossible.

Ann Hunter Small, the great missionary teacher had a favourite saying: 'A church which is alive dares to do anything.' That daring only becomes possible to the individual and to the church that takes God at his word.

Matthew 9:9–13, 18–26

Matthew tells the story of the ruler's daughter much more briefly than the other gospel writers do. If we want further details of it, we must read it in Mark 5:21–43 and in Luke 8:40–56. There we discover that the ruler's name was Jairus, and that he was a ruler of the synagogue (Mark 5:22; Luke 8:41).

The ruler of the synagogue was a very important person. He was elected from among the elders. He was not a teaching or a preaching official; he had 'the care of the external order in public worship, and the supervision of the concerns of the synagogue in general'. He appointed those who were to read and to pray in the service, and invited those who were to preach. It was his duty to see that nothing unfitting took place within the synagogue; and the care of the synagogue buildings was in his oversight. The whole practical administration of the synagogue was in his hands.

It is clear that such a man would come to Jesus only as a last resort. He would be one of those strictly orthodox Jews who regarded Jesus as a dangerous heretic; and it was only when everything else had failed that he turned in desperation to Jesus. Jesus might well have said to him: 'When things were going well with you, you wanted to kill me; now that things are going badly, you are appealing for my help.' And Jesus might well have refused help to a man who came like that. But he bore no grudge; here was a man who needed him, and Jesus' one desire was to help. Injured pride and the unforgiving spirit had no part in the mind of Jesus.

It is probable that when Jesus said the girl was asleep, he meant exactly what he said. In Greek as in English, a dead person was often said to be asleep. In fact, the word *cemetery* comes from the Greek word *koimētērion* and means *a place where people sleep*. In Greek there are two words for *to sleep*: the one is *koimasthai*, which is very commonly used both of natural sleep and of the sleep of death;

the other is *katheudein*, which is not used nearly so frequently of the sleep of death, but which much more usually means natural sleep. It is *katheudein* which is used in this passage.

In this part of the world, cataleptic coma was by no means uncommon. Burial in the Middle East follows death very quickly, because the climate makes it necessary. Henry Baker Tristram, who travelled extensively in the Bible lands, writes: 'Interments always take place at latest on the evening of the day of death, and frequently at night, if the deceased have lived till after sunset.' Because of the commonness of this state of coma, and because of the commonness of speedy burial, not infrequently people were buried alive. It may well be that here we have an example not so much of divine healing as of divine diagnosis; and that Jesus saved this girl from a terrible end. One thing is certain: Jesus that day in Capernaum rescued a young Jewish girl from the grasp of death.

Beyond doubt, the ruler came to Jesus when everything else had failed. He was a ruler of the synagogue, he was a pillar of Jewish orthodoxy. He was one of the men who despised and hated Jesus, and who would have been glad to see him eliminated. No doubt he tried every kind of doctor, and every kind of cure; and only in sheer desperation, and as a last resort, did he come to Jesus at all.

That is to say, *the ruler came to Jesus from a very inadequate motive.* He did not come to Jesus as a result of an outflow of the love of his heart; he came to Jesus because he had tried everything and everyone else, and because there was nowhere else to go. The hymn writer F. W. Faber makes God say of a straying child of God:

If goodness lead him not,
Then weariness may toss him to my breast.

The ruler came to Jesus with an *inadequate motive.* Here we see a tremendous thing. It does not matter how we come to Christ, if only we come. No matter how inadequately and how imperfectly we come, his love and his arms are open to receive us.

There is a double lesson here. It means that we do not wait to ask Christ's help until our motives, our faith and our theology are perfect; we may come to him exactly as we are. And it means that we have no right to criticize others whose motives we suspect, whose faith we question and whose theology we believe to be mistaken. It is not how we come to Christ that matters; it is that we should come at all, for he is willing to accept us as we are, and able to make us what we ought to be.

The Sunday between 12 and 18 June
At Home with God *and* The Waiting Harvest

Romans 5:1–8

Here is one of Paul's great lyrical passages in which he almost sings the intimate joy of his confidence in God. Trusting faith has done what the labour to produce the works of the law could never do: it has given us peace with God. Before Jesus came, no one could ever be really close to God. Some have seen him as the complete stranger, the utterly untouchable. Some, indeed, have seen him not as the supreme good but as the supreme evil. Swinburne wrote in 'Anactoria':

> His hidden face and iron feet,
> Hath not man known and felt them in their way
> Threaten and trample all things every day?
> Hath he not sent us hunger? Who hath cursed
> Spirit and flesh with longing? Filled with thirst
> Their lips that cried to him?

It is only when we realize that God is the Father of our Lord Jesus Christ that there comes into life that closeness to him, that new relationship, which Paul calls justification. Through Jesus, says Paul, we have an introduction to this grace in which we stand. The word he uses for *introduction* is *prosagōgē*. It is a word which conjures up two great images.

(1) It is the word normally used for introducing or ushering some-one into the presence of royalty; and it is the word for the approach of the worshipper to God. It is as if Paul was saying: 'Jesus ushers us into the very presence of God. He opens the door for us to the presence of the King of kings; and when that door is opened what we find is *grace*; not condemnation, not judgement, not vengeance, but the sheer, undeserved, incredible kindness of God.'

(2) But *prosagōgē* brings to mind another picture. In late Greek, it is the word for the place where ships come in, a *harbour* or a *haven*. If we take it in that sense, it means that as long as we tried to depend on our own efforts we were tempest-tossed, like sailors striving with a sea which threatened to overwhelm them completely; but, now that we have heard the word of Christ, we have reached at last the haven of God's grace, and we know the calm of depending not on what we can do for ourselves but on what God has done for us.

Because of Jesus, we have entry to the presence of the King of kings and entry to the haven of God's grace. No sooner has Paul said this than the other side of the matter strikes him. All this is true, and it is glory; but the fact remains that, in this life, Christians are up against it. It is hard to be a Christian in Rome. Remembering that, Paul produces a great climax. 'Trouble', he said, 'produces fortitude.'

The word he uses for *trouble* is *thlipsis*, which literally means *pressure*. All kinds of things may press in upon a Christian – want and difficult circumstances, sorrow, persecution, unpopularity and lone-liness. All that pressure, says Paul, produces fortitude. The word he uses for *fortitude* is *hupomonē*, which means more than endurance. It means the spirit which can overcome the world; it means the spirit which does not passively endure but which actively overcomes the trials and tribulations of life.

When Beethoven was threatened with deafness, that most ter-rible of troubles for a musician, he said: 'I will take life by the throat.' That is *hupomonē*. When the poet W. E. Henley was lying in Edinburgh Infirmary with one leg amputated, and the prospect that he would lose the other leg as well, he wrote 'Invictus'.

> Out of the night that covers me,
> Black as the Pit from pole to pole,
> I thank whatever gods may be
> For my unconquerable soul.

That is *hupomonē*. *Hupomonē* is not the spirit which lies down and lets the floods go over it; it is the spirit which meets things head on and overcomes them.

'Fortitude', Paul goes on, 'produces character.' The word he uses for *character* is *dokimē*. *Dokimē* is used of metal which has been passed through the fire so that everything base has been purged out of it. It is used of coinage as we use the word *sterling*. When affliction is met with fortitude, out of the battle we emerge stronger, purer, better and nearer to God.

'Character', Paul goes on, 'produces hope.' Two people can meet the same situation. It can drive one of them to despair, and it can spur the other to triumphant action. To the one, it can be the end of hope; to the other, it can be a challenge to greatness. 'I do not like crises,' said the Director General of the BBC, Lord Reith, 'but I like the opportunities which they supply.' The difference corresponds to the difference between individuals. If we allow circumstances to beat us, if we allow ourselves to whine and grovel under affliction, we make ourselves the kind of people who, when the challenge of the crisis comes, cannot do anything but despair. If, on the other hand, if we have always faced and, by facing, conquered things; then, when the challenge comes, we meet it with eyes alight with hope. The character that has endured the test always emerges in hope.

Then Paul makes one last great statement: 'The Christian hope never proves an illusion, for it is founded on the love of God.' *The Rubaiyat of Omar Khayyam* speaks wistfully of human hopes:

The Worldly Hope men set their hearts upon
Turns Ashes – or it prospers; and anon,
Like Snow upon the Desert's dusty Face
Lighting a little Hour or two – is gone.

When our hope is in God, it cannot turn to dust and ashes. When our hope is in God, it cannot be disappointed. When our hope is in the love of God, it can never be an illusion, for God loves us with an everlasting love backed by an everlasting power.

Matthew 9:35–10:8

In verses 37–38 we have one of the most characteristic things Jesus ever said. When he and the orthodox religious leaders of his day looked on the crowd of ordinary men and women, they saw them in quite different ways. The Pharisees saw the masses as chaff to be destroyed and burned up; Jesus saw them as a harvest to be reaped and to be saved. The Pharisees in their pride looked for the destruction of sinners; Jesus in love died for the salvation of sinners.

But here also is one of the great Christian truths and one of the supreme Christian challenges. That harvest will never be reaped unless there are reapers to reap it. It is one of the blazing truths of Christian faith and life that *Jesus Christ needs us*. When he was upon this earth, his voice could reach so few. He was never outside Palestine, and there was a world which was waiting. He still wants the world to hear the good news of the gospel; but they will never hear unless others tell them. He wants all men and women to hear the good news; but they will never hear it unless there are those who are prepared to cross the seas and the mountains and bring the good news to them.

Nor is prayer enough. Some people might say: 'I will pray for the coming of Christ's kingdom every day in life.' But in this, as in so many things, prayer without works is dead. Martin Luther had a friend who felt about the Christian faith as he did. The friend was also a monk. They came to an agreement. Luther would go down into the dust and heat of the battle for the Reformation in the world; the friend would stay in the monastery and uphold Luther's hands in prayer. So they began that way. Then, one night, the friend had a dream. He saw a vast field of corn as big as the world; and one solitary man was seeking to reap it – an impossible and a heartbreaking task. Then he caught a glimpse of the reaper's face; and the reaper was Martin Luther; and Luther's friend saw the truth in a flash. 'I must leave my prayers', he said, 'and get to work.' And so he left his pious solitude and went down to the world to labour in the harvest.

It is the dream of Christ that we should all be missionaries and reapers. There are those who cannot do other than pray, because of physical limitations, and their prayers are indeed the strength of the labourers. But that is not the way for most of us, for those of us who have strength of body and health of mind. Not even the giving of our money is enough. If the harvest of men and women is ever to be reaped, then every one of us must be a reaper, for there is someone whom each one of us could – and must – bring to God.

The Sunday between 19 and 25 June

Dying to Live *and* The Warfare and the Cost of Jesus' Messengers

Romans 6:1b–11

As he has so often done in this letter, Paul is once again carrying on an argument against a kind of imaginary opponent. The argument springs from the great saying at the end of the last chapter: 'Where sin abounded, grace superabounded.' It runs something like this.

The objector: You have just said that God's grace is great enough to find forgiveness for every sin.

Paul: That is so.

The objector: You are, in fact, saying that God's grace is the most wonderful thing in all this world.

Paul: That is so.

The objector: Well, if that is so, let us go on sinning. The more we sin, the more grace will abound. Sin does not matter, for God will forgive anyway. In fact, we can go further than that and say that sin is an excellent thing, because it gives the grace of God a chance to operate. The conclusion of your argument is that sin produces grace; therefore sin is bound to be a good thing if it produces the greatest thing in the world.

Paul's first reaction is to recoil from that argument in sheer horror. 'Do you suggest', he demands, 'that we should go on sinning in order to give grace more chance to operate? God forbid that we should pursue such an incredible course.' Then, having recoiled like that, he goes on to something else. Have you never thought, he demands, 'what happened to you when you were baptized?'

Now, when we try to understand what Paul goes on to say, we must remember that baptism in his time differed from the common practice today.

(1) It was adult baptism. That is not to say that the New Testament is opposed to infant baptism; but infant baptism is the result of the Christian family, and the Christian family could hardly be said to have come into being as early as the time of Paul. Men and women came to Christ as individuals in the early Church, often leaving their families behind.

(2) Baptism in the early Church was closely connected with confession of faith. People were baptized when they entered the Church; and many were entering the Church direct from the religion of the state. In baptism, they came to a decision which cut their lives in two, a decision which often meant that they had to tear themselves up by the roots, a decision which was so definite that it often meant nothing less than beginning life all over again.

(3) Usually, baptism was by total immersion, and that practice lent itself to a symbolism to which sprinkling does not so readily lend itself. When those being baptized descended into the water and the water closed over their heads, it was like being buried. When they emerged from the water, it was like rising from the grave. Baptism was symbolically like dying and rising again. The new Christians died to one kind of life and rose to another; they died to the old life of sin and rose to the new life of grace.

If we are fully to understand this, we must remember that Paul was using language and pictures that almost anyone of his day and generation would understand. It may seem strange to us, but it was not at all strange to his contemporaries.

The Jews would understand it. When a Gentile entered the Jewish religion, it involved three things – sacrifice, circumcision and baptism. He entered the Jewish faith by baptism. The effect of this baptism was held to be complete regeneration; he was called a little child just born, the child of one day. All his sins were cancelled because God could not punish sins committed before he was born. The completeness of the change was seen in the fact that certain Rabbis held that a man's child born after baptism was his first-born, even if he had older children. Any Jew would fully understand Paul's words about the necessity of those who were baptized being completely new.

The Greeks would understand. At this time, the only real Greek religion was found in the mystery religions. They were wonderful things. They offered release from the cares and sorrows and fears of this earth; and the release was by union with some god. All the mysteries were passion plays. They were based on the story of some god who suffered and died and rose again. The story was played out as a drama. Before a man could see the drama, he had to be initiated. He had to undergo a long course of instruction on the inner meaning of the drama. He had to undergo a course of ascetic discipline. He was carefully prepared. Any Greek who had been through this would have no difficulty in understanding what Paul meant by dying and rising again in baptism, and, in so doing, becoming one with Christ.

Paul was using words and pictures that both Jew and Gentile would recognize and understand. In this passage lie three great permanent truths.

(1) It is a terrible thing to seek to trade on the mercy of God and to make it an excuse for sinning. Think of it in human terms. How despicable it would be for children to consider themselves free to sin because they knew that their parents would forgive. That would be taking advantage of love to break love's heart.

(2) Those who enter upon the Christian way are committed to a different kind of life. They have died to one kind of life and been born to another. In recent years, we may have tended to stress

the fact that acceptance of the Christian way need not make so very much difference in a person's life. Paul would have said that it ought to make all the difference in the world.

(3) But there is more than a mere ethical change in our lives when we accept Christ. There is a real identification with Christ. It is, in fact, the simple truth that the ethical change is not possible without that union. We are *in Christ*. One great scholar has suggested this analogy for that phrase. We cannot live our physical life unless we are in the air and the air is in us; unless we are in Christ, and Christ is in us, we cannot live the life of God.

Matthew 10:24–39

Nowhere is the sheer honesty of Jesus more vividly displayed than it is in the final verses of this passage. Here he sets the Christian demand in its most forceful and uncompromising form. He tells his disciples exactly what they may expect if they accept the commission to be his messengers. Here in this passage, Jesus offers four things.

(1) He offers a *warfare*; and in that warfare it will often be true that the enemy will be members of a person's own household.

When some great cause emerges, it is bound to divide people; there are bound to be those who answer, and those who refuse, the challenge. To be confronted with Jesus is necessarily to be confronted with the choice whether to accept him or to reject him; and the world is always divided into hose who have accepted Christ and those who have not. The bitterest thing about this warfare was that people's enemies would be from their own households. It can happen that people love their family so much that they may refuse some great adventure, some avenue of service, some call to sacrifice, either because they do not wish to leave them, or because to accept it would involve them in danger. It is possible for loved ones to become in effect enemies, if the thought of them keeps us from doing what we know God wants us to do.

(2) He offers a *choice*; and we have to choose sometimes between the closest ties of earth and loyalty to Jesus Christ. John Bunyan knew all about that choice. The thing which troubled him most about his imprisonment was the effect it would have upon his wife and children. What was to happen to them, bereft of his support? 'The parting with my wife and poor children hath often been to me in this place, as the pulling the flesh from my bones; and that not only because I am somewhat too fond of these great mercies, but also because I should have often brought to my mind the many hardships, miseries, and wants that my poor family was like to meet with, should I be taken from them, *especially my poor blind child*, who lay nearer my heart than all I had besides. O the thought of the hardship I thought my blind one might go under, would break up my heart to pieces . . . But yet, recalling myself, thought I, I must venture you all with God, though it goeth to the quick to leave you; O I saw in this condition, I was a man who was pulling down his house upon the head of his wife and children; yet thought I, I must do it, I must do it.'

Once again, this terrible choice will come very seldom, in God's mercy to many of us it may never come; but the fact remains that all loyalties must give place to loyalty to God.

(3) Jesus offers a *cross*. People in Galilee knew very well what a cross was. When the Roman general Varus had broken the revolt of Judas of Galilee, he crucified 2,000 Jews, and placed the crosses by the wayside along the roads to Galilee. In the ancient days, the criminal did actually carry the crossbeam of his cross to the place of crucifixion, and the men to whom Jesus spoke had seen people staggering under the weight of their crosses and dying in agony upon them. The truly great, whose names are on the honour roll of faith, knew very well what they were doing. After his trial in Scarborough

Castle, the Quaker George Fox wrote: 'And the officers would often be threatening me, that I should be hanged over the wall . . . they talked much then of hanging me. But I told them, "If that was it they desired, and it was permitted them, I was *ready*." '

Christians may have to sacrifice their personal ambitions, the ease and the comfort that they might have enjoyed, the career that they might have achieved; they may have to lay aside their dreams, to realize that shining things of which they have caught a glimpse are not for them. They will certainly have to sacrifice their will, for Christians can never again do what they like; they must do what Christ likes. In Christianity there is always some cross, for it is the religion of the cross.

(4) He offers *adventure*. He told them that those who found life would lose it; and those who lost life would find it. Again and again, that has been proved true in the most literal way. It has always been true that many people might easily have saved their lives; but, if their lives had been saved, they would also have been lost, for no one would ever have heard of them, and the place they hold in history would have been lost to them.

There is no place for a policy of safety first in the Christian life. Those who seek first ease and comfort and security and the fulfilment of personal ambition may well get all these things – but they will not be happy; for we were sent into this world to serve God and one another. It is possible to hoard life if we wish to do so. But that way, we will lose all that makes life valuable to others and worth living for ourselves. The way to serve others, the way to fulfil God's purpose for us, the way to true happiness is to spend life selflessly, for only thus will we find life, here and hereafter.

The Sunday between 26 June and 2 July
The Exclusive Possession *and* The Reward of Those Who Welcome Jesus' Messengers
Romans 6:12–23

To a certain type of mind, the doctrine of free grace is always a temptation to say: 'If forgiveness is as easy and as inevitable as all that, if God's one desire is to forgive, and if his grace is wide enough to cover every spot and stain, why worry about sin? Why not do as we like? It will be all the same in the end.'

Paul counters this argument by using a vivid picture. He says: 'Once you gave yourselves to sin as its slave; when you did that, righteousness had no claim over you. But now you have given yourselves to God as the slaves of righteousness; and so sin has no claim over you.'

To understand this, we must understand the status of the slave. Every single moment of a slave's time belonged to their master. They were their master's absolutely exclusive possession. That is the picture that is in Paul's mind. He says: 'At one time, you were the slave of sin. Sin had exclusive possession of you. At that time, you could not talk of anything else but sinning. But now, you have taken God as your master and he has exclusive possession of you. Now you cannot even talk about sinning; you must talk about nothing but holiness.'

Paul actually apologizes for using this picture. He says: 'I am only using a human analogy so that your human minds can understand it.' He apologized because he did not like to compare the Christian life to any kind of slavery. But the one thing that this picture does show is that Christians can have no master but God. They cannot give a part of their lives to God and another part to the world. With God, it is all – or nothing. As long as people keep some part of their lives without God, they are not really Christians. Christians are men and women who have given complete control of their lives to Christ, holding nothing back. No one who has done that can ever think of using grace as an excuse for sin. But Paul has something more to say: 'You took a spontaneous decision to obey the pattern of the teaching to which you were committed.' In other words, he is saying: 'You knew what you were doing, and you did it of your own free will.'

This passage has arisen from a discussion of baptism. This therefore means that baptism was instructed baptism. Baptism in the early Church was adult baptism and confession of faith. It is, then, quite clear that no one was ever allowed into the Christian Church on an emotional impulse. Everyone was instructed; they had to know what they were doing; they were shown what Christ offered and demanded.

Jesus does not want followers who have not stopped to count the cost. He does not want anyone to express loyalty that will not last or make commitment on the crest of a wave of emotion. The Church has a duty to present the faith in all the riches of its offer and the heights of its demands to those who wish to become its members.

Paul draws a distinction between the old life and the new. The old life was characterized by *uncleanness* and *lawlessness*. The world of the Roman Empire was lawless in the sense that people's lusts were their only laws; and that lawlessness produced more lawlessness. That, indeed, is the law of sin. Sin creates even more sin. The first time we do a wrong thing, we may do it with hesitation and a tremor and a shudder. The second time we do it, it is easier; and, if we go on doing it, it becomes effortless; sin loses its terror. The first time we allow ourselves some indulgence, we may be satisfied with very little of it; but the time comes when we need more and more of it to produce the same thrill. Sin leads on to sin; lawlessness produces lawlessness. To start on the path of sin is to go on to more and more.

The new life is different; it is life which is righteous. Now, the Greeks defined righteousness as *giving to others and to God their due*. The Christian life is one which gives God his proper place and which respects the rights of human personality. Christians will never disobey God nor ever use a human being to gratify their desire for pleasure. The Christian life leads to what the Revised Standard Version calls *sanctification*. The word in Greek is *hagiasmos*. All Greek nouns which end in *-asmos* describe not a completed state but a *process*. Sanctification is the road to holiness. When people give their lives to Christ, they do not then become perfect; the struggle is by no means over. But Christianity has always regarded the direction in which we are facing as more important than the particular stage we have reached. Once we are Christ's, we have started on the process of sanctification, the road to holiness. As Mary Butler's hymn has it:

Leaving every day behind
Something which might hinder;
Running swifter every day;
Growing purer, kinder.

The writer Robert Louis Stevenson said: 'To travel hopefully is a better thing than to arrive.' What is true is that it is a great thing to set out to a great goal, even if we never get the whole way.

Paul finishes with a great saying that contains a double metaphor. 'Sin's pay is death,' he says, 'but God's free gift is eternal life.' Paul uses two military words. For *pay*, he uses *opsōnia*. *Opsōnia* was the soldier's pay, something that he earned with the risk of his body and the sweat of his brow, something that was due to him and could not be taken from him. For *gift*, he uses *charisma*. The *charisma*, or in Latin the *donativum*, was a totally unearned gift which the army sometimes received. On special occasions, for instance on his birthday, or on his accession to the throne, or the anniversary of it, an emperor handed out a free gift of money to the army. It had not been earned; it was a gift of the emperor's kindness and grace. So, Paul says: 'If we got the pay we had earned, it would be death; but, out of his grace, God has given us life.'

Matthew 10:40–42

Here Jesus is using a way of speaking which the Jews regularly used. The Jews always felt that to receive a person's envoy or messenger was the same as to receive that person. To pay respect to an ambassador was the same as to pay respect to the king who had sent him. To welcome with love the messenger of a friend was the same as to welcome the friend. The Jews always felt that to honour a person's representative was the same as to honour the person who had sent the representative. This was particularly so in regard to wise men and to those who taught God's truth. The Rabbis said: 'He who shows hospitality to the wise is as if he brought the first fruits of his produce unto God.' 'He who greets the learned is as if he greeted God.' If people are truly of God, to receive them is to receive the God who sent them.

This passage sets out the four links in the chain of salvation. (1) There is God, out of whose love the whole process of salvation began. (2) There is Jesus, who brought that message to men and women. (3) There are the human messengers, the prophets who speak, the good people who are examples, the disciples who learn, who in turn all pass on to others the good news which they themselves have received. (4) There are the believers, who welcome God's messengers and God's message and who thus find life to their souls.

In this passage, there is something very lovely for every simple and humble individual.

(1) We cannot all be prophets, and preach and proclaim the word of God; but those who give God's messenger the simple gift of hospitality will receive no less a reward than that prophet. There are many who have been great public figures; there are many whose voices have kindled the hearts of thousands of people; there are many who have carried an almost intolerable burden of public service and public responsibility, all of whom would gladly have borne witness that they could never have survived the effort and the demands of their task, were it not for the love and the care and the sympathy and the service of someone at home, who was never in the public eye at all. When true greatness is measured up in the sight of God, it will be seen again and again that those who greatly moved the world were entirely dependent on someone else who, as far as the world is concerned, remained unknown. Even prophets must eat and be clothed. Let those who have the often thankless task of making a home, cooking meals, washing clothes, shopping for household necessities or caring for children never think of it as a dreary and weary chore. It is God's greatest task; and they will be far more likely to receive the prophet's reward than those whose days are filled with committees and whose homes are comfortless.

(2) We cannot all be shining examples of goodness; we cannot all stand out in the world's eye as righteous; but those who help such people in their work will receive equal reward. The folklorist and writer of short stories, H. L. Gee, has a lovely story. There was a young boy in a country village who, after a great struggle, reached the ministry. His helper in his days of study had been the village cobbler. The cobbler, like so many of his trade, was a man of wide reading and far thinking, and he had done much for the boy. In

due time, the young man was licensed to preach. And on that day, the cobbler said to him: 'It was always my desire to be a minister of the gospel, but the circumstances of my life made it impossible. But you are achieving what was closed to me. And I want you to promise me one thing – I want you to let me make and cobble your shoes – for nothing – and I want you to wear them in the pulpit when you preach, and then I'll feel you are preaching the gospel that I always wanted to preach standing in my shoes.' Beyond a doubt, the cobbler was serving God as the preacher was, and his reward would one day be the same.

(3) We cannot all teach the child; but there is a real sense in which we can all serve the child. We may not have either the knowledge or the technique to teach, but there are simple duties to be done, without which the child cannot live. It may be that in this passage it is not so much *children in age* of whom Jesus is thinking as *children in the faith*. It seems very likely that the Rabbis called their disciples *the little ones*. It may be that in the technical, academic sense we cannot teach, but there is a teaching by life and example which we can all offer.

The great beauty of this passage is its stress on simple things. The Church and Christ will always need their great orators, their great shining examples of sainthood, their great teachers, those whose names are household words; but the Church and Christ will also always need those in whose homes there is hospitality, on whose hands there is all the service which makes a home, and in whose hearts there is the caring which is Christian love; and, as Robert Browning wrote in 'Pippa Passes', 'All service ranks the same with God.'

The Sunday between 3 and 9 July
The Human Situation *and* The Accent of Compassion

Romans 7:15–25a

Paul is baring his very soul; and he is telling us of an experience which lies at the heart of the human situation. He knew what was right and wanted to do it; and yet, somehow, he never could. He knew what was wrong and the last thing he wanted was to do it; and yet, somehow, he did. He felt himself to be a split personality. It was as if two men were inside the one skin, pulling in different directions. He was haunted by this feeling of frustration – his ability to see what was good and his inability to do it, his ability to recognize what was wrong and his inability to refrain from doing it.

Paul's contemporaries knew this feeling well, as, indeed, we know it ourselves. The Roman philosopher Seneca talked of 'our helplessness in necessary things'. He talked about how people hate their sins and love them at the same time. Ovid, the Roman poet, had penned the famous saying: 'I see the better things, and I approve them, but I follow the worse.'

No one knew this problem better than the Jews. They had solved it by saying that in every individual there were two natures, called the *Yetser hatob* and the *Yetser hara*. It was the Jewish conviction that God had made human beings like that with a good impulse and an evil impulse inside them.

There were Rabbis who believed that that evil impulse was present in the embryo in the womb, there even before birth. It was 'a malevolent second personality'. It was the ever-present, unyielding enemy. It was there waiting, if need be for a lifetime, for a chance to ruin a person. But the Jews were equally clear, in theory, that no one need ever succumb to that evil impulse. It was all a matter of choice.

Ben Sirach wrote of God's creation of human life:

It was he who created humankind in the beginning,
and he left them in the power of their own choice.
If you choose, you can keep the commandments,
and to act faithfully is a matter of your own choice.
He has placed before you fire and water;
stretch out your hand for whichever you choose.
Before each person are life and death,
and whichever one chooses will be given . . .
He has not commanded anyone to be wicked,
and he has not given anyone permission to sin.
(Ecclesiasticus [Sirach] 15:14–20)

There were certain things which would keep people from falling prey to the evil impulse. There was *the law*. They thought of God as saying:

I created for you the evil impulse; I created for you the
law as an antiseptic.
If you occupy yourself with the law, you will not fall
into the power of the evil impulse.
There was *the will and the mind*.
When God created man, he implanted in him his affections
and his dispositions; and then, over all, he
enthroned the sacred, ruling mind.

When the evil impulse attacked, the Jews held that wisdom and reason could defeat it; to be occupied with the study of the word of the Lord was safety; the law was a means of preventing the advance of evil; at such a time, the good impulse could be called up in defence.

Paul knew all that; and knew, too, that, while it was all theoretically true, in practice it was not true. There were things in human nature – that is what Paul meant by *this fatal body* – which responded to the seduction of sin. It is part of the human situation that we know what is right and yet do wrong, that we are never as good as we know we ought to be. At one and the same time, our minds turn to goodness and they turn also to sin.

From one point of view, this passage might be called a demonstration of inadequacies.

(1) It demonstrates *the inadequacy of human knowledge*. If to know the right thing was to do it, life would be easy. But knowledge by itself does not make us good. It is the same in every walk of life. We may know exactly how golf should be played; but that is very far from being able to play it. We may know how poetry ought to be written; but that is very far from being able to write it. We may know how we ought to behave in any given situation; but that is very far from being able to behave in the right way. That is the difference between religion and morality. Morality is knowledge of a code; religion is knowledge of a person; and it is only when we know Christ that we are able to do what we know we ought.

(2) It demonstrates the inadequacy of *human resolution*. To resolve to do a thing is very far from doing it. There is in human nature an essential weakness of the will. The will comes up against the problems, the difficulties, the opposition – and it fails. Once, Peter made a great resolution. 'Even though I must die with you,' he said, 'I will not deny you' (Matthew 26:35); and yet he failed badly when it came to the point. The human will that does not receive strength from Christ is bound to crack.

(3) It demonstrates *the limitations of diagnosis*. Paul knew quite clearly what was wrong; but he was unable to put it right. He was like a doctor who could accurately diagnose a disease but was pow-

erless to prescribe a cure. Jesus is the one person who not only knows what is wrong, but who can also put right that wrong. It is not criticism he offers, but help.

Matthew 11:16–19, 25–30

At the end of this passage, Jesus is speaking to people desperately trying to find God and desperately trying to be good, who were finding the tasks impossible and who were driven to weariness and to despair. He says: 'Come to me all you who are exhausted.' His invitation is to those who are exhausted with the search for the truth. The Greeks had said: 'It is very difficult to find God, and, when you have found him, it is impossible to tell anyone else about him.' Zophar demanded of Job: 'Can you find out the deep things of God?' (Job 11:7). It is Jesus' claim that the weary search for God ends in Jesus himself. W. B. Yeats, the great Irish poet and mystic, wrote: 'Can one reach God by toil? He gives himself to the pure in heart. He asks nothing but our attention.' The way to know God is not by mental search, but by giving attention to Jesus Christ, for in him we see what God is like.

He says: 'Come to me all you who are weighted down beneath your burdens.' For orthodox Jews, religion was a thing of burdens. Jesus said of the scribes and Pharisees: 'They tie up heavy burdens, hard to bear, and lay them on the shoulders of others' (Matthew 23:4). To the Jews, religion was a thing of endless rules. People lived their lives in a forest of regulations which dictated every action. They must listen forever to a voice which said: 'You shall not.'

Jesus invites us to take his yoke upon our shoulders. The Jews used the phrase *the yoke* for *entering into submission to*. They spoke of the yoke of the law, the yoke of the commandments, the yoke of the kingdom and the yoke of God. But it may well be that Jesus took the words of his invitation from something much nearer home than that.

He says: 'My yoke is *easy*.' The word *easy* is in Greek *chrēstos*, which can mean *well-fitting*. In Palestine, ox-yokes were made of wood; the ox was brought, and the measurements were taken. The yoke was then roughed out, and the ox was brought back to have the yoke tried on. The yoke was carefully adjusted, so that it would fit well, and not chafe the neck of the patient animal. The yoke was tailor-made to fit the ox.

There is a legend that Jesus made the best ox-yokes in all Galilee, and that from all over the country people came to him to buy the best yokes that skill could make. In those days, as now, shops had their signs above the door; and it has been suggested that the sign above the door of the carpenter's shop in Nazareth may well have been: 'My yokes fit well.' It may well be that Jesus is here using a picture from the carpenter's shop in Nazareth where he had worked.

Jesus says: 'My yoke fits well.' What he means is: 'The life I give you is not a burden to cause you pain; your task is made to measure to fit you.' Whatever God sends us is made to fit our needs and our abilities exactly.

Jesus says: 'My burden is light.' As a Rabbi had it: 'My burden is become my song.' It is not that the burden is easy to carry; but it is laid on us in love; it is meant to be carried in love; and love makes even the heaviest burden light. When we remember the love of God, when we know that our burden is to love God and to love one another, then the burden becomes a song. There is an old story which tells how a man came upon a little boy carrying a still smaller boy, who was lame, upon his back. 'That's a heavy burden for you to carry,' said the man. 'That's no' a burden,' came the answer. 'That's my wee brother.' The burden which is given in love and carried in love is always light.

The Sunday between 10 and 16 July
The Liberation of our Human Nature *and* The Sower Went out to Sow

Romans 8:1–11

In this chapter two words keep recurring again and again – *flesh* (*sarx*) and *spirit* (*pneuma*). We will not understand the passage at all unless we understand the way in which Paul is using these words.

(1) *Sarx* literally means *flesh*. Broadly speaking, Paul uses it in three different ways. (a) He uses it quite literally. He speaks of physical circumcision, literally 'in the flesh' (Romans 2:28). (b) Over and over again, he uses the phrase *kata sarka*, literally *according to the flesh*, which most often means *looking at things from the human point of view*. For instance, he says that Abraham is our ancestor *kata sarka, from the human point of view* (Romans 4:1). He says that Jesus is the son of David *kata sarka* (Romans 1:3), that is to say, on the human side of his descent. (c) But he has his own way of using this word sarx. When he is talking of the Christians, he talks of the days when we were *in the flesh* (*en sarki*) (Romans 7:5). He speaks of those *who walk according to the flesh* as distinct from those who live the Christian life (Romans 8:4–5). He says that *the mind of the flesh* is death, and that it is hostile to God (Romans 8:6, 8). He talks about *living according to the flesh* (Romans 8:12). He says to his Christian friends: 'You are not *in the flesh*' (Romans 8:9).

It is quite clear, especially from the last instance, that Paul is not using *flesh* simply in the sense of the body, as we say *flesh and blood*. He really means human nature in all its weakness, and he means human nature in its vulnerability to sin; that part of human beings which offers sin a way in. He means sinful human nature, apart from Christ, everything that attaches people to the world instead of to God. *To live according to the flesh* is to live a life dominated by the dictates and desires of sinful human nature instead of a life dominated by the dictates and the love of God. The flesh is the lower side of human nature.

It is to be carefully noted that, when Paul thinks of the kind of life lived by those dominated by the sarx, he is not by any means thinking exclusively of sexual and bodily sins. The flesh to him was not a physical thing but spiritual. It was human nature in all its sin and weakness; it was all that human beings are without God and without Christ.

(2) There is the word *spirit*; in this single chapter, it occurs no fewer than twenty times. This word has a very definite Old Testament background. In Hebrew, it is *ruach*, and behind it there are two basic ideas. (a) It is not only the word for *spirit*; it is also the word for *wind*. It always contains the idea of power, power as of a mighty rushing wind. (b) In the Old Testament, it always includes the idea of something that is more than human. *Spirit*, to Paul, represented a power which was divine.

Paul says that there was a time when Christians were at the mercy of their own sinful human nature. In that state, the law simply became something that moved them to sin, and they went from bad to worse, defeated and frustrated men and women. But, when they became Christians, into their lives came the surging power of the Spirit of God, and, as a result, they entered into victorious living.

He speaks of the effect of the work of Jesus on us. What Paul is getting at is this. He had already explained that all humanity sinned in Adam (Romans 5). The Jewish conception of solidarity made it possible for Paul to argue that, quite literally, all were involved in Adam's sin and in its consequence – death. But there is another side to this picture. Into this world came Jesus, with a completely human nature; and he brought to God a life of perfect obedience, of perfect fulfilment of God's law. Now, because Jesus was fully a man, just as we were one with Adam, we are now one with him; and, just as we were involved in Adam's sin, we are now involved in Jesus' perfection. In him, humanity brought to God the perfect obedience, just as, in Adam, humanity brought to God the fatal disobedience. Men and women are saved because they were once involved in Adam's sin but are now involved in Jesus' goodness.

Because of what Jesus did, there opens out to Christians a life dominated no longer by the flesh but by that Spirit of God, which fills us with a power that is not our own. The penalty of the past is removed, and strength for our future is assured.

Matthew 13:1–9, 18–23

Here is a picture which anyone in Palestine would understand. Here we actually see Jesus using the here and now to get to the there and then. What in all likelihood happened was that, as Jesus was using the boat by the lakeside as a pulpit, in one of the fields near the shore a sower was actually sowing, and Jesus took the sower, whom they could all see, as a text, and began: 'Look at the sower there sowing his seed in that field!' Jesus began from something which at the moment they could actually see to open their minds to truth which as yet they had never seen.

In Palestine, the fields were in long narrow strips; and the ground between the strips was always a right of way. It was used as a common path; and therefore it was beaten as hard as a pavement by the feet of countless passers-by. That is what Jesus means by the wayside. If seed fell there – and some was bound to fall there in whatever way it was sown – there was no more chance of its penetrating into the earth than if it had fallen on the road.

The stony ground was not ground filled with stones; it was what was common in Palestine, a thin skin of earth on top of an underlying shelf of limestone rock. The earth might be only a very few inches deep before the rock was reached. On such ground, the seed would certainly germinate; and it would germinate quickly, because the ground grew speedily warm with the heat of the sun. But there was no depth of earth; and, when it sent down its roots in search of nourishment and moisture, it would meet only the rock, and would be starved to death and quite unable to withstand the heat of the sun.

The thorny ground was deceptive. When the sower was sowing, the ground would look clean enough. It is easy to make a garden look clean by simply turning it over; but in the ground still lay the fibrous roots of the couch grass and the ground elder and all the perennial pests, ready to spring to life again. Every gardener knows that the weeds grow with a speed and a strength that few good seeds can equal. The result was that the good seed and the dormant weeds grew together; but the weeds were so strong that they throttled the life out of the seed.

The good ground was deep and clean and soft; the seed could gain an entry; it could find nourishment; it could grow unchecked; and in the good ground it brought forth an abundant harvest.

The parable is aimed at the *hearers of the word*. If we take the parable as a warning to hearers, it means that there are different ways of accepting the word of God, and the fruit which it produces depends on the hearts of those who accept it. The fate of any spoken word depends on the hearers. Who then are the hearers described and warned in this parable?

(1) There are the hearers *with shut minds*. There are people into whose minds the word has no more chance of gaining entry than the seed has of settling into the ground that has been beaten hard by many feet. There are many things which can shut people's minds. Prejudice can make them blind to everything they do not

wish to see. There may be truth which condemns the things that an individual loves and which accuses the things that he or she does; and many refuse to listen to or to recognize the truth which condemns them, for there are none so blind as those who deliberately will not see.

(2) There are the hearers with minds like the shallow ground. These are people who *fail to think things out and think them through.* Some people are at the mercy of every new craze. They take a thing up quickly and just as quickly drop it. They must always be in fashion. It is possible to be like that with the word. When people hear it, they may be swept off their feet with an emotional reaction; but no one can live on an emotion. We all have minds, and it is a moral obligation to have an intelligent faith. Christianity has its demands, and these demands must be faced before it can be accepted. The Christian offer is not only a privilege, it is also a responsibility. A sudden enthusiasm can always so quickly become a dying fire.

(3) There are the hearers who have *so many interests in life that often the most important things get crowded out.* It is characteristic of modern life that it becomes increasingly crowded and increasingly fast. We become too busy to pray; we become so preoccupied with many things that we forget to study the word of God. We can become so involved in committees and charitable services that we leave ourselves no time for him from whom all love and service come. Our work can take such a hold that we are too tired to think of anything else. It is not even that we deliberately banish prayer and the Bible and the Church from our lives; it can be that we often think of them and intend to make time for them, but somehow in our crowded lives never get round to it. We must be careful to see that Christ is not pushed into the sidelines of life.

(4) There are people who are like the good ground. In their reception of the word, there are four stages. Like the good ground, *their minds are open.* They are at all times willing to learn. They are prepared *to hear.* They are never either too proud or too busy to

listen. Many of us would have been saved all kinds of heartbreak if we had simply stopped to listen to the voice of a wise friend or to the voice of God. *Such people understand.* They have thought the thing out and know what this means for them, and are prepared to accept it. *They translate their hearing into action.* They produce the good fruit of the good seed. The real hearers are those who listen, who understand and who obey.

The Sunday between 17 and 23 July

Entry into the Family of God *and* The Act of an Enemy

Romans 8:12–25

Paul is here introducing us to another of the great metaphors in which he describes the new relationship of Christians to God. He speaks of Christians being adopted into the family of God. It is only when we understand how serious and complicated a step Roman adoption was that we really understand the depth of meaning in this passage.

Roman adoption was always rendered more serious and more difficult by the Roman *patria potestas*. This was the father's power over his family; it was the power of absolute disposal and control, and in the early days it was actually the power of life and death. In relation to his father, a Roman son never came of age. No matter how old he was, he was still under the *patria potestas*, in the absolute possession and under the absolute control of his father. Obviously, this made adoption into another family a very difficult and serious step. In adoption, a person had to pass from one patria potestas to another.

There were two steps. The first was known as *mancipatio*, and was carried out by a symbolic sale, in which copper and scales were symbolically used. Three times the symbolism of sale was carried out. Twice the father symbolically sold his son, and twice he bought him back; but the third time he did not buy him back, and thus the *patria potestas* was held to be broken. There followed a ceremony called *vindicatio*. The adopting father went to the *praetor*, one of the

Roman magistrates, and presented a legal case for the transference of the person to be adopted into his *patria potestas*. When all this had been done, the adoption was complete. Clearly, this was a serious and an impressive step.

But it is the consequences of adoption which are most significant for the picture that is in Paul's mind. There were four main ones.

(1) The adopted person lost all rights in his old family and gained all the rights of a legitimate son in his new family. In the most binding legal way, he got a new father.

(2) It followed that he became heir to his new father's estate. Even if other sons were born afterwards, it did not affect his rights. He was co-heir with them, and no one could deny him that right.

(3) In law, the old life of the adopted person was completely wiped out; for instance, all debts were cancelled. He was regarded as a new person entering into a new life in which the past had no part.

(4) In the eyes of the law, he was absolutely the son of his new father. Roman history provides an outstanding case of how completely this was held to be true. The Emperor Claudius adopted Nero in order that he might succeed him to the throne; they were not in any sense blood relatives. Claudius already had a daughter, Octavia. To cement the alliance, Nero wished to marry her. Nero and Octavia were not blood relatives; yet, in the eyes of the law, they were brother and sister; and before they could marry, the Roman senate had to pass special legislation.

That is what Paul is thinking of. He uses yet another picture from Roman adoption. He says that God's spirit witnesses with our spirit that we really are his children. The adoption ceremony was carried out in the presence of seven witnesses. Now, suppose the adopting father died and there was some dispute about the right of the adopted son to inherit, one or more of the seven witnesses stepped forward and swore that the adoption was genuine. Thus the right of the adopted person was guaranteed, and he entered into his inheritance. So, Paul is saying, it is the Holy Spirit who is the witness to our adoption into the family of God.

So, we see that every step of Roman adoption was meaningful in the mind of Paul when he transferred the picture to our adoption into the family of God. Once, we were in the absolute control of our own sinful human nature; but God, in his mercy, has brought us into his absolute possession.

The old life has no more rights over us; God has an absolute right. The past is cancelled and its debts are wiped out; we begin a new life with God and become heirs of all his riches. If that is so, we become joint heirs with Jesus Christ, God's own Son. Whatever Christ inherits, we also inherit. If Christ had to suffer, we also inherit that suffering; but, if Christ was raised to life and glory, we also inherit that life and glory.

After speaking of the glory of adoption into the family of God, Paul comes to the troubled state of this present world. He draws a great picture. He speaks with a poet's vision. He sees all nature waiting for the glory that shall be. The world is one where beauty fades and loveliness decays; it is a dying world; but it is waiting for its liberation from all this, and the coming of the state of glory (for discussion of this section see The Second Sunday before Lent, p.72).

It was Paul's picture that when people became Christians they entered into the very family of God. They did nothing to deserve it; God, the great Father, in his amazing love and mercy, has taken lost, helpless, poverty-stricken, debt-laden sinners and adopted them into his own family, so that the debts are cancelled and the glory inherited.

Matthew 13:24–30, 36–43

The pictures in this parable would be clear and familiar to a Palestinian audience. Tares were one of the curses against which a farmer had to labour. They were a weed called bearded darnel (*lo-lium temulentum*). In their early stages, the tares so closely resembled the wheat that it was impossible to distinguish the one from the other. When both had produced seed heads it was easy to distinguish them; but by that time their roots were so intertwined that the tares could not be weeded out without tearing the wheat out with them.

W. M. Thomson in *The Land and the Book* tells how he saw the tares in the Wadi Hamam: 'The grain is just in the proper stage of development to illustrate the parable. In those parts where the grain has headed out [produced seed heads], the tares have done the same, and there a child cannot mistake them for wheat or barley; but when both are less developed, the closest scrutiny will often fail to detect them. I cannot do it at all with any confidence. Even the farmers, who in this country generally weed their fields, do not attempt to separate the one from the other. They would not only mistake good grain for them, but very commonly the roots of the two are so intertwined that it is impossible to separate them without plucking up both. Both, therefore, must be left to grow together until the time of harvest.'

The wheat and tares could not be safely separated when both were growing, but in the end they had to be separated, because the grain of the bearded darnel is slightly poisonous. It causes dizziness and sickness and is narcotic in its effects, and even a small amount has a bitter and unpleasant taste. In the end, it was usually separated by hand. The scholar N. Levison describes the process: 'Women have to be hired to pick the darnel grain out of the seed which is to be milled . . . As a rule the separation of the darnel from the wheat is done after the threshing. By spreading the grain out on a large tray which is set before the women, they are able to pick out the darnel, which is a seed similar in shape and size to wheat, but slate-grey in colour.'

So, the darnel in its early stages was indistinguishable from the wheat, but in the end it had to be laboriously separated from it, or the consequences were serious.

The picture of a man deliberately sowing darnel in someone else's field is by no means only imagination. That was actually sometimes done. In codified Roman law, this crime is forbidden and its punishment laid down. The whole series of pictures within this parable was familiar to the people of Galilee who heard it for the first time.

It may well be said that in its lessons this is one of the most practical parables that Jesus ever told.

(1) It teaches us that there is always a hostile power in the world, seeking and waiting to destroy the good seed. Our experience is that both kinds of influence act upon our lives – the influence which helps the seed of the word to flourish and to grow, and the influence which seeks to destroy the good seed before it can produce fruit at all. The lesson is that we must be forever on our guard.

(2) It teaches us how hard it is to distinguish between those who are in the kingdom and those who are not. Some people may appear to be good and may in fact be bad; and others may appear to be bad and may yet be good. We are much too quick to classify people and label them good or bad without knowing all the facts.

(3) It teaches us not to be so quick with our judgements. If the reapers had had their way, they would have tried to tear out the darnel and they would have torn out the wheat as well. Judgement had to wait until the harvest came. In the end, we will be judged, not by any single act or stage in our lives, but by our whole lives. Judgement cannot come until the end. It is possible to make a great mistake, and then redeem ourselves and, by the grace of God, atone for it by making the rest of life a lovely thing. It is also possible to live an honourable life and then in the end wreck it all by a sudden collapse into sin. No one who sees only part of a thing can judge

the whole; and no one who knows only part of an individual's life can judge the whole person.

(4) It teaches us that judgement does come in the end. Judgement is not hasty, but judgement comes. It may be that, humanly speaking, in this life the sinner seems to escape the consequences – but there is a life to come. It may be that, humanly speaking, goodness never seems to enter into its reward – but there is a new world to redress the balance of the old.

(5) It teaches us that the only person with the right to judge is God. It is God alone who can discern the good and the bad; it is God alone who sees all of an individual and all of a person's life. It is God alone who can judge.

So, ultimately this parable is two things – it is a warning not to judge people at all, and it is a warning that in the end there comes the judgement of God.

The Sunday between 24 and 30 July

The Love from Which Nothing Can Separate Us *and* The Transforming Power of Christ

Romans 8:26–39

In verses 31–39 we have one of the most lyrical passages Paul ever wrote. In verse 32, there is a wonderful allusion which would stand out to any Jew who knew the Old Testament well. Paul says in effect: 'God for us did not spare his own Son; surely that is the final guarantee that he loves us enough to supply all our needs.' The words Paul uses of God are the very words God used of Abraham when Abraham proved his utter loyalty by being willing to sacrifice his son Isaac at God's command. God said to Abraham: 'You have not withheld your son, your only son, from me' (Genesis 22:12). Paul seems to say: 'Think of the greatest human example in the world of an individual's loyalty to God; God's loyalty to you is like that.' Just as Abraham was so loyal to God that he was prepared to sacrifice his dearest possession, God is so loyal to men and women that he is prepared to sacrifice his only Son for them. Surely we can trust a loyalty like that for anything.

Paul goes on with a poet's fervour and a lover's rapture to sing of how nothing can separate us from the love of God in our risen Lord.

(1) No affliction, no hardship, no peril can separate us (verse 35). The disasters of the world do not separate us from Christ; they bring us closer.

(2) In verses 38–9, Paul makes a list of terrible things. Neither *life nor death* can separate us from Christ. In life we live with Christ; in death we die with him; and because we die with him, we also rise with him. Death, far from being a separation, is only a step into his nearer presence; not the end but 'the gate on the skyline' leading to the presence of Jesus Christ.

The angelic powers cannot separate us from him. At this particular time, the Jews had a highly developed belief in angels. Everything had its angel. There was an angel of the winds, of the clouds, of the snow and hail and hoar frost, of the thunder and the lightning, of cold and heat and of the seasons. The Rabbis said that there was nothing in the world, not even a blade of grass, that did not have its angel. According to the Rabbis, there were three ranks of angels. The first included thrones, cherubim and seraphim. The second included powers, lordships and mights. The third included angels, archangels and principalities. More than once, Paul speaks of these angels (Ephesians 1:21, 3:10, 6:12; Colossians 2:10, 2:15; 1 Corinthians 15:24). Now, the Rabbis – and Paul had once been a Rabbi – believed that they were grudgingly hostile to men and women. They believed that they had been angry when God created human life. It was as if they did not want to share God with anyone and had grudged human beings their share in him. The Rabbis had a legend that, when God appeared on Sinai to give Moses the law, he was attended by his hosts of angels; and the angels grudged Israel the law, and assaulted Moses on his way up the mountain and would have stopped him had not God intervened. So Paul, thinking in terms of his own day, says: 'Not even the grudging, jealous angels can separate us from the love of God, much as they would like to do so.'

No age in time can separate us from Christ. Paul speaks of *things present and things to come*. We know that the Jews divided all time into *this present age* and *the age to come*. Paul is saying: 'In this present world, nothing can separate us from God in Christ; the day will come when this world will be shattered and the new age will dawn. It does not matter; even then, when this world has passed and the new world come, the bond is still the same.'

No malign influences (powers) will separate us from Christ. Paul speaks about *height and depth*. These are astrological terms. The ancient world was haunted by the tyranny of the stars. It was generally believed that everyone was born under a certain star and thereby an individual's destiny was settled. There are some who still believe that; but the ancient world was really haunted by this supposed domination of people's lives by the influence of the stars. *Height* (*hupsōma*) was the time when a star was at its zenith and its influence was greatest; *depth* (*hathos*) was the time when a star was at its lowest, waiting to rise and to put its influence on someone. Paul says to these haunted people of his age: 'The stars cannot hurt you. In their rising and their setting, they are powerless to separate you from God's love.'

No other world can separate us from God. The word that Paul uses for *other* (*heteros*) has really the meaning of *different*. He is saying: 'Suppose that by some wild flight of imagination there emerged another and a different world, you would still be safe; you would still be enfolded in the love of God.'

Here is a vision to take away all loneliness and all fear. Paul is saying: 'You can think of every terrifying thing that this or any other world can produce. Not one of them is able to separate the Christian from the love of God which is in Jesus Christ, Lord of every terror and Master of every world.'

Of what then shall we be afraid?

Matthew 13:31–33, 44–52

In this chapter, there is nothing more significant than the sources from which Jesus drew his parables. In every case, he drew them from the scenes and activities of everyday life.

He began with things which were entirely familiar to his hearers in order to lead them to things which had never yet entered their minds. He took the parable of the sower from the farmer's field and the parable of the wheat and the tares from the perennial problem which confronted the farmer in his struggle with the weeds. He took the parable of the hidden treasure from the everyday task of digging in a field, and the parable of the pearl of great price from the world of commerce and trade. But in the parable of the leaven, Jesus came nearer home than in any other, because he took it from the kitchen of an ordinary house.

In Palestine, bread was baked at home; three measures of meal was just the average amount which would be needed for a baking for a fairly large family, like the family at Nazareth. Jesus took his parable of the kingdom from something that he had often seen his mother, Mary, do. Leaven was a little piece of dough kept over from a previous baking, which had fermented in the keeping.

In Jewish language and thought, leaven is almost always connected with an *evil* influence; the Jews connected fermentation with putrefaction, and leaven stood for that which is evil (cf. Matthew 16:6; 1 Corinthians 5:6–8; Galatians 5:9). One of the ceremonies of preparation for the Passover Feast was that every scrap of leaven had to be sought out from the house and burned. It may well be that Jesus chose this illustration of the kingdom deliberately. There would be a certain shock in hearing the kingdom of God compared to leaven; and the shock would arouse interest and rivet attention, as an illustration from an unusual and unexpected source always does.

The whole point of the parable lies in one thing – *the transforming power of the leaven*. Leaven changed the character of a whole baking. Unleavened bread is like a water biscuit, hard, dry, unappetizing and uninteresting; bread baked with leaven is soft and porous and spongy, tasty and good to eat. The introduction of the leaven causes a transformation in the dough; and the coming of the kingdom causes a transformation in life.

Let us gather together the characteristics of this transformation.

(1) Christianity transformed life for *the individual*. In 1 Corinthians 6:9–10, Paul gathers together a list of the most terrible and disgusting kinds of sinners; and then, in the next verse, there comes the tremendous statement: 'And such were some of you.' We must never forget that the function and the power of Christ is to make bad people good. The transformation of Christianity begins in the individual life, for through Christ the victim of temptation can become the victor over it.

(2) There are four great social directions in which Christianity transformed life. Christianity transformed life for *women*. The Jew in his morning prayer thanked God that he had not made him a Gentile, a slave or a woman. In Greek civilization, women lived lives of utter seclusion, with nothing to do beyond the household tasks. In the lands of the Middle East, it was often possible to see a family on a journey. The father would be mounted on a donkey; the mother would be walking, and probably bent beneath a burden. One demonstrable historical truth is that Christianity transformed life for women.

(3) Christianity transformed life for *the weak and the ill*. In pagan life, the weak and the ill were considered a nuisance. In Sparta, children, when they were born, were submitted to the examiners; if they were fit, they were allowed to live; if they were weakly or deformed, they were exposed to death on the mountainside. The first blind asylum was founded by Thalasius, a Christian monk; the

first free dispensary was founded by Apollonius, a Christian merchant; the first hospital of which there is any record was founded by Fabiola, a Christian lady. Christianity was the first faith to be interested in the broken things of life.

(4) Christianity transformed life for *the elderly*. Like the weak, the elderly were a nuisance. Cato, the Roman writer on agriculture, gives advice to anyone who is taking over a farm: 'Look over the livestock and hold a sale. Sell your oil, if the price is satisfactory, and sell the surplus of your wine and grain. Sell worn-out oxen, blemished cattle, blemished sheep, wool, hides, an old wagon, old tools, *an old slave, a sickly slave*, and whatever else is superfluous.' The old, whose day's work was done, were fit for nothing else than to be discarded on the rubbish heaps of life. Christianity was the first faith to regard men and women as persons and not instruments capable of doing so much work.

(5) Christianity transformed life for *the child*. In the immediate background of Christianity children could often be considered a disaster and the custom of simply exposing children to death was tragically common. There is a well-known letter from a man Hilarion, who had gone off to Alexandria, to his wife Alis, whom he had left at home. He writes to her: 'If – good luck to you – you bear a child, if it is a boy, let it live; if it is a girl, throw it out.' In modern civilization, life is almost built round the child; in ancient civilization, children had a very good chance of dying before they had begun to live.

Those who ask the question 'What has Christianity done for the world?' have delivered themselves into a Christian debater's hands. There is nothing in history so unanswerably demonstrable as the transforming power of Christianity and of Christ on the individual life and on the life of society.

The Sunday between 31 July and 6 August
The Tragic Failure *and* Compassion and Power

Romans 9:1–5

Paul begins to explain the Jewish rejection of Jesus Christ. He begins not in anger but in sorrow. Here is no tempest of anger and no outbreak of enraged condemnation; here is the poignant sorrow of the broken heart. Paul was like the God whom he loved and served: he hated the sin, but he loved the sinner. No one will ever even begin to try to save men and women without first loving them.

Paul sees the Jews not as people to be lashed with anger but as people whose salvation he yearns and longs for out of love. He says that for the sake of his own people he would consent to be accursed if it would do any good. The dearest thing in all Paul's life was the fact that nothing could separate him from the love of God in Christ Jesus; but, if it would do anything to save his own people, he would even accept banishment from God.

Here again is the great truth that those who would save sinners must love them. When a son or a daughter has done something wrong and incurred punishment, many parents would gladly bear that punishment if only they could. As F. W. H. Myers makes Paul say in his poem 'Saint Paul':

Then with a thrill the intolerable craving,
Shivers throughout me like a trumpet call;
O to save these, to perish for their saving –
Die for their life, be offered for them all.

That is what God felt; that is what Paul felt; and that is what we must feel.

Paul did not for a moment deny the place of the Jews in God's plan. He lists their privileges.

(1) In a special sense, they were children of God, specially chosen, specially adopted into the family of God. 'You are children of the Lord your God' (Deuteronomy 14:1). 'Is not he your father, who created you?' (Deuteronomy 32:6). 'Israel is my firstborn son' (Exodus 4:22). 'When Israel was a child, I loved him, and out of Egypt I called my son' (Hosea 11:1). The Bible is full of this idea of the special sonship of Israel and of Israel's refusal to accept it in the fullest sense. Israel's rejection was deliberate and open-eyed, and to God it was heartbreaking. It is a terrible thing to break the heart of God.

(2) Israel had the glory. The *shekinah* or *kaboth* occurs again and again in Israel's history. It was the divine splendour of light which descended when God was visiting his people (Exodus 16:10, 24:16–17, 29:43, 33:18–22). Israel had seen the glory of God and yet had rejected him. To us, it has been given to see the glory of God's love and mercy in the face of Jesus Christ; it is a terrible thing if we then choose the ways of earth.

(3) Israel had the covenants. A covenant is a relationship entered into between two people, a bargain for mutual profit, an engagement for mutual friendship. Again and again, God had approached the people of Israel and entered into a special relationship with them. He did so with Abraham, with Isaac, with Jacob and on Mount Sinai when he gave the law.

Irenaeus, the second-century Bishop of Lyons, distinguishes four great occasions when God entered into agreement with his people. The first was the covenant with Noah after the flood, and the sign was the rainbow in the heavens which stood for God's promise that the floods would not come again. The second was the covenant with Abraham, and its sign was the sign of circumcision.

The third was the covenant with the nation entered into on Mount Sinai, and its basis was the law. The fourth is the new covenant in Jesus Christ.

It is an amazing thing to think of God approaching men and women and entering into a pledged relationship with them. It is the simple truth that God has never left human beings alone. He did not make one approach and then abandon them. He has made approach after approach; and he still makes approach after approach to the individual human soul. He stands at the door and knocks; and it is the fearful responsibility of human will that we can refuse to open.

(4) They had the law. Israel could never plead ignorance of God's will; God had told them what he wanted them to do. If they sinned, they sinned in knowledge and not in ignorance; and the sin of knowledge is the sin against the light which is worst of all.

(5) They had the worship of the Temple. Worship is in essence the approach of the soul to God; and God in the Temple-worship had given to the Jews a special road of approach to himself. If the door to God was shut, they had shut it on themselves.

(6) They had the promises. Israel could never say that it did not know its destiny. God had told them of the task and the privilege which were in store for them in his purpose. They knew that they were destined for great things in God's plan.

(7) They had the ancestors. They had a tradition and a history; and anyone who can dare to be false to tradition and to shame the heritage into which he or she has entered is in a poor state.

(8) Then comes the culmination. From them, there came the Anointed One of God. Everything else had been a preparation for this; and yet, when he came, they rejected him. The biggest grief that parents can have is to give their children every chance of success, to sacrifice and save and toil to give them the opportunity, and then to find that the children, through disobedience or rebelliousness or self-indulgence, have failed to grasp it. Therein lies tragedy,

for therein is the waste of love's labour and the defeat of love's dream. The tragedy of Israel was that God had prepared people for the day of the coming of his Son – and all the preparation was frustrated. It was not that God's law had been broken; it was that God's love had been spurned. It is not the anger, but the broken heart of God, which lies behind Paul's words.

Matthew 14:13–21

There were three perfectly simple and natural reasons why Jesus should seek to be alone. He was human and he needed rest. He never recklessly ran into danger, and it was best to withdraw. And, most of all, Jesus knew that he must meet with God before he met with men and women. He was seeking rest for his body and strength for his soul in the lonely places.

But he was not to get it. It would be easy to see the boat set sail and to deduce where it was going; and the crowds flocked round the top of the lake and were waiting for him at the other side when he arrived. So Jesus healed them and, when the evening came, he fed them before they took the long road home. Few of Jesus' miracles are so revealing as this.

(1) It tells us of the compassion of Jesus. When he saw the crowds, he was moved with compassion to the depths of his being. That is a very wonderful thing. Jesus had come to find peace and quiet and loneliness; instead, he found a vast crowd eagerly demanding what he could give. He might so easily have resented them. What right had they to invade his privacy with their continual demands? But Jesus was not like that. So far from finding them a nuisance, he was moved with compassion for them.

(2) In this story, we see Jesus witnessing that all gifts are from God. He took the food and he said a blessing. The Jewish grace

before meals was very simple: 'Blessed art thou, Yahweh our God, King of the universe, who bringest forth bread from the earth.' That would be the grace which Jesus said, for that was the grace which every Jewish family used. Here we see Jesus showing that it is God's gifts which he brings to men and women. The grace of gratitude is rare enough towards others; it is rarer still towards God.

(3) This miracle informs us very clearly of the place of the disciple in the work of Christ. The story tells that Jesus gave to the disciples and the disciples gave to the crowd. Jesus worked through the hands of his disciples that day, and he still does.

Again and again, we come face to face with this truth which is at the heart of the Church. It is true that disciples are helpless without their Lord, but it is also true that the Lord is helpless without his disciples. Jesus Christ needs disciples through whom he can work and through whom his truth and his love can enter into the lives of others. Without such men and women, he cannot get things done, and it is our task to be the people he needs.

It would be easy to be daunted and discouraged by a task of such magnitude. But there is another thing in this story that may lift up our hearts. When Jesus told the disciples to feed the crowd, they told him that all they had was five loaves and two fishes; and yet with what they brought to him, Jesus achieved his miracle. Jesus sets every one of us the tremendous task of communicating himself to others; but he does not demand from us splendours and magnificences that we do not possess. He says to us: 'Come to me as you are, however ill-equipped; bring to me what you have, however little, and I will use it greatly in my service.' Little is always much in the hands of Christ.

(4) At the end of the miracle, there is that strange little touch that the fragments were gathered up. Even when a miracle could feed people sumptuously, there was no waste. There is something to note here. God gives to us with munificence, but a wasteful extrava-

gance is never right. God's generous giving and our wise using must go hand in hand.

Miracles are not isolated events in history; they are demonstrations of the always and forever operative power of Jesus Christ. There are three ways in which we can look at this miracle.

(1) We may look at it as a simple multiplication of loaves and fishes. That would be very difficult to understand, and would be something which happened once and never repeated itself. If we regard it that way, let us be content; but let us not be critical and condemnatory of those who feel that they must find another way.

(2) Many people see in this miracle a sacrament. They have felt that those who were present received only the smallest morsel of food, and yet with that were strengthened for their journey and were content. They have felt that this was not a meal where people satisfied their physical appetite, but a meal where they ate the spiritual food of Christ. If that is so, this is a miracle which is re-enacted every time we sit at the table of our Lord; for there comes to us the spiritual food which sends us out to walk with firmer feet and greater strength the way of life which leads to God.

(3) There are those who see in this miracle something which in a sense is perfectly natural, and yet which in another sense is a real miracle, and which in any sense is very precious. Was it really likely that the vast majority of the crowd would set out around the lake without any food at all? Would they not take something with them, however little? Now it was evening and they were hungry. *But they were also selfish.* And they would not produce what they had, in case they had to share it and left themselves without enough. Then Jesus took the lead. Such as he and his disciples had, he began to share with a blessing and an invitation and a smile. And thereupon all began to share, and before they knew what was happening, there was enough and more than enough for all.

If this is what happened, it was not the miracle of the multiplication of loaves and fishes; it was the miracle of the changing of selfish people into generous people at the touch of Christ. If that is so, then in the realest sense Christ fed them with himself and sent his Spirit to dwell within their hearts. It does not matter how we understand this miracle. One thing is sure – when Christ is there, the weary find rest and the hungry soul is fed.

The Sunday between 7 and 13 August
Mistaken Zeal *and* In the Hour of Trouble

Romans 10:5–15

Paul was entirely ready to admit that the Jews were zealous for God; but he also saw that their enthusiasm was misdirected. Jewish religion was based on meticulous obedience to the law, and by this kind of obedience to the law, they earned credit with God. Nothing shows better the Jewish attitude than the three classes into which they divided people. There were those who were good, whose balance was on the right side; there were those who were bad, whose balance was on the debit side; there were those who were in between, who, by doing one more good work, could become good. It was all a matter of law and achievement.

To this, in verse 4, Paul has answered: 'Christ is the end of the law.' What he meant was: 'Christ is the end of legalism.' The relationship between God and his people is no longer the relationship between a creditor and a debtor, between an earner and an assessor, between a judge and a criminal waiting to receive judgement. Because of Jesus Christ, we are no longer faced with the task of satisfying God's justice; we need only to accept his love. We no longer have to win God's favour; we need simply to take the grace and love and mercy which he freely offers.

To make his point, Paul uses two Old Testament quotations. First, he quotes Leviticus 18:5, where it says that, if people meticulously obey the commandments of the law, they will find life. That is true – *but no one ever has*. Then he quotes Deuteronomy 30:12–13.

Moses is saying that God's law is not inaccessible and impossible; it is there in a person's mouth and life and heart. Paul allegorizes that passage. It was not our effort which brought Christ into the world or raised him from the dead. It is not our effort which wins us goodness. It is all done for us, and we have only to accept.

Verses 9–10 are of prime importance. They give us the basis of the first Christian creed.

(1) We must say *Jesus Christ is Lord*. The word for *Lord* is *kurios*. This is the keyword of early Christianity. It has four stages of meaning. (a) It is the normal title of respect like the English *sir*, the French *monsieur*, the German *Herr*. (b) It is the normal title of the Roman emperors. (c) It is the normal title of the Greek gods, placed before the god's name. *Kurios Serapis* is Lord Serapis. (d) In the Greek translation of the Hebrew Scriptures, it is the regular translation of the divine name, Yahweh or Jehovah. So, to call Jesus *kurios* was to place him on a level with the emperor and with God; it was to give him the supreme place in a person's life and so to pledge him implicit obedience and reverent worship. To call Jesus *kurios* was to count him unique. First, in order to be Christians, we must have a sense of the utter *uniqueness* of Jesus Christ.

(2) We must believe that Jesus has risen from the dead. The resurrection was an essential of Christian belief. Christians must believe not only that Jesus *lived*, but also that he *lives*. We must not only know *about Christ*; we must *know* him. We are not studying a figure in history, however great; we are living with a real presence. We must know not only Christ the *martyr*; we must know Christ the *victor*, too.

(3) But we must not only believe in our hearts; we must confess with our lips. Christianity is belief plus confession; it involves witness before others. Not only God, but also our fellow men and women, must know what side we are on. The Jews would find it hard to believe that the way to God was not through the law; this

way of trust and of acceptance was shatteringly and incredibly new to them. Further, they would have real difficulty in believing that the way to God was open to *everybody*. The Gentiles did not seem to them to be in the same position as the Jews at all. So, in verses 11 and 13, Paul concludes his argument by citing two Old Testament texts to prove his case. First, he cites Isaiah 28:16: 'No one who *believes* in him will be put to shame.' There is nothing about law there; it is all based on faith. Second, he cites Joel 2:32: '*Everyone* who calls on the name of the Lord shall be saved.' There is no limitation there; the promise is to *everyone*; therefore, there is no difference between Jew and Greek.

In essence, this passage is an appeal to the Jews to abandon the way of legalism and accept the way of grace. It is an appeal to them to recognize that their single-minded enthusiasm is misplaced. It is an appeal to listen to the prophets who long ago declared that faith is the only way to God, and that that way is open to all.

Matthew 14:22–33

The lesson of this passage is abundantly clear, but what actually happened is not. First of all, let us set the scene. After the feeding of the multitude, Jesus sent his disciples away. Matthew says that he *compelled* them to embark on the boat and go on ahead. At first sight, the word *compelled* sounds strange; but if we turn to John's account of the incident, we will most likely find the explanation. John tells us that after the feeding of the multitude, the crowd wished to come and to make him a king by force (John 6:15). There was a surge of popular acclamation, and in the excited state of Palestine a revolution might well have begun there and then. It was a dangerous situation, and the disciples might well have complicated it, for they, too, were still thinking of Jesus in terms of earthly power. Jesus sent away his disciples because a situation had arisen with which he could best deal alone, and in which he did not wish them to become involved.

When he was alone, he went up into a mountain to pray; and by this time the night had come. The disciples had set out back across the lake. One of the sudden storms, for which the lake was notorious, had come down, and they were struggling against the winds and the waves, and making little progress. As the night wore on, Jesus began to walk round the head of the lake to reach the other side.

There are two possible interpretations of this passage. It may describe a miracle in which Jesus actually walked on the water. Or, it may mean that the disciples' boat was driven by the wind to the northern shore of the lake, that Jesus came down from the mountain to help them when he saw them struggling in the moonlight, and that he came walking through the surf and the waves towards the boat, and came so suddenly upon them that they were terrified when they saw him. Both of these interpretations are equally valid. Some will prefer one, and some the other.

But, whatever interpretation we choose, the significance is perfectly clear. *In the hour of the disciples' need, Jesus came to them.* When the wind was contrary and life was a struggle, Jesus was there to help. No sooner had a need arisen than Jesus was there to help and to save. In life, the wind is often contrary. There are times when we are up against it and life is a desperate struggle with ourselves, with our circumstances, with our temptations, with our sorrows and with our decisions. At such a time, no one need struggle alone, for Jesus comes to us across the storms of life, with hand stretched out to save, and with his calm, clear voice bidding us take heart and have no fear.

It does not really matter how we take this incident; it is in any event far more than the story of what Jesus once did in a storm in far-off Palestine; it is the sign and the symbol of what he always does for his people, when the wind is contrary and we are in danger of being overwhelmed by the storms of life.

There is no passage in the New Testament in which Peter's character is more fully revealed than this. It tells us three things about him.

(1) Peter was given to acting upon impulse and without thinking of what he was doing. It was his mistake that again and again he acted without fully facing the situation and without counting the cost. He was to do exactly the same when he affirmed undying and unshakable loyalty to Jesus (Matthew 26:33–5), and then denied his Lord's name. And yet there are worse sins than that, because Peter's whole trouble was that he was ruled by his heart; and, however he might sometimes fail, his heart was always in the right place and the instinct of his heart was always love.

(2) Because Peter acted on impulse, he often failed and came to grief. It was always Jesus' insistence that people should look at a situation in all its bleak grimness before they acted (Luke 9:57–8; Matthew 16:24–5). Jesus was completely honest with people; he always urged them to see how difficult it was to follow him before they set out upon the Christian way. A great deal of Christian failure is due to acting upon an emotional moment without counting the cost.

(3) But Peter never finally failed, for always in the moment of his failure he clutched at Christ. The wonderful thing about him is that every time he fell, he rose again; and that it must have been true that even his failures brought him closer and closer to Jesus Christ. As has been well said, a saint is not someone who never fails; a saint is someone who after a fall gets up and goes on again every time. Peter's failures only made him love Jesus Christ the more.

These verses finish with another great and permanent truth. When Jesus got into the boat, the wind sank. The great truth is that, wherever Jesus Christ is, the wildest storm becomes a calm. In every time of storm and stress, the presence of Jesus and the love which flows from the cross bring peace and serenity and calm.

The Sunday between 14 and 20 August

That Mercy May be for All *and* Faith Tested and Faith Answered

Romans 11:1–2a, 29–32

Somehow, Paul had to find an explanation of the fact that God's people rejected his Son when he came into the world. Paul never shut his eyes to that tragic fact, but he found a way in which the whole tragic situation could be fitted into the plan of God.

In verse 32 Paul has a strange thought. 'God', he says, 'shut up all to disobedience that he may have mercy upon all.' The one thing Paul cannot conceive of is that individuals of any nation could in any way merit their own salvation. Now, if the Jews had observed complete obedience to God's will, they might well have reckoned that they had earned the salvation of God as a right. So, Paul is saying that God involved the Jews in disobedience in order that, when his salvation did come to them, it might be unmistakably an act of his mercy and due in no way to their own merit. Neither Jew nor Gentile could ever be saved except through the mercy of God.

In many ways, Paul's argument may seem strange to us, and the 'proofs' he brings forward may seem unconvincing. Our minds and hearts may even shudder at some of the things he says. But the argument is not irrelevant, for the tremendous thing behind it is *a philosophy of history*. To Paul, *God was in control*. Nothing was entirely without purpose. Not even the most heartbreaking event was outside the purpose of God. Events could never run out of control. The purposes of God could never be frustrated.

It is told that a child once stood at the window on a night when the gale was terrifying in its savage force. 'God', she said, 'must have lost grip of his winds tonight.' To Paul, that was precisely what never happened. Nothing was ever out of God's control; everything was serving his purpose.

To that, Paul would have added another tremendous conviction. He would have insisted that, in it and through it all, *God's purpose was a purpose of salvation and not of destruction.* It may well be that Paul would even have gone to the lengths of saying that God's arranging of things was designed to save men and women *even against their will.* In the last analysis, it was not the wrath of God which was pursuing them, but the love of God which was tracking them down.

The situation of Israel was exactly that which Francis Thompson so movingly portrayed in 'The Hound of Heaven':

I fled Him down the nights and down the days;
I fled Him down the arches of the years;
I fled Him down the labyrinthine ways
Of my own mind; and in the mist of tears
I hid from Him, and under running laughter . . .
But with unhurrying chase,
And unperturbèd pace,
Deliberate speed, majestic instancy,
They beat – and a Voice beat
More instant than the Feet –
'All things betray thee, who betrayest Me.'
Then comes the time when the fugitive is beaten.
Naked I wait Thy love's uplifted stroke!
My harness piece by piece Thou hast hewn from me,
And smitten to my knee,
I am defenceless utterly.
Then comes the end:
Halts by me that footfall;

Is my gloom, after all,
Shade of His hand, outstretched caressingly?
'Ah, fondest, blindest, weakest,
I am He Whom thou seekest!
Thou dravest love from thee, who dravest Me!'

That was exactly Israel's situation. They fought their long battle against God; they are still fighting it. But God's pursuing love is always after them.

Matthew 15:[10–20] 21–28

There are tremendous implications in this passage. Apart from anything else, it describes the only occasion on which Jesus was ever outside of Jewish territory. The supreme significance of the passage is that it foreshadows the going out of the gospel to the whole world; it shows us the beginning of the end of all the barriers.

For Jesus, this was a time of deliberate withdrawal. The end was coming near; and he wished some time of quiet when he could prepare for the end. It was not so much that he wished to prepare himself, although that purpose was also in his mind, but rather that he wished for some time in which he could prepare his disciples for the day of the cross. There were things which he must tell them, and which he must compel them to understand.

There was no place in Palestine where he could be sure of privacy; wherever he went, the crowds would find him. So he went right north through Galilee until he came to the land of Tyre and Sidon where the Phoenicians dwelt. There, at least for a time, he would be safe from the hostility of the scribes and Pharisees, and from the dangerous popularity of the people; for no Jew would be likely to follow him into Gentile territory.

This passage shows us Jesus seeking a time of quiet before the turmoil of the end. This is not in any sense a picture of him running away; it is a picture of him preparing himself and his disciples for the final and decisive battle which lay so close ahead.

But even in these foreign parts, Jesus was not to be free from the demand of human need which cried out to him. There was a woman who had a daughter who was seriously ill. She must have heard somehow of the wonderful things which Jesus could do; and she followed him and his disciples, crying desperately for help. At first, Jesus seemed to pay no attention to her. The disciples were embarrassed. 'Give her what she wants,' they said, 'and be rid of her.' The reaction of the disciples was not really compassion at all; it was the reverse – to them the woman was a nuisance, and all they wanted was to be rid of her as quickly as possible. To grant a request to get rid of a person who is, or may become, a nuisance is a common enough reaction; but it is very different from the response of Christian love and pity and compassion.

But to Jesus there was a problem here. That he was moved with compassion for this woman we cannot for a moment doubt. But she was a Gentile. Not only was she a Gentile; she belonged to the old Canaanite stock, and the Canaanites were the ancestral enemies of the Jews. Even at that very time, or not much later, Josephus could write: 'Of the Phoenicians, the Tyrians have the most ill-feeling towards us.' We have already seen that if Jesus was to have any effect, he had to limit his objectives like a wise general. He had to begin with the Jews; and here was a Gentile crying for mercy. There was only one thing for him to do; he must awaken true faith in the heart of this woman.

So Jesus at last turned to her: 'It is not right to take the children's bread and to throw it to the pet dogs.' To call a person a dog was a deadly and a contemptuous insult. The Jews spoke with arrogant insolence about 'Gentile dogs', 'infidel dogs' and later 'Christian dogs'. In those days, the dogs were the unclean scavengers of the street – lean, savage, often diseased. But there are two things to remember. The tone and the look with which a thing is said make all the difference. A thing which seems hard can be said with a disarming smile. We can call a friend 'an old villain' or 'a rogue', with a smile and a tone which take all the sting out of it and fill it with affection. We can be quite sure that the smile on Jesus' face and the compassion in his eyes robbed the words of all insult and bitterness. Second, it is the diminutive word for *dogs* (*kunaria*) which is used, and the *kunaria* were not the street dogs, but the little household pets, very different from the stray dogs that roamed the streets and probed in the refuse heaps.

The woman was a Greek; she was quick to see, and she had all a Greek's ready wit. 'True,' she said, 'but even the dogs get their share of the crumbs which fall from their master's table.' And Jesus' eyes lit up with joy at such an indomitable faith; and he granted her the blessing and the healing which she so much desired.

The Sunday between 21 and 27 August
Members of One Body *and* The Inadequacies of Human Categories

Romans 12:1–8

One of Paul's favourite thoughts is of the Christian Church as a body (cf. 1 Corinthians 12:12–27). The members of the body neither argue with one another nor envy each other nor dispute about their relative importance. Each part of the body carries out its own function, however prominent or however humbly unseen that function may be. It was Paul's conviction that the Christian Church should be like that. Each member has a task to do; and it is only when all contribute the help of their own tasks that the body of the Church functions as it ought.

Beneath this passage lie very important rules for life.

(1) First of all, it urges us to know ourselves. One of the first basic commandments of the Greek wise men was: 'Know yourself.' We do not get very far in this world until we know what we can and what we cannot do. An honest assessment of our own capabilities, without conceit and without false modesty, is one of the first essentials of a useful life.

(2) Second, it urges us to accept ourselves and to use the gift God has given us. We are not to envy someone else's gift and regret that some other gift has not been given to us. We are to accept ourselves as we are, and use the gift we have. The result may be that we have to accept the fact that service for us means some humble sphere and some almost unseen part.

It was one of the great basic beliefs of the Stoics that there was a spark of God in every living creature. The Sceptics laughed at this doctrine. 'God in worms?' demanded the Sceptic. 'God in dung beetles?' The Stoic replied: 'Why not? Cannot an earthworm serve God? Do you suppose that it is only a general who is a good soldier? Cannot the lowest member of the ranks fight his best and give his life for the cause? Happy are you if you are serving God and carrying out the great purpose as truly as an earthworm.'

The efficiency of the life of the universe depends on the humblest creatures. Paul is here saying that we must accept ourselves; and, even if we find that the contribution we have to offer will be unseen, without praise and without prominence, we must make it, certain that it is essential and that without it the world and the Church can never be what they are meant to be.

(3) Third, Paul is really saying that whatever gift any individual has comes from God. He calls gifts *charismata*. In the New Testament, a *charisma* is something given by God to people as individuals and which they could never have acquired or attained for themselves.

In point of fact, life is like that. One person might practice for a lifetime and yet never play the violin like Yehudi Menuhin. He had more than practice; he had the something plus, the *charisma*, which is a gift of God. One person might toil for a lifetime and still be clumsy in the use of tools and wood and metals; another can carve wood and mould metal with a special skill, and tools become an extension of that person who has the something plus, the *charisma*, which is a gift of God. Others might practise speaking forever and a day, and still never acquire that magic something which moves an audience or a congregation; but someone else steps on to a platform or climbs into a pulpit, and the audience is in the hollow of that person's hand. There is that something plus, that *charisma*, which is a gift of God. It is possible to work for a lifetime and never acquire the gift of putting thoughts on paper in a vivid and intelligible way; but there are people who, without effort, see their thoughts grow on the paper in front of them; these people have the something plus, the *charisma*, which is the gift of God.

We all have our own *charisma*. It may be for writing sermons, building houses, sowing seeds, carving wood, working with figures, playing the piano, singing songs, teaching children, or playing football or golf. It is a something plus given to each one of us by God.

(4) Fourth, whatever gift we have, we must use it, and the motive of use must be not our personal prestige but the conviction that it is at one and the same time our duty and our privilege to make our own contribution to the common good.

Matthew 16:13–20

At Caesarea Philippi, Jesus determined to demand a verdict from his disciples. He had to know before he set out for Jerusalem and the cross if anyone had even dimly grasped who and what he was. He did not ask the question directly; he led up to it. He began by asking what people were saying about him, and who they took him to be.

Some said that he was John the Baptist. Herod Antipas was not the only man who felt that John the Baptist was so great a figure that it might well be that he had come back from the dead.

Others said that he was Elijah. In doing so, they were saying two things about Jesus. They were saying that he was as great as the greatest of the prophets, for Elijah had always been looked on as the summit and the prince of the prophetic line. They were also saying that Jesus was the forerunner of the Messiah. As Malachi had it, the promise of God was: 'Lo, I will send you the

prophet Elijah before the great and terrible day of the Lord comes'
(Malachi 4:5).

To this day, the Jews expect the return of Elijah before the coming of the Messiah, and to this day they leave a chair vacant for
Elijah when they celebrate the Passover; for when Elijah comes, the
Messiah will not be far away. So the people looked on Jesus as the
herald of the Messiah and the forerunner of the direct intervention of God.

Some said that Jesus was Jeremiah. Jeremiah had a curious
place in the expectations of the people of Israel. It was believed
that, before the people went into exile, Jeremiah had taken the ark
and the altar of incense out of the Temple, and hidden them away
in a lonely cave on Mount Nebo; and that, before the coming of
the Messiah, he would return and produce them, and the glory of
God would come to the people again (2 Maccabees 2:1–12). In 4
Ezra [2 Esdras] 2:18, the promise of God is: 'I will send you help,
my servants Isaiah and Jeremiah.'

When the people identified Jesus with Elijah and with Jeremiah,
they were, according to their understanding, paying him a great
compliment and setting him in a high place, for Jeremiah and
Elijah were none other than the expected forerunners of the
Anointed One of God. When they arrived, the kingdom would be
very near indeed.

When Jesus had heard the verdicts of the crowd, he asked the
all-important question: 'And *you* – who do you say I am?' At that
question, there may well have been a moment's silence, while into
the minds of the disciples came thoughts which they were almost
afraid to express in words; and then Peter made his great discovery
and his great confession; and Jesus knew that his work was safe
because there was at least someone who understood.

It is interesting to note that each of the three gospels has its own
version of the saying of Peter. Matthew has:

You are the Messiah, the Son of the living God.
Mark is briefer (8:29):
You are the Messiah.
Luke is clearest of all (9:20):
The Messiah of God.

Jesus knew now that there was at least someone who had recognized him for the Messiah, the Anointed One of God, the Son of the living God. The word *Messiah* and the word *Christ* are the same; the one is the Hebrew and the other is the Greek for *the Anointed One*. Kings were ordained to office by anointing, as they still are. The Messiah, the Christ, the Anointed One is God's King over all people.

Within this passage, there are two great truths.

(1) Essentially, Peter's discovery was that human categories, even the highest, are inadequate to describe Jesus Christ. When the people described Jesus as Elijah or Jeremiah or one of the prophets, they thought they were setting Jesus in the highest category they could find. It was the belief of the Jews that for 400 years the voice of prophecy had been silent; and they were saying that in Jesus men and women heard again the direct and authentic voice of God. These were great tributes; but they were not great enough; for there are no human categories which are adequate to describe Jesus Christ.

Once, Napoleon gave his verdict on Jesus. 'I know men,' he said, 'and Jesus Christ is more than a man.' Doubtless Peter could not have given a theological account and a philosophic expression of what he meant when he said that Jesus was the Son of the living God; the one thing of which Peter was quite certain was that no merely human description was adequate to describe him.

(2) This passage teaches that our discovery of Jesus Christ must be a *personal discovery*. Jesus' question is: '*You* – what do *you* think of me?' When Pilate asked him if he was the king of the Jews, his answer was: 'Do you ask this on your own, or did others tell you

about me?' (John 18:34). Our knowledge of Jesus must never be at second hand.

We might know every verdict ever passed on Jesus; we might know every Christology that human minds have ever thought out; we might be able to give a competent summary of the teaching about Jesus of every great thinker and theologian – and still not be Christians. Christianity never consists in *knowing about* Jesus; it always consists in *knowing Jesus*. Jesus Christ demands a personal verdict. He did not ask only Peter, he asks every one of us: '*You* – what do *you* think of me?'

The Sunday between 28 August and 3 September
Christians and Their Neighbours *and* Losing and Finding Life

Romans 12:9–21

Paul first presents his people with twelve concise rules for ordinary, everyday life. And then offers a series of rules and principles which should guide our relationships with our neighbours.

(1) Christians must meet persecution with a prayer for those who persecute them. When Christians are hurt, and insulted, and badly treated, they have the example of their Master before them, for he, upon his cross, prayed for forgiveness for those who were killing him.

There has been no greater force to move people into Christianity than this serene forgiveness which the martyrs in every age have shown. Stephen died praying for forgiveness for those who stoned him to death (Acts 7:60). Among those who killed him was a young man named Saul, who afterwards became Paul, the apostle to the Gentiles and the slave of Christ. There can be no doubt that the death scene of Stephen was one of the things that turned Paul to Christ. As St Augustine said, 'The Church owes Paul to the prayer of Stephen.' Many persecutors have become followers of the faith they once sought to destroy, because they have seen how Christians can forgive.

(2) We are to rejoice with those who rejoice, and to weep with those who weep. There are few bonds like that of a common sorrow. The bond of tears is the strongest of all. And yet it is much easier to weep with those who weep than it is to rejoice with those who rejoice. It

is more difficult to congratulate others on their success, especially if their success involves disappointment to us, than it is to sympathize with their sorrow and their loss. It is only when self is dead that we can take as much joy in the success of others as in our own.

(3) We are to live in harmony with one another. Robert Leighton, the seventeenth-century Bishop of Glasgow, once wrote: 'The mode of Church government is unconstrained; but peace and concord, kindness and good will are indispensable.' When strife enters into any Christian society, the hope of doing any good work is gone.

(4) We are to avoid all pride and snobbishness. We always have to remember that the standards by which the world judges people are not necessarily the standards by which God judges them. Saintliness has nothing to do with rank, or wealth, or birth. Dr James Black of the United Presbyterian Church in Dundee, in his own vivid way, described a scene in an early Christian congregation. A notable convert has been made, and the great man comes to his first Church service. He enters the room where the service is being held. The Christian leader points to a place. 'Will you sit there, please?' 'But,' says the man, 'I cannot sit there, for that would be to sit beside my slave.' 'Will you sit there, please?' repeats the leader. 'But,' says the man, 'surely not beside my slave.' 'Will you sit there, please?' repeats the leader once again. And the man at last crosses the room, sits beside his slave, and gives him the kiss of peace. That is what Christianity did; and that is what it alone could do in the Roman Empire. The Christian Church was the only place where master and slave sat side by side. It is still the place where all earthly distinctions are gone, for with God there is no respect for individual status.

(5) We are to make our conduct fair for all to see. Paul was well aware that Christian conduct must not only be good; it must also look good. So-called Christianity can be presented in the hardest and most unlovely way; but real Christianity is something which is fair for all to see.

(6) We are to live at peace with all. But Paul adds two qualifications. (a) He says: *if it is possible*. There may come a time when the claims of courtesy have to submit to the claims of principle. Christianity is not an easy-going tolerance which will accept anything and shut its eyes to everything. There may come a time when some battle has to be fought – and, when it does, Christians will not shirk it. (b) He says: *as far as you can*. Paul knew very well that it is easier for some to live at peace than for others. He knew that one person can be compelled to control as much temper in an hour as someone else in a whole lifetime. We would do well to remember that goodness is a great deal easier for some than for others; that will keep us both from criticism and from discouragement.

(7) We are to keep ourselves from all thought of taking revenge. Paul gives three reasons for that. (a) Vengeance belongs not to us but to God. In the last analysis, no human being has a right to judge any other; only God can do that. (b) To treat people with kindness rather than vengeance is the way to move them. Vengeance may break the spirit; but kindness will break people's hearts. 'If we are kind to our enemies,' says Paul, 'it will heap coals of fire on their heads.' That means not that it will store up further punishment for them but that it will move them to burning shame. (c) To stoop to vengeance is to be ourselves conquered by evil. Evil can never be conquered by evil. If hatred is met with more hatred, it is only increased; but, if it is met with love, an antidote for the poison is found. The only real way to destroy an enemy is to make that person a friend.

Matthew 16:21–28

Here we have one of the dominant and constantly recurring themes of Jesus' teaching. Again and again he confronted them with the challenge of the Christian life. There are three things which people must be prepared to do if they are to live the Christian life.

(1) They must *deny themselves*. Ordinarily we use the word *self-denial* in a restricted sense. We use it to mean giving up something. For instance, a week of self-denial may be a week when we do without certain pleasures or luxuries in order to contribute to some good cause. But that is only a very small part of what Jesus meant by self-denial. To deny oneself means in every moment of life to say no to self and yes to God. The life of constant self-denial is the life of constant assent to God.

(2) They must *take up a cross*. That is to say, they must take up the burden of sacrifice. The Christian life is the life of sacrificial service. Christians may have to abandon personal ambition to serve Christ; it may be that they will discover that the place where they can render the greatest service to Jesus Christ is somewhere where the reward will be small and the prestige non-existent. They will certainly have to sacrifice time and leisure and pleasure in order to serve God through the service of others.

(3) They must *follow Jesus Christ*. That is to say, they must render to Jesus Christ a perfect obedience. When we were young, many of us used to play a game called 'Follow my Leader'. Everything the leader did, however difficult, and, in the case of the game, however ridiculous, we had to copy. The Christian life is a constant following of our leader, a constant obedience in thought and word and action to Jesus Christ. Christians walk in the footsteps of Christ, wherever he may lead.

There is all the difference in the world between *existing* and *living*. To exist is simply to have the lungs breathing and the heart beating; to live is to be alive in a world where everything is worth while, where there is peace in the soul, joy in the heart and a thrill in every moment. Jesus here gives us the recipe for *life* as distinct from *existence*.

(1) People who play for safety love life. Matthew was writing somewhere between AD 80 and 90. He was therefore writing in some of the bitterest days of persecution. He was saying: 'The time may well come when you can save your life by abandoning your faith; but if you do, so far from saving life, in the real sense of the term you are losing life.' Those who are faithful may die, but they die to live; those who abandon their faith for safety may live, but they live to die.

In our day and generation, it is not likely to be a question of martyrdom, but it still remains a fact that if we meet life in the constant search for safety, security, ease and comfort, we are losing all that makes life worthwhile. Life becomes an earthbound thing when it might have been reaching for the stars. Someone once wrote a bitter epitaph on a man: 'He was born a man and died a grocer.' Any trade or profession might be substituted for the word grocer. Those who play for safety cease to be truly human, for human beings are made in the image of God.

(2) People who risk all for Christ – and maybe look as if they had lost all – find life. It is the simple lesson of history that it has always been the adventurous men and women, bidding farewell to security and safety, who wrote their names on history and greatly assisted human progress. Unless there had been those prepared to take risks, many medical cures would not exist. Unless there had been those prepared to take risks, many of the machines which make life easier would never have been invented. It is the people who are prepared 'to bet their lives that there is a God' who in the end find life.

(3) Then Jesus speaks with warning: 'Suppose people play for safety; suppose they gain the whole world; then suppose that they find that life is not worth living – what can they give to get life back again?' And the grim truth is that they cannot get life back again. It is perfectly possible to gain all the things we have set our

hearts upon, and then to wake up one morning to find that we have missed the most important things of all.

(4) Finally, Jesus asks about those who would follow him: 'What will they give in exchange for their life?' The Greek is: 'What *antallagma* will they give for their life?' *Antallagma* is an interesting word. In the book of Ecclesiasticus, it says: 'There is no *antallagma* for a faithful friend,' and: 'There is no *antallagma* for a disciplined soul' (cf. Ecclesiasticus 6:15, 26:14). It means that there is no price which will buy a faithful friend or a disciplined soul. So, this final saying of Jesus can mean two things. (a) It can mean: once we have lost the fundamental value of life, because of our desire for security and for material things, there is no price that we can pay to get it back again. We have done something to ourselves which cannot ever be fully obliterated. (b) It can mean: We owe ourselves and everything else to Jesus Christ; and there is nothing that we can give to Christ in place of our lives. It is quite possible to try to give our money to Christ and to withhold our lives. It is even more possible to give lip-service to Christ and to withhold our lives. The only possible gift to Christ is our whole life. There is no substitute for it. Nothing less will do.

The Sunday between 4 and 10 September
The Debt Which Can Never Be Paid *and*
The Power of the Presence

Romans 13:8–14

The previous passage (verses 1–7) dealt with what might be called public debts. Verse 7 mentions two of these. There is what Paul calls *tribute*, and what he calls *taxes*. By *tribute*, he means the tribute that must be paid by those who are members of a nation that is under the rule of another. The standard contributions that the Roman government levied on such nations were three. There was a *ground tax* by which people had to pay, either in cash or in kind, one-tenth of all the grain, and one-fifth of the wine and fruit produced by their land.

There was *income tax*, which was one per cent of a man's income. There was a *poll tax*, which had to be paid by everyone between the ages of 14 and 65. By *taxes*, Paul means the local taxes that had to be paid. There were customs duties, import and export taxes, taxes for the use of main roads, for crossing bridges, for entry into markets and harbours, for the right to possess an animal or to drive a cart or wagon. Paul insists that Christians must pay their tribute and their taxes to state and to local authority, however galling it might be.

Then he turns to *private* debts. He says: 'Owe no one anything.' It seems almost unnecessary to say such a thing; but there were some who even twisted the petition of the Lord's Prayer, 'Forgive us our debts, as we forgive our debtors,' into a reason for claiming to be absolved from all money obligations. Paul had to remind his people that Christianity is not an excuse for refusing our obligations to other people; it is a reason for fulfilling them to the utmost.

He goes on to speak of the one debt that must be paid every day, and yet, at the same time, must continue to be owed every day – the debt to love one another. Origen, the great third-century biblical scholar, said: 'The debt of love remains with us permanently and never leaves us; this is a debt which we both discharge every day and forever owe.' It is Paul's claim that if people honestly seek to discharge this debt of love, they will automatically keep all the commandments.

They will not commit adultery, for, when two people allow their physical passions to sweep them away, the reason is not that they love each other too much but that they love each other too little. In real love, there is at the same time respect and restraint, which saves from sin. Christians will not kill, for love never seeks to destroy, but always to build up; it is always kind and will always seek to destroy enemies not by killing them, but by seeking to make friends of them. Christians will never steal, for love is always more concerned with giving than with getting. They will not covet, for covetousness (*epithumia*) is the uncontrolled desire for what is forbidden, and love cleanses the heart, until that desire is gone.

St Augustine famously said: 'Love God, and do what you like.' If love is the motivation within the heart, if a person's whole life is dominated by love for God and love for other people, that person needs no other law.

Matthew 18:15–20

In verses 19–20 we have on of the sayings of Jesus whose meaning we need to probe, or else we will be left with heartbreak and great disappointment. Jesus says that if two upon earth agree upon any matter for which they are praying, they will receive it from God. If that is to be taken literally, and without any qualification, it is manifestly untrue. On countless occasions, two people have agreed to pray for the physical or the spiritual welfare of a loved one – and their prayer has not, in the literal sense, been answered.

Time after time, God's people have agreed to pray for the conversion of their own land or the conversion of unbelievers and the coming of the kingdom, and even today that prayer is far from being fully answered. People agree to pray – and pray desperately – and do not receive that for which they pray. There is no point in refusing to face the facts of the situation, and nothing but harm can result from teaching people to expect what does not happen. But when we come to see what this saying means, there is a precious depth in it.

(1) First and foremost, it means that prayer must never be selfish and that selfish prayer cannot find an answer. We are not meant to pray only for our own needs, thinking of nothing and no one but ourselves; we are meant to pray as members of a fellowship, in agreement, remembering that life and the world are arranged not for us as individuals but for the fellowship as a whole. It would often happen that if our prayers were answered, the prayers of someone else would be disappointed. Often, our prayers for our success would necessarily involve someone else's failure. Effective prayer must be the prayer of agreement, from which the element of selfish concentration on our own needs and desires has been quite cleansed away.

(2) When prayer is unselfish, it is always answered. But here, as everywhere, we must remember the basic law of prayer – that law is that in prayer we receive not the answer which we desire, but the answer which God in his wisdom and his love knows to be best. Simply because we are human beings, with human hearts and fears and hopes and desires, most of our prayers are prayers for escape. We pray to be saved from some trial, some sorrow, some disap-

pointment, some hurting and difficult situation. And always God's answer is the offer not of escape, but of victory.

God does not give us escape from a human situation; he enables us to accept what we cannot understand; he enables us to endure what without him would be unendurable; he enables us to face what without him would be beyond all facing. The perfect example of all this is Jesus in Gethsemane. He prayed to be released from the fearful situation which confronted him. He was not released from it; but he was given power to meet it, to endure it and to conquer it. When we pray unselfishly, God sends his answer – but the answer is always his answer and not necessarily ours.

(3) Jesus goes on to say that where two or three are gathered in his name, he is there in the midst of them. The Jews themselves had a saying: 'Where two sit and are occupied with the study of the law, the glory of God is among them.' We may take this great promise of Jesus into two spheres.

(a) We may take it into the sphere of the *Church*. Jesus is just as much present in the little congregation as in the great mass meeting. He is just as much present at the prayer meeting or the Bible study circle with their handful of people as in the crowded arena. He is not the slave of numbers. He is there wherever faithful hearts meet, however few they may be; for he gives all of himself to each individual person.

(b) We may take it into the sphere of the *home*. One of the earliest interpretations of this saying of Jesus was that *the two or three are father, mother and child*, and that it means that Jesus is there, the unseen guest in every home. There are those who never give of their best except on the so-called great occasion; but, for Jesus Christ, every occasion where even two or three are gathered in his name is a great occasion.

The Sunday between 11 and 17 September

The Impossibility of Isolation and Under Judgement *and* How to Forgive

Romans 14:1–12

Paul lays down the great fact that it is impossible in the nature of things to live an isolated life. There is no such thing in this world as a completely detached individual. That, in fact, is doubly true. 'Man', said the English poet William Macneile Dixon, 'has an affair with the gods and an affair with the mortals.' We can never disentangle ourselves either from other people or from God.

In three directions as individuals, we cannot disentangle ourselves from other people.

(1) We cannot isolate ourselves from *the past*. No one is self-made. 'I am a part', said Ulysses, 'of all that I have met.' We are receivers of a tradition. Each one of us is a mixture of all that our ancestors made us. True, we contribute something to that blend; but we do not start from nothing. For good or for ill, we start with what all the past has made us. The unseen cloud of witnesses does not only surround us; they dwell within us. We cannot dissociate ourselves from the roots from which we have grown and from the rock from which we are hewn.

(2) We cannot isolate ourselves from *the present*. We live in a civilization in which people are becoming more and more closely bound together every day. Nothing we do affects only ourselves. We have the terrible power of making others happy or sad by our conduct; we have the still more terrible power of making others good or bad. Each one of us has an influence which makes it easier for others

to take the high way or the low way. All our actions have consequences which affect others more or less closely. We are all bound up in the bundle of life, and from that bundle we cannot escape.

(3) We cannot isolate ourselves from *the future*. As we receive life, so we hand life on. We hand on to our children a heritage of physical life and of spiritual character. We are not self-contained individual units; we are links in a chain. The story is told of a youth, who lived carelessly, who began to study biology. Through a microscope, he was watching certain of these living things that you can actually see living and dying and creating others in a moment of time. He looked up from the microscope. 'Now I see it,' he said. 'I am a link in the chain, and I will not be a weak link any more.' It is our terrible responsibility that we leave something of ourselves in the world by leaving something of ourselves in others. Sin would be a far less terrible thing if it affected only the person involved in it. The terror of every sin is that it starts a new train of evil in the world.

Still less can we disentangle ourselves from Jesus Christ.

(1) In this life, Christ is forever a living presence. We do not need to speak of living as if Christ saw us; he does see us. All life is lived under his gaze. We can no more escape from the risen Christ than we can from our own shadows. There is no place where we can leave Christ behind, and there is nothing which we can do unseen.

(2) Not even death breaks that presence. In this world, we live in the unseen presence of Christ; in the next, we shall see him in his visible presence. Death is not the chasm that ends in obliteration; it is the gateway that leads to Christ. No human being can follow a policy of isolation. We are bound to one another and to Christ by ties that neither time nor eternity can break. We can neither live nor die for ourselves alone.

Paul has been thinking of the impossibility of the isolated life. But there is one situation in which every individual is isolated, and that is when standing before the judgement seat of God. We have no right to judge anyone else because we ourselves are under judgement. It is the very essence of humanity that we are not the judges but the judged. The only person who has the right to judge anyone is God; we who stand before God's judgement have no right to judge others who also stand before him.

When Paul wrote, the Roman magistrates sat dispensing justice in the great basilicas, and in the colonnaded porches around the forum. The Romans knew well the sight of someone standing before the judge's judgement seat. That is what happens to everyone; and it is a judgement which must be faced alone. Naked we come into the world, and naked we leave it. We stand before God in the awful loneliness of our own souls; to him we can take nothing but the character which in life we have been building up.

Yet that is not the whole truth. We do not stand alone at the judgement seat of God, for we stand with Jesus Christ. We do not need to go stripped of everything; we may go dressed in the merits that are his. Collin Brooks, writer and journalist, writes in one of his books: 'God may be kinder than we think. If he cannot say, "Well done! good and faithful servant," it may be that he will say at last, "Don't worry, my bad and faithless servant: I don't altogether dislike you."' That was one man's whimsical way of stating his faith; but there is more to it than that. It is not that God merely does not dislike us; it is that, sinners as we are, he loves us for the sake of Jesus Christ. True, we must stand before God's judgement seat in the naked loneliness of our own souls; but, if we have lived with Christ in life, we shall stand with him in death, and before God he will be the advocate to plead our cause.

Matthew 18:21–35

We owe a very great deal to the fact that Peter had a quick tongue. Again and again, he rushed into speech in such a way that his impetuosity drew from Jesus teaching which is immortal. On this occasion, Peter thought that he was being very generous. He asked Jesus how often he ought to forgive someone, and then answered his own question by suggesting that he should forgive seven times.

Peter was not without warrant for this suggestion. It was Rabbinic teaching that a person must forgive another *three* times. Rabbi Jose ben Hanina said: 'He who begs forgiveness from his neighbour must not do so more than three times.' Rabbi Jose ben Jehuda said: 'If a man commits an offence once, they forgive him; if he commits an offence a second time, they forgive him; if he commits an offence a third time, they forgive him; the fourth time they do not forgive.' The biblical proof that this was correct was taken from Amos. In the opening chapters of Amos, there is a series of condemnations on the various nations *for three transgressions and for four* (1:3, 6, 9, 11, 13; 2:1, 4, 6). From this, it was deduced that God's forgiveness extends to three offences and that he visits the sinner with punishment at the fourth. It was not to be thought that people could be more gracious than God, so forgiveness was limited to three times.

Peter thought that he was going very far, for he takes the Rabbinic three times, multiplies it by two, for good measure adds one, and suggests, with eager self-satisfaction, that it will be enough if he forgives seven times. Peter expected to be warmly commended; but Jesus' answer was that the Christian must forgive seventy times seven. In other words, there is no reckonable limit to forgiveness.

Jesus then told the story of the servant forgiven a great debt who went out and dealt mercilessly with a fellow servant who owed him a debt that was an infinitesimal fraction of what he himself had owed, and who for his mercilessness was utterly condemned. This parable teaches certain lessons which Jesus never tired of teaching.

(1) It teaches that lesson which runs through all the New Testament – we must forgive in order to be forgiven. Those who will not forgive others cannot hope that God will forgive them.

'Blessed are the merciful,' said Jesus, 'for they will receive mercy' (Matthew 5:7). No sooner had Jesus taught his disciples his own prayer than he went on to expand and explain one petition in it: 'For if you forgive others their trespasses, your heavenly Father will also forgive you; but if you do not forgive others, neither will your Father forgive your trespasses' (Matthew 6:14–15). As James had it: 'For judgement will be without mercy to anyone who has shown no mercy' (James 2:13). Divine and human forgiveness go hand in hand.

(2) Why should that be so? One of the great points in this parable is the contrast between the two debts. The first servant owed his master 10,000 talents – and a talent was the equivalent of fifteen years' wages. That is an incredible debt. It was more than the total budget of the ordinary province. The total revenue of the province which contained Idumaea, Judaea and Samaria was only 600 talents; the total revenue of even a wealthy province like Galilee was only 300 talents. Against that background, this debt is staggering. It was this that the servant was forgiven. The debt which a fellow servant owed him was a trifling thing; it was 100 denarii, and a denarius was the usual day's wage for a working man. It was therefore a mere fraction of his own debt.

The biblical scholar A. R. S. Kennedy drew this vivid picture to contrast the debts. Suppose they were paid in small coins (he suggested sixpences; we might think in terms of 5-pence pieces or dimes). The 100-denarii debt could be carried in one pocket. The 10,000-talent debt would take an army of about 8,600 carriers to carry it, each carrying a sack of coins 60 lb in weight; and they would form, at a distance of a yard apart, a line five miles long! The contrast between the debts is staggering. The point is that nothing that others can do to us can in any way compare with what we have done to God; and if God has forgiven us the debt we owe to him, we must forgive our neighbours the debts they owe to us. Nothing that we have to forgive can even faintly or remotely compare with what we have been forgiven. As A. M. Toplady's great hymn 'Rock of Ages' has it:

Not the labours of my hands
Can fulfil thy law's demands;
Could my zeal no respite know,
Could my tears for ever flow,
All for sin could not atone.

We have been forgiven a debt which is beyond all paying – for human sin brought about the death of God's own Son – and if that is so, we must forgive others as God has forgiven us, or we can hope to find no mercy.

The Sunday between 18 and 24 September

Citizens of the Kingdom *and* Work and Wages in the Kingdom of God

Philippians 1:21–30

Paul was in prison awaiting trial and had to face the fact that it was quite uncertain whether he would live or die. His desire to live is not for his own sake, but for the sake of those whom he can continue to help. So, if Paul is spared to come and see the Philippians again, they will have in him grounds to boast in Jesus Christ. That is to say, they will be able to look at him and see in him a shining example of how, through Christ, they can face the worst standing tall and unafraid. It is the duty of every Christian to trust in this way so that others will be able to see what Christ can do for those who have given their lives to him.

One thing is essential – the Philippians must live in a manner that is worthy of their faith and the belief they declare. Paul chooses his words very carefully. The Authorized Version has it: 'Let your conversation be as it become the gospel of Christ.' Nowadays this is misleading. To us, *conversation* means *talk*; but it is derived from the Latin word *conversari*, which means *to conduct oneself*. In the seventeenth century, *conversation* was not only a person's way of speaking to other people; it was that individual's whole behaviour. The phrase means: 'Let your behaviour be worthy of those who are pledged to Christ.'

But, on this occasion, Paul uses a word which he very seldom uses in order to express his meaning. The word he would normally use for *to conduct oneself* in the ordinary affairs of life is *peripatein*, which literally means *to walk about*; here he uses *politeuesthai*, which means *to be a citizen*. Paul was writing from the very centre of the Roman Empire, from Rome itself; it was the fact that he was a Roman citizen that had brought him there. Philippi was a Roman colony; and Roman colonies were little bits of Rome planted throughout the world, where the citizens never forgot that they were Romans. They spoke the Latin language, wore the usual Latin clothes and called their magistrates by the Latin names, however far they might be from Rome. So, what Paul is saying is: 'You and I know full well the privileges and the responsibilities of being a Roman citizen. You know full well how even in Philippi, so many miles from Rome, you must still live and act as a Roman does. Well then, remember that you have an even higher duty than that. Wherever you are, you must live as befits a citizen of the kingdom of God.'

What does Paul expect from them? He expects them *to stand fast*. The world is full of Christians on the retreat, who, when things become difficult, play down their Christianity. True Christians stand fast, unashamed in any company. He expects *unity*; they are to be bound together in one spirit. Let the world quarrel; Christians must be united. He expects a certain *unconquerability*. Often, evil seems invincible; but Christians must never abandon hope or give up the struggle. He expects a *cool, calm courage*. In times of *crisis*, others may be nervous and afraid; Christians will still be serene, in control of themselves and of the situation.

If they can be like that, they will set such an example that those who are not Christians will be disgusted with their own way of life, will realize that the Christians have something they do not possess, and will seek out of a sense of self-preservation to share it.

Paul does not suggest that this will be easy. When Christianity first came to Philippi, they saw him fight his own battle. They saw him beaten and imprisoned for the faith (Acts 16:19). They know what he is now going through. But let them remember that a general chooses the best soldiers for the hardest tasks, and that it is an honour to suffer for Christ. There is a story about a veteran French soldier who, in a desperate situation, found a young recruit trembling with fear. 'Come, son,' said the veteran, 'and you and I will do something fine for France.' So Paul says to the Philippians: 'For you and for me the battle is on; let us do something fine for Christ.'

Matthew 20:1–16

This parable has been called 'one of the greatest and most glorious of all'. It may indeed have had a comparatively limited application when it was spoken for the first time; but it contains truth which goes to the very heart of the Christian religion. We begin with the significance it originally had.

(1) It is in one sense a warning to the disciples. It is as if Jesus said to them: 'You have received the great privilege of coming into the Christian Church and fellowship very early, right at the beginning. In later days, others will come in. You must not claim a special honour and a special place because you were Christians before they were. All men and women, no matter when they come, are equally precious to God.' There are people who think that, because they have been members of a church for a long time, the Church practically belongs to them and they can dictate its policy. Such people resent what seems to them the intrusion of new blood or the rise of a new generation with different plans and different ways. In the Christian Church, seniority does not necessarily mean honour.

(2) There is an equally definite warning to the Jews. They knew that they were the chosen people, nor would they ever willingly forget that choice. As a consequence, they looked down on the Gentiles. Usually they hated and despised them, and hoped for nothing but their destruction. This attitude threatened to be carried forward into the Christian Church. If the Gentiles were to be

allowed into the fellowship of the Church at all, they must come in as inferiors. Christianity knows nothing of such a conception of superiority. It may well be that we who have been Christian for so long have much to learn from those younger churches who are late-comers to the fellowship of the faith.

(3) These are the original lessons of this parable; but it has very much more to say to us.

In it, there is *the comfort of God*. It means that no matter when people enter the kingdom – late or soon, in the first flush of youth, in the strength of the middle of the day, or when the shadows are lengthening – they are equally dear to God. The Rabbis had a saying: 'Some enter the kingdom in an hour; others hardly enter it in a lifetime.' In the picture of the holy city in the Book of Revelation, there are twelve gates. There are gates on the *east* which is the direction of the dawn, and whereby people may enter in the glad morning of their days; there are gates on the *west* which is the direction of the setting sun, and whereby people may enter in their age. No matter when they come to Christ, they are equally dear to him.

(4) Here, also, is the infinite *compassion* of God. There is an element of human tenderness in this parable. There is nothing more tragic in this world than men and women who are unemployed, those whose talents are rusting in idleness because there is nothing for them to do. One great teacher used to say that the saddest words in all Shakespeare's plays are the words: 'Othello's occupation's gone.' In that market place, men stood waiting because no one had hired them; in his compassion, the master gave them work to do. He could not bear to see them idle.

Further, in strict justice, the fewer hours a man worked, the less pay he should have received. But the master knew perfectly well that one denarius a day was no great wage; he knew that if a workman went home with less, there would be a worried wife and hungry children; and therefore he went beyond justice and gave them more than was their due. This parable states implicitly two great truths which are the very charter of all those who work – the right of everyone to work and the right of everyone to a living wage for that work.

(5) Here also is the *generosity* of God. These men did not all do the same work; but they did receive the same pay. There are two great lessons here. The first is it is not the amount of service given, but the love in which it is given which matters. God does not look on the amount of our service. As long as it is all we have to give, all service ranks the same with God.

The second lesson is even greater – all God gives is of grace. We cannot earn what God gives us; we cannot deserve it; what God gives us is given out of the goodness of his heart; what God gives is not pay, but a gift; not a reward, but a grace.

(6) Surely that brings us to the supreme lesson of the parable – *the whole point of work is the spirit in which it is done.* The servants are clearly divided into two classes. The first came to an agreement with the master; they had a contract; they said: 'We work, if you give us so much pay.' As their conduct showed, all they were concerned with was to get as much as possible out of their work. But in the case of those who were engaged later, there is no word of contract; all they wanted was the chance to work, and they willingly left the reward to the master.

We are not Christians if our first concern is pay. Christians work for the joy of serving God and others. That is why the first will be last and the last will be first. Many in this world, who have earned great rewards, will have a very low place in the kingdom because rewards were their sole thought. Many who, as the world counts it, are poor, will be great in the kingdom, because they never thought in terms of reward but worked for the thrill of working and for the joy of serving. It is the paradox of the Christian life that those who aim at reward lose it, and those who forget reward find it.

The Sunday between
25 September and 1 October
The Cure for Disunity *and*
The Expedient Ignorance

Philippians 2:1–13

The one danger which threatened the Philippian church was that of disunity. There is a sense in which that is the danger of every healthy church. It is when people are really serious and their beliefs really matter to them that they are apt to come into conflict with one another. The greater their enthusiasm, the greater the danger that they may collide. It is against that danger Paul wishes to safeguard his friends.

In verses 3–4, he gives us the three great causes of disunity. There is *selfish ambition*. There is always the danger that people might work not to advance the work but to advance themselves.

There is the desire for *personal prestige*. Prestige is for many people an even greater temptation than wealth. To be admired and respected, to have a seat on the platform, to have one's opinion sought, to be known by name and appearance, even to be flattered, are for many people most desirable things. But the aim of Christians ought to be not self-display but self-obliteration. We should do good deeds, not in order that others may glorify us, but that they may glorify our Father in heaven. Christians should desire to focus people's eyes not upon themselves but on God.

There is *concentration on self*. If we are always concerned first and foremost with our own interests, we are bound to come into conflict with others. If for us life is a competition whose prizes we must win, we will always think of other human beings as enemies or at least as opponents who must be pushed out of the way. Concentration on self inevitably means elimination of others, and the object of life becomes not to help others up but to put them down.

Faced with this danger of disunity, Paul sets down five considerations which ought to prevent disharmony.

(1) The fact that we are all in Christ should keep us in unity. No one can walk in disunity with other people and in unity with Christ. If we have Christ as a companion on the way, we inevitably become companions of others. The relationships we hold with other people are no bad indication of our relationship with Jesus Christ.

(2) The power of Christian love should keep us in unity. Christian love is that unconquered goodwill which never knows bitterness and never seeks anything but the good of others. It is not a mere reaction of the heart, as human love is; it is a victory of the will, achieved by the help of Jesus Christ. It does not mean loving only those who love us, or those whom we like, or those who are lovable. It means an unconquerable goodwill even to those who hate us, to those whom we do not like, to those who are unlovely. This is the very essence of the Christian life; and it affects us in the present time and in eternity.

(3) The fact that they share in the Holy Spirit should keep Christians from disunity. The Holy Spirit binds individuals to God and to one another. It is the Spirit who enables us to live that life of love, which is the life of God; if we live in disunity with others, we thereby show that the gift of the spirit is not ours.

(4) The existence of human compassion should keep people from disunity. As Aristotle had it long ago, human beings were never meant to be snarling wolves but were meant to live in fellowship together. Disunity breaks the very structure of life.

(5) Paul's last appeal is the personal one. There can be no happiness for him as long as he knows that there is disunity in the church which is dear to him. If they want to bring him perfect joy, they must perfect their fellowship. It is not with a threat that Paul speaks to

the Christians of Philippi but with the appeal of love, which ought always to be the tone used by the pastor, as it was the tone of our Lord.

The appeal that Paul makes to the Philippians is more than an appeal to live in unity in a given situation; it is an appeal to live a life which will lead to the salvation of God in time and in eternity. Nowhere in the New Testament is the work of salvation more succinctly stated. As the Revised Standard Version has it in verses 12–13, 'Work out your own salvation with fear and trembling; for God is at work in you, both to will and to work for his good pleasure.' As always with Paul, the words are meticulously chosen.

Work out your own salvation; the word he uses for *work out* is *katergazesthai*, which always has the idea of bringing to completion. It is as if Paul says: 'Don't stop half-way; go on until the work of salvation is fully achieved in you.' No Christian should be satisfied with anything less than the total benefits of the gospel.

'For God is at work in you both to will and *to work* for his good pleasure.' The word Paul uses for *work* is the verb *energein*. There are two significant things about it; it is always used of *the action of God*, and it is always used of *effective action*. God's action cannot be frustrated, nor can it remain half-finished; it must be fully effective.

Salvation is of God. It is God who works in us the desire to be saved. Without his help, there can be no progress in goodness; without his help, no sin can be conquered and no virtue achieved. The end of the process of salvation is with God, for its end is friendship with God, in which we are his and he is ours. The work of salvation is begun, continued and ended in God.

(For the discussion of verses 5–11, see Palm Sunday, p. 109.)

Matthew 21:23-32

When we think of the extraordinary things Jesus had been doing, we cannot be surprised that the Jewish authorities asked him what right he had to do them. At the moment, Jesus was not prepared to give them the direct answer that his authority came from the fact that he was the Son of God. To do so would have been to precipitate the end. There were actions still to be done and teaching still to be given. It sometimes takes more courage to bide one's time and to await the necessary moment than it does to throw oneself on the enemy and invite the end. For Jesus, everything had to be done in God's time; and the time for the final crisis had not yet come.

So he countered the question of the Jewish authorities with a question of his own, one which placed them in a dilemma. He asked them whether John's ministry came 'from heaven or from men', whether it was divine or merely human in its origin. Were those who went out to be baptized at the Jordan responding to a merely human impulse, or were they in fact answering a divine challenge? The dilemma of the Jewish authorities was this. If they said that the ministry of John was from God, then they had no alternative to admitting that Jesus was the Messiah, for John had borne definite and unmistakable witness to that fact. On the other hand, if they denied that John's ministry came from God, then they would have to bear the anger of the people, who were convinced that he was the messenger of God.

For a moment, the Jewish chief priests and elders were silent. Then they gave the lamest of all lame answers. They said: 'We do not know.' If ever anyone stood self-condemned, these men did. They ought to have known; it was part of the duty of the Sanhedrin, of which they were members, to distinguish between true and false prophets; and they were saying that they were unable to make that distinction. Their dilemma drove them into a shameful self-humiliation.

There is a grim warning here. There is such a thing as the deliberately assumed ignorance of cowardice. If we consult *expediency* rather than *principle*, our first question will be not 'What is the truth?' but 'What is it safe to say?' Again and again, the worship of expediency will drive us to a cowardly silence. We will lamely say: 'I do not know the answer,' when we know perfectly well the answer, but are afraid to give it. The true question is not 'What is it safe to say?' but 'What is it right to say?'

The deliberately assumed ignorance of fear and the cowardly silence of expediency are shameful things. If we know the truth, we are under obligation to tell it, though the heavens should fall.

The meaning of the parable that follows is crystal clear. The Jewish leaders are the people who said they would obey God and then did not. The tax-gatherers and the prostitutes are those who said that they would go their own way and then took God's way.

The key to the correct understanding of this parable is that it is not really praising anyone. It is setting before us a picture of two very imperfect sets of people, of whom one set were nonetheless better than the other. Neither son in the story was the kind of son to bring full joy to his father. Both were unsatisfactory; but the one who in the end obeyed was incalculably better than the other. The ideal son would be the son who accepted the father's orders with obedience and with respect and who unquestioningly and fully carried them out. But there are truths in this parable which go far beyond the situation in which it was first spoken.

It tells us that there are two very common classes of people in this world. First, there are the people whose promises are much better than their practice. They will promise anything; they make great protestations of piety and fidelity; but their practice lags far behind. Second, there are those whose practice is far better than their promises. They claim to be tough, hard-headed materialists, but somehow they are found out doing kindly and generous things, almost in secret, as if they were ashamed of it. They profess to have no interest in the Church and in religion, and yet in reality they live more Christian lives than many professing Christians.

We have all of us met these people, those whose practice is far away from the almost sanctimonious piety of their professed beliefs, and those whose practice is far ahead of the sometimes cynical, and sometimes almost irreligious, declarations which they make about what they believe. The real point of the parable is that, while the second class are infinitely to be preferred to the first, neither is anything like perfect. The really good man or woman is the one in whom professed belief and practice meet and match.

Further, this parable teaches us that promises can never take the place of performance, and fine words are never a substitute for fine deeds. The son who said he would go, and did not, had all the outward marks of courtesy. In his answer, he called his father 'sir' with all respect. But a courtesy which never gets beyond words is a totally illusory thing. True courtesy is obedience, willingly and graciously given.

On the other hand, the parable teaches us that a good thing can easily be spoiled by the way it is done. A fine thing can be done with a lack of graciousness and a lack of charm which spoil the whole deed. Here, we learn that the Christian way is in performance and not promise, and that the mark of a Christian is obedience graciously and courteously given.

The Sunday between 2 and 8 October
What it Means to Know Christ *and*
The Vineyard of the Lord

Philippians 3:4b–14

Paul first states the privileges which came to him by birth and goes on to state his achievements in the Jewish faith. All these things Paul might have claimed to set down on the credit side of the balance; but, when he met Christ, he wrote them off as nothing more than bad debts. The things that he had believed to be his glories were in fact quite useless. All human achievement had to be laid aside, in order that he might accept the free grace of Christ. He had to strip himself of every human claim of honour in order that he might accept in complete humility the mercy of God in Jesus Christ.

So he says: 'Out of my experience I tell you that the Jewish way is wrong and futile. You will never get into a right relationship with God by your own efforts in keeping the law. You can get into a right relationship with God only by taking Jesus Christ at his word, and by accepting what God himself offers to you.' Paul had discovered that a right relationship with God is based not on law but on faith in Jesus Christ. It is not *achieved* by any individual but *given* by God, not *won* by *works* but accepted in *trust*. The basic thought of this passage is the uselessness of law and the sufficiency of knowing Christ and accepting the offer of God's grace.

Paul then defines more closely what he means by the supreme value above all else of the knowledge of Christ. It is important to note the verb which he uses for *to know*. It is part of the verb *ginōskein*, which almost always indicates personal knowledge. It is not simply intellectual knowledge, the knowledge of certain facts or even principles. It is the personal experience of another person. We may see the depth of this word from a fact of Old Testament usage. The Old Testament uses *to know* of sexual intercourse. 'Now the man *knew* his wife Eve, and she conceived and bore Cain' (Genesis 4:1). In Hebrew, the verb is *yada*, and in Greek it is translated by *ginōskein*. This verb indicates the most intimate knowledge of another person. It is not Paul's aim *to know about Christ*, but personally *to know him*. To know Christ means for him certain things.

(1) It means to know *the power of his resurrection*. For Paul, the resurrection was not simply a past event in history, however amazing. It was not simply something which had happened to Jesus, however important it was for him. It was a dynamic power which operated in the life of the individual Christian. We cannot know everything that Paul meant by this phrase; but the resurrection of Christ is the great dynamic, the driving force in at least three different directions.

(a) It is the guarantee of the importance of this life and of this body in which we live. It was in the body that Christ rose, and it is this body which he sanctifies (1 Corinthians 6:13ff.).

(b) It is the guarantee of the life to come (Romans 8:11; 1 Corinthians 15:14ff.). Because Christ lives, we shall live also; his victory is our victory.

(c) It is the guarantee that in life and in death and beyond death the presence of the risen Lord is always with us. It is the proof that his promise to be with us always to the end of the world is true. The resurrection of Christ is the guarantee that this life is worth living and that the physical body is sacred; it is the guarantee that death is not the end of life and that there is a world beyond; it is the guarantee that nothing in life or in death can separate us from him.

(2) It means to know *the fellowship of his sufferings*. Again and again, Paul returns to the thought that, when Christians have to suffer,

they are in some strange way sharing the very suffering of Christ and are even filling up that suffering (2 Corinthians 1:5, 4:10–11; Galatians 6:17; Colossians 1:24). To suffer for the faith is not a penalty; it is a privilege, for thereby we share the very work of Christ.

(3) It means to *be so united with Christ that day by day we come more to share in his death, so that finally we share in his resurrection.* To know Christ means that we share the way he walked; we share the cross he bore; we share the death he died; and finally we share the life he lives for evermore.

To know Christ is not to be skilled in any theoretical or theological knowledge; it is to know him with such intimacy that in the end we are as united with him as we are with those whom we love on earth, and that, just as we share their experiences, so we also share his.

Matthew 21:33–46

In interpreting a parable, it is normally a first principle that every parable has only one point and that the details are not to be stressed. Normally, to try to find a meaning for every detail is to make the mistake of treating the parable as an allegory. But in this case it is different. In this parable, the details do have a meaning.

Before we treat it in detail, let us set these identifications down. The vineyard is the nation of Israel, and its owner is God. The cultivators are the religious leaders of Israel, who, as it were, had charge for God of the welfare of the nation. The messengers who were sent successively are the prophets sent by God and so often rejected and killed. The son who came last is none other than Jesus himself. Here, in a vivid story, Jesus set out at one and the same time the history and the doom of Israel.

This parable has much to tell us in three directions.

(1) It has much to tell us about God.

(a) It tells of God's *trust* in human beings. The owner of the vineyard entrusted it to the cultivators. He did not even stand over them to exercise a police-like supervision. He went away and left them with their task. God pays us the compliment of entrusting us with his work. Every task we receive is a task given us to do by God.

(b) It tells of God's *patience*. The master sent messenger after messenger. He did not come with sudden vengeance when one messenger had been abused and ill-treated. He gave the cultivators chance after chance to respond to his appeal. God bears with us in all our sinning and will not cast us off.

(c) It tells of God's *judgement*. In the end, the master of the vineyard took the vineyard from the cultivators and gave it to others. God's sternest judgement is when he takes out of our hands the task which he meant us to do. To become useless to God is to sink to the lowest level.

(2) It has much to tell us about human nature.

(a) It tells of human *privilege*. The vineyard was equipped with everything – the hedge, the wine press, the tower – which would make the task of the cultivators easy and enable them to discharge it well. God does not only give us a task to do; he also gives us the means whereby to do it.

(b) It tells of *human freedom*. The master left the cultivators to do the task as they liked. God is no tyrannical taskmaster; he is like a wise leader who allocates tasks and then trusts people to do them.

(c) It tells of human *answerability*. To everybody comes a day of reckoning. We are answerable for the way in which we have carried out the task God gave us to do.

(d) It tells of the *deliberateness of human sin*. The cultivators carry out a deliberate policy of rebellion and disobedience towards the master. Sin is deliberate opposition to God; it is the taking of our own way when we know quite well what the way of God is.

(3) It has much to tell us about Jesus.

(a) It tells of the *claim of Jesus*. It shows us quite clearly Jesus lifting himself out of the succession of the prophets. Those who came before him were the messengers of God; no one could deny them that honour; but they were *servants*; he was the *Son*. This parable contains one of the clearest claims Jesus ever made to be unique, to be different from even the greatest of those who went before.

(b) It tells of the *sacrifice of Jesus*. It makes it clear that Jesus knew what lay ahead. In the parable, the hands of wicked men killed the son. Jesus was never in any doubt of what lay ahead. He did not die because he was compelled to die; he went willingly and with open eyes to death.

The Sunday between 9 and 15 October

The True Teaching and the True God
and Joy and Judgement

Philippians 4:1–9

In the final verses of this passage, Paul lays down the way of true teaching. He speaks of the things which the Philippians have *learned*. These are the things in which he personally instructed them. This stands for the personal interpretation of the gospel, which Paul brought to them. He speaks of the things which the Philippians have *received*. The word is *paralambanein*, which characteristically means to accept a fixed tradition. This, then, stands for the accepted teaching of the Church, which Paul had handed on to them.

From these two words, we learn that teaching consists of two things. It consists of handing on to others the accepted body of truth and doctrine which the whole Church holds; and it consists of illuminating that body of doctrine by the personal interpretation and instruction of the teacher. If we would teach or preach, we must know the accepted body of the Church's doctrine; and then we must pass it through our own minds and hand it on to others, both in its own simplicity and in the significances which our own experiences and our own thinking have given to it.

Paul goes further than that. He tells the Philippians to copy what they have heard and seen in himself. Tragically few teachers and preachers can speak like that; and yet it remains true that personal example is an essential part of teaching. Teachers must demonstrate in action the truth which they express in words.

Finally, Paul tells his Philippian friends that, if they faithfully do all this, the God of peace will be with them. It is of great interest to study Paul's titles for God.

(1) He is *the God of peace*. This, in fact, is his favourite title for God (Romans 16:20; 1 Corinthians 14:33; 1 Thessalonians 5:23). To a Jew, peace was never merely a negative thing, never merely the absence of trouble. It was everything which makes for a person's highest good. Only in the friendship of God is it possible to find life as it was meant to be.

But also, to a Jew, this peace led especially to *right relationships*. It is only by the grace of God that we can enter into a right relationship with him and with one another. The God of peace is able to make life what it was meant to be by enabling us to enter into fellowship with himself and with other people.

(2) He is *the God of hope* (Romans 15:13). Belief in God is the only thing which can keep us from the ultimate despair. Only the sense of the grace of God can keep us from despairing about ourselves; and only the sense of the providence of God which rules over all things can keep us from despairing about the world. The psalmist sang: 'Why are you cast down, O my soul? . . . Hope in God; for I shall again praise him, my help and my God' (Psalm 42:11, Psalm 43:5). The hymn-writer F. W. Faber wrote:

For right is right, since God is God,
And right the day must win;
To doubt would be disloyalty,
To falter would be sin.

The hope of Christians is indestructible because it is founded on the eternal God.

(3) He is *the God of patience, of comfort and of consolation* (Romans 15:5; 2 Corinthians 1:3). Here, we have two great words. Patience is in Greek *hupomonē*, which never means simply the ability to sit

down and bear things but the ability to rise up and conquer them. God is the one who gives us the power to use any experience to lend greatness and glory to life. God is the one in whom we learn to use joy and sorrow, success and failure, achievement and disappointment alike, to enrich and to ennoble life, to make us more useful to others and to bring us nearer to himself. *Consolation* and *comfort* are the same Greek word – *paraklēsis*. *Paraklēsis* is far more than soothing sympathy; it is encouragement. It is the help which not only puts an arm round someone but sends that person out to face the world; it not only wipes away the tears but makes it possible to face the world with steady eyes. *Paraklēsis* is comfort and strength combined. God is the one in whom any situation becomes our glory and in whom people find strength to go on gallantly when life has collapsed.

(4) He is *the God of love and peace* (2 Corinthians 13:11). Here, we are at the heart of the matter. Behind everything is that love of God which will never let us go, which puts up with all our sinning, which will never cast us off, which never sentimentally weakens but always vigorously strengthens us for the battle of life. Peace, hope, patience, comfort, love – these were the things which Paul found in God. Indeed, 'our competence is from God' (2 Corinthians 3:5).

Matthew 22:1–14

This chapter is in the form of not one parable, but two.

The events of the first were completely in accordance with normal Jewish customs. When the invitations to a great feast, like a wedding feast, were sent out, the time was not stated; and when everything was ready, the servants were sent out with a final summons to tell the guests to come. So, the king in this parable had long ago sent out his invitations; but it was not until everything was prepared that the final summons was issued – and insultingly refused. This parable has two meanings.

(1) It has a purely local meaning – an accusation directed at the Jews. The invited guests, who when the time came refused to come, stand for the Jews. Ages ago, they had been invited by God to be his chosen people; yet when God's Son came into the world, and they were invited to follow him, they contemptuously refused. The result was that the invitation of God went out directly to the highways and the byways; and the people in the highways and the byways stand for the sinners and the Gentiles, who never expected an invitation into the kingdom.

(2) This parable also has much to say on a much wider scale.

(a) It reminds us that the invitation of God is to a feast as joyous as a wedding feast. His invitation is to joy. To think of Christianity as a gloomy giving up of everything which brings laughter and sunshine and happy fellowship is to mistake its whole nature. It is to joy that Christians are invited; and it is joy they miss, if they refuse the invitation.

(b) It reminds us that the things which make people deaf to the invitation of Christ are not necessarily bad in themselves. In the parable, one man went to his estate: the other to his business. They did not go off on a wild binge or an immoral adventure. They went off on the, in itself, excellent task of efficiently administering their business life. It is very easy to be so busy with the things of the present that the things of eternity are forgotten, to hear so insistently the claims of the world that the soft invitation of the voice of Christ cannot be heard. The tragedy of life is that it is things which are good in themselves which shut out the things that are supreme. We can be so busy making a living that we fail to make a life; we can be so busy with the administration and the organization of life that we forget life itself.

(c) It reminds us that the appeal of Christ is not so much to consider how we will be punished as it is to see what we will miss if we do not take his way of things. Those who would not come were punished, but their real tragedy was that they lost the joy of the wedding feast. If we refuse the invitation of Christ, some day our greatest pain will lie not in the things we suffer but in the realization of the precious things we have missed.

(d) It reminds us that in the last analysis God's invitation is the invitation of grace. Those who were gathered in from the highways and the byways had no claim on the king at all; they could never have expected an invitation to the wedding feast; still less could they ever have deserved it. It came to them from nothing other than the wide-armed, open-hearted, generous hospitality of the king. It was grace which offered the invitation and grace which gathered them in.

The second parable is a very close continuation and amplification of the first. It is the story of a guest who appeared at a royal wedding feast without a wedding garment. This parable also contains both a local and a universal lesson.

(1) The local lesson is this. Jesus has just said that the king, to supply his feast with guests, sent his messengers out into the highways and byways to gather people in. That was the parable of the open door. It told how the Gentiles and the sinners would be gathered in. This parable strikes the necessary balance. It is true that the door is open to everyone, but when people come they must bring a life which seeks to fit the love which has been given to them. Grace is not only a gift; it is a grave responsibility. We cannot go on living the life we lived before we met Jesus Christ. We must be clothed in a new purity and a new holiness and a new goodness. The door is open, but the door is not open for the sinner to come and remain a sinner, but for the sinner to come and become a saint.

(2) This is the permanent lesson. The way in which people come to anything demonstrates the spirit in which they come. If we go to visit in a friend's house, we know very well that it is not our clothes which matter to the friend, but it is a matter of respect that we should present ourselves in our friend's house as neatly as we can. The fact that we prepare ourselves to go there is the way in which

we outwardly show our affection and our esteem for our friend. So it is with God's house. This parable has nothing to do with the *clothes* in which we go to church; it has everything to do with the *spirit* in which we go to God's house. It is profoundly true that church-going must never be a fashion parade. But there are garments of the mind and of the heart and of the soul – the garment of expectation, the garment of humble penitence, the garment of faith, the garment of reverence – and these are the garments without which we ought not to approach God. Too often, we go to God's house with no preparation at all; if every man and woman in our congregations came to church *prepared to worship*, after a little prayer, a little thought and a little self-examination, then worship would be worship indeed – the worship in which and through which things happen in the souls of men and women and in the life of the Church and in the affairs of the world.

The Sunday between 16 and 22 October

Love's Introduction *and* Human and Divine Right

1 Thessalonians 1:1–10

Paul sends this letter to the church of the Thessalonians *which is in God and the Lord Jesus Christ.* God was the very atmosphere in which the Church lived and moved and had its being. Just as the air is in us and we are in the air and cannot live without it, so the true Church is in God and God is in the true Church, and there is no true life for the Church without God. Further, the God in whom the Church lives is the God and Father of our Lord Jesus Christ; and, therefore, the Church does not shiver in the icy fear of a God who is a tyrant but basks in the sunshine of a God who is love.

In this opening chapter, we see Paul at his most attractive. In a short time, he was going to deal out warning and rebuke; but he begins with unmixed praise. Even when he rebuked, it was his aim never to discourage but always to uplift. In every individual there is something fine, and often the best way to rid a person of the lower things is to praise the higher things. The best way to eradicate faults is to praise someone's virtues so that they will flower all the more; we all react better to encouragement than to rebuke. It is told that once the Duke of Wellington's cook gave notice and left him. He was asked why he had left so honourable and well-paid a position. His answer was: 'When the dinner is good, the Duke never praises me, and when it is bad, he never blames me; it was just not worth while.' Encouragement was lacking. Paul, like a good psychologist and with true Christian tact, begins with praise even when he means to move on to rebuke.

In verse 3, Paul picks out three great ingredients of the Christian life.

(1) There is *work which is inspired by faith*. Nothing tells us more about people than the way in which they work. They may work in fear of being reprimanded; they may work for hope of gain; they may work from a grim sense of duty; or they may work inspired by faith. Their faith is that their tasks have been given by God and that they are working in the last analysis not for others but for God. It has been said that the sign of true dedication to God is to be able to find glory in drudgery.

(2) There is *the labour which is prompted by love*. The First World War veteran and writer, Bernard Newman, tells how he once stayed in a Bulgarian peasant's house. All the time he was there, the daughter was stitching away at a dress. He said to her: 'Don't you ever get tired of that eternal sewing?' 'Oh no!' she said. 'You see, this is my wedding dress.' Work done out of love always has a glory.

(3) There is *the endurance which is founded on hope*. When Alexander the Great was setting out on his campaigns, he divided all his possessions among his friends. Someone said: 'But you are keeping nothing for yourself.' 'Oh yes, I am,' he said. 'I have kept my hopes.' It is possible to put up with anything as long as we have hope, for then we are walking not to the night but to the dawn.

In verse 4, Paul speaks of the Thessalonians as being *beloved by God*. The phrase *beloved by God* was a phrase which the Jews applied only to supremely great figures like Moses and Solomon, and to the nation of Israel itself. Now the greatest privilege of the greatest among God's chosen people has been extended to the humblest of the Gentiles.

Verse 8 speaks of the faith of the Thessalonians sounding forth like *a trumpet*; the word could also mean crashing out like *a roll of thunder*. There is something tremendous about the sheer defiance of early Christianity. When all prudence would have dictated a way of life that would escape notice and so avoid danger and persecution, the

Christians broadcast their faith. They were never ashamed to show whose they were and whom they sought to serve.

In verses 9–10, two words are used which are characteristic of the Christian life. The Thessalonians *served* God and *waited* for the coming of Christ. The Christian is called upon to serve in the world and to wait for glory. The loyal service and the patient waiting were the necessary preludes to the glory of heaven.

Matthew 22:15–22

We see here the Jewish leaders launching their attack on Jesus; and they do so by directing at Jesus carefully formulated questions. They ask these questions in public, while the crowd look on and listen, and their aim is to make Jesus discredit himself by his own words in the presence of the people. Here, then, we have the question of the Pharisees, and it was subtly framed. Palestine was an occupied country, and the Jews were subject to the Roman Empire; and the question was: 'Is it, or is it not, lawful to pay tribute to Rome?'

The question set Jesus a very real dilemma. If he said that it was unlawful to pay the tax, they would promptly report him to the Roman government officials as a seditious person, and his arrest would certainly follow. If he said that it was lawful to pay the tax, he would stand discredited in the eyes of many of the people. Not only did the people resent the tax as everyone resents taxation; they resented it even more for religious reasons. To the Jews, God was the only king; their nation was a theocracy; to pay tax to an earthly king was to admit the validity of his kingship and thereby to insult God. Whichever way Jesus might answer – so his questioners thought – he would lay himself open to trouble.

This question of tax-paying was not merely of historical interest. Matthew was writing between AD 80 and 90. The Temple had been destroyed in AD 70. So long as the Temple stood, every

Jew had been bound to pay the half-shekel Temple tax. After the destruction of the Temple, the Roman government demanded that that tax should be paid to the temple of Jupiter Capitolinus in Rome. It is obvious how bitter a regulation that was for the Jews to stomach. The matter of taxes was a real problem in the actual ministry of Jesus; and it was still a real problem in the days of the early Church. But Jesus was wise. He asked to see a denarius, which was stamped with the emperor's head. In the ancient days, coinage was the sign of kingship. As soon as a king came to the throne, he struck his own coinage and that coinage was held to be the property of the king whose image it bore. Jesus asked whose image was on the coin. The answer was that Caesar's head was on it. 'Well then,' said Jesus, 'give it back to Caesar; it is his. Give to Caesar what belongs to him, and give to God what belongs to him.'

With his unique wisdom, Jesus never laid down rules and regulations; that is why his teaching is timeless and never goes out of date. He always lays down principles. Here he lays down a very great and very important one.

Every Christian has a double citizenship. Christians are citizens of the country in which they happen to live. To it they owe many things. They owe the safety against lawless people which only settled government can give; they owe all public services. In a welfare state, citizens owe still more to the state – education, medical services, provision for unemployment and old age. This places them under a debt of obligation.

Because Christians are men and women of honour, they must be responsible citizens; failure in good citizenship is also failure in Christian duty. Untold troubles can descend upon a country or an industry when Christians refuse to take their part in the administration and leave it to selfish, self-seeking, partisan and un-Christian men and women. The Christians had a duty to Caesar in return for the privileges which the rule of Caesar brought to them.

But Christians are also citizens of heaven. There are matters of religion and of principle in which the responsibility of Christians is to God. It may well be that the two citizenships will never clash; they do not need to. But when Christians are convinced that it is God's will that something should be done, it must be done; or, if they are convinced that something is against the will of God, they must resist it and take no part in it. Where the boundaries between the two duties lie, Jesus does not say. That is for our own consciences to test. But real Christians – and this is the permanent truth which Jesus here lays down – are at one and the same time good citizens of their country and good citizens of the kingdom of heaven. They will fail in their duty neither to God nor to society. They will, as Peter said, 'Fear God. Honour the emperor' (1 Peter 2:17).

The Sunday between 23 and 29 October
Paul on His Defence *and* Duty to God and Duty to Others

1 Thessalonians 2:1–8

Beneath the surface of this passage run the slanders which Paul's opponents at Thessalonica attached to him.

(1) Verse 2 refers to the imprisonment and abuse that he had received at Philippi (Acts 16:16–40). There were, no doubt, those in Thessalonica who said that this man Paul had a police record, that he was nothing less than a criminal on the run from justice and that obviously no one should listen to a man like that. A really malicious mind will twist anything into a slander.

(2) Behind verse 3, there are no fewer than three charges.

(a) It was being said that Paul's preaching came from sheer delusion. Anyone with a really original mind will always run the risk of being called mad. Later on, Festus thought that Paul was mad (Acts 26:24). There was a time when Jesus' friends came and tried to take him home because they thought that he was mad (Mark 3:21). Christian standards can be so different from the standards of the world that those who follow them with single-minded purpose and a burning enthusiasm can appear to others to be off their heads.

(b) It was being said that Paul's preaching sprang from impure motives. The word used for *impurity* (*akatharsia*) often has to do with sexual impurity. There was one Christian custom which non-Christians often and deliberately misinterpreted; that was the kiss of peace (1 Thessalonians 5:26). When the Christians spoke of the Love Feast and the kiss of peace, it was not difficult for an evil mind to read into these phrases meaning that was never there. It is often the case that a truly unpleasant mind will see a similar unpleasantness everywhere.

(c) It was being said that Paul's preaching was cunningly aimed at deluding others. The propagandists of Hitler's Germany discovered that if a lie is repeated often enough and loudly enough it will in the end be accepted as the truth. That was the charge which was levelled at Paul.

(3) Verse 4 indicates that Paul was accused of seeking to please people rather than to please God. No doubt that rose from the fact that he preached the liberty of the gospel and the freedom of grace as against the slavery of legalism. There are always people who do not think that they are being religious unless they are being unhappy; and anyone who preaches a gospel of joy will be subject to misrepresentation, which is exactly what happened to Jesus.

(4) Verse 6 indicates that Paul was accused of seeking personal prestige. It is a constant danger for preachers that they should seek to promote themselves and not the message. In 1 Thessalonians 1:5, there is a thought-provoking phrase. Paul does not say: '*I* came to you.' He says: '*Our gospel* came to you.' The man was lost in his message.

(5) Verse 7 indicates that Paul was charged with being something of a dictator. His gentleness was that of a wise father. His was the love which knew how to be firm. To him, Christian love was in no way easy or sentimental; he knew that people needed discipline, not for their punishment but for the good of their souls.

Matthew 22:34–46

The question here, 'What commandment in the law is greatest?' looks like a return to the attack on the part of the Pharisees; but in Mark's Gospel, the atmosphere is different. As Mark tells the story

(Mark 12:28–34), the scribe did not ask Jesus this question to trip him up. He asked it to enable Jesus to demonstrate how well he could answer; and the passage ends with the scribe and Jesus very close to each other.

We may well say that here Jesus laid down the complete definition of religion.

(1) Religion consists in loving God. The verse which Jesus quotes is Deuteronomy 6:5. That verse was part of the *Shema*, the basic and essential creed of Judaism, the sentence with which every Jewish service still opens, and the first text which every Jewish child commits to memory. It means that to God we must give a total love, a love which dominates our emotions, a love which directs our thoughts, and a love which is the dynamic of our actions. All religion starts with the love which is total commitment of life to God.

(2) The second commandment which Jesus quotes comes from Leviticus 19:18. Our love for God must issue in love for others. But it is to be noted in which order the commandments come; it is love of God first, and love of others second. It is only when we love God that other people become lovable. The biblical teaching about human beings is not that we are collections of chemical elements, not that we are part of the brute creation, but that men and women are made in the image of God (Genesis 1:26–7). It is for that reason that human beings are lovable. The true basis of all democracy is in fact the love of God. Take away the love of God, and we can look at human nature and become angry at those who cannot be taught; we can become pessimistic about those who cannot make progress; we can become callous to those who are cold and calculating in their actions. The love of humanity is firmly grounded in the love of God.

To be truly religious is to love God and to love those whom God made in his own image; and to love God and other people, not with a vague sentimentality, but with that total commitment which issues in devotion to God and practical service of others.

To us, verses 41–46 may seem to contain one of the most obscure things which Jesus ever said. This may be so, but nonetheless it is a most important statement. Even if, at first sight, we do not fully grasp its meaning, we can still feel the air of awe and astonishment and mystery which it has about it.

Again and again Jesus refused to allow his followers to proclaim him as the Messiah until he had taught them what Messiahship meant. Their ideas of Messiahship needed the most radical change.

The most common title of the Messiah was *Son of David*. Behind it lay the expectation that there would one day come a great prince of the line of David who would shatter Israel's enemies and lead the people to the conquest of all nations. The Messiah was most commonly thought of in nationalistic, political, military terms of power and glory. This is another attempt by Jesus to alter that conception.

He asked the Pharisees whose son they understood the Messiah to be; they answered, as he knew they would: 'David's son'. Jesus then quotes Psalm 110:1: 'The Lord says to my lord, "Sit at my right hand."' All accepted that as a messianic text. In it, the first *Lord is* God; the second *lord is* the Messiah. That is to say, David calls the Messiah *lord*. But, if the Messiah is David's son, how could David call his own son *lord*?

The clear result of the argument is that *it is not adequate to call the Messiah Son of David*. He is not David's son; he is David's lord. When Jesus healed the blind men, they called him Son of David (Matthew 20:30). When he entered Jerusalem, the crowds hailed him as Son of David (Matthew 21:9). Jesus is here saying: 'It is not enough to call the Messiah Son of David. It is not enough to think of him as a prince of David's line and an earthly conqueror. You must go beyond that, for the Messiah is David's *lord*.'

What did Jesus mean? He can have meant only one thing – that the true description of him is *Son of God*. *Son of David* is not an adequate title; only *Son of God* will do. And, if that is so, Messiahship is not to be thought of in terms of Davidic conquest, but in terms of divine and sacrificial love. Here, then, Jesus makes his greatest claim. In him, there came not the earthly conqueror who would repeat the military triumphs of David, but the Son of God who would demonstrate the love of God upon his cross.

There would be few that day who caught anything like all that Jesus meant; but when Jesus spoke these words, even the densest of them felt a shiver in the presence of the eternal mystery. They had the awed and uncomfortable feeling that they had heard the voice of God; and for a moment, in this man Jesus, they glimpsed God's very face.

The Last Sunday after Trinity (Bible Sunday)

The Garments of Christian Grace *and* The Coming of the King

Colossians 3:12–17

Paul here gives his list of the great graces with which the Colossians must clothe themselves.

There is kindness (*chrēstotēs*). R. C. Trench, the nineteenth-century Archbishop of Dublin, calls this a lovely word for a lovely quality. The ancient writers defined *chrēstotēs* as the virtue of those whose neighbours' good is as dear to them as their own. Josephus, the Jewish historian, uses it as a description of Isaac, the man who dug wells and gave them to others because he would not fight about them (Genesis 26:17–25). It is used of wine which has grown mellow with age and lost its harshness. It is the word used when Jesus said: 'My yoke is easy' (Matthew 11:30). Goodness by itself can be stern; but *chrēstotēs* is the goodness which is kind, that type of goodness which Jesus used to the sinning woman who anointed his feet (Luke 7:37–50). No doubt Simon the Pharisee was a good man; but Jesus was more than good, he was *chrēstotēs*. The Rheims version of the Bible translates it as *benignity*. Christians are marked by a goodness which is kindly.

There is *humility* (*tapeinophrosunē*). It has often been said that humility was a virtue created by Christianity. In classical Greek, there is no word for *humility* which does not have some suggestion of servility; but Christian humility carries no sense of cringing sub-mission. It is based on two things. First, on the divine side, it is based on the awareness of the *creatureliness* of humanity. God is the

Creator, men and women are the creatures, and in the presence of the Creator the creatures cannot feel anything but humility. Second, on the human side, it is based on the belief that we are all children of God; and there is no room for arrogance when we are living among men and women who are all of royal lineage.

There is *gentleness* (*praotēs*). Long ago, Aristotle had defined *praotēs* as the happy mid-point between too much and too little anger. The person who has *praotēs* is someone who is so self-controlled, because of being God-controlled, that anger is always expressed at the right time and never at the wrong time. Such a person has at one and the same time the strength and the sweetness of true gentleness.

There is *patience* (*makrothumia*). This is the spirit which never loses its patience with others. Their foolishness and their unteachability never drive it to cynicism or despair; their insults and their ill-treatment never drive it to bitterness or wrath. Human patience is a reflection of the divine patience which tolerates all our sinning and never casts us off.

There is the *tolerant and the forgiving spirit*. Christians forbear and forgive; and they do so because those who have been forgiven must always be forgiving. As God forgave them, so they must forgive others, for only the forgiving can be forgiven.

To the virtues and the graces, Paul adds one more – what he calls *the perfect bond of love*. Love is the binding power which holds the whole Christian body together. The tendency of any body of people is sooner or later to fly apart; love is the one bond which will hold them together in unbreakable fellowship.

Then Paul paints a vivid picture. 'Let the peace of Christ be the decider of all things within your heart.' Literally, what he says is: 'Let the peace of Christ be the umpire in your heart.' He uses a verb from the athletic arena; it is the word that is used of the umpire who settled things in any matter of dispute. If the peace of Jesus Christ is the umpire in anyone's heart, then, when feelings clash and we are pulled in two directions at the same time, the decision of Christ will keep us in the way of love, and the Church will remain the one body it is meant to be. The way to right action is to appoint Jesus Christ as the one who decides between the conflicting emotions in our hearts; and, if we accept his decisions, we cannot go wrong.

It is interesting to see that, from the beginning, the Church was a singing Church. It inherited that from the Jews, for the Jewish philosopher Philo tells us that they would often spend the whole night in hymns and songs. One of the earliest descriptions of a church service we possess is that of Pliny, the Roman governor of Bithynia, who sent a report of the activities of the Christians to Trajan, the Roman emperor, in which he said: 'They meet at dawn to sing a hymn to Christ as God.' The gratitude of the Church has always gone up to God in praise and song.

Finally, Paul gives the great principle for living that everything we do or say should be done and said in the name of Jesus. One of the best tests of any action is: 'Can we do it, calling upon the name of Jesus? Can we do it, asking for his help?' One of the best tests of any word is: 'Can we speak it and in the same breath name the name of Jesus? Can we speak it, remembering that he will hear?' If we bring every word and deed to the test of the presence of Jesus Christ, we will not go wrong.

Matthew 24:30–35

An essential part of the Jewish thought of the future was the *day of the Lord*, that day when God was going to intervene directly in history, and when the present age, with all its incurable evil, would begin to be transformed into the age to come.

Very naturally, the New Testament writers to a very great extent identified the second coming of Jesus and the day of the Lord; and they took over all the imagery which had to do with the day of the

Lord and applied it to the second coming. None of these pictures is to be taken literally; they *are* pictures, and they *are* visions; they are attempts to put the indescribable into human words and to find some kind of picture for happenings for which human language has no picture.

The value of these pictures is not in their details, which at best are only symbolic and which use the only pictures which the minds of men and women could conceive, but in the eternal truth which they conserve; and the basic truth in them is that whatever the world is like, God has not abandoned it.

Verses 32–5 seem to indicate that, just as it is possible to tell by the signs of nature when summer is on the way, so it will be possible to tell by the signs of the world when the second coming is on the way. Then it seems to go on to say that the second coming will happen within the lifetime of the generation listening to Jesus at that moment.

Let us take as our starting point verse 34: 'This is the truth I tell you – this generation shall not pass away, until these things have happened.' When we consider that saying, three possibilities emerge.

(1) If Jesus said it in reference to the second coming, he was mistaken, for he did not return within the lifetime of the generation listening to his words. Many accept that point of view, believing that Jesus in his humanity had limitations of knowledge and did believe that within that generation he would return. We can readily accept that in his humanity Jesus had limitations of knowledge; but it is difficult to believe that he was in error regarding so great a spiritual truth as this.

(2) It is possible that Jesus said something like this which was changed in the transmitting. In Mark 9:1, Jesus is reported as saying: 'Truly I tell you, there are some standing here who will not taste death until they see that the kingdom of God has come with power.' That was gloriously and triumphantly true. Within that

generation, the kingdom of God did spread mightily until there were Christians throughout the known world.

Now the early Christians did look for the second coming immediately. In their situation of suffering and persecution, they looked and longed for the release that the coming of their Lord would bring, and sometimes they took sayings which were intended to speak of the *kingdom* and attached them to the *second coming*, which is a very different thing. Something like that may have happened here. What Jesus may have said was that his *kingdom* would come in power and might before that generation had passed away.

(3) But there is a third possibility. What if the phrase *until these things have happened* has no reference to the second coming? What if their reference is, in fact, to the prophecy with which the chapter began (verses 1–2), the siege and fall of Jerusalem? If we accept that, there is no difficulty. What Jesus is saying is that these grim warnings of his regarding the doom of Jerusalem will be fulfilled within that very generation – and they were, in fact, fulfilled forty years later.

The Fourth Sunday before Advent
Paul on His Defence *and* Threats to Faith

1 Thessalonians 2:9–13

Beneath the surface of this chapter run the slanders which Paul's opponents at Thessalonica attached to him. Verse 9 indicates that there were those who said that Paul was in this business of preaching the gospel for what he could get out of it.

The trouble in the early Church was that there were people who did attempt to cash in on their Christianity. The first Christian book of order is called the *Didache: The Teaching of the Twelve Apostles*, and in it there are some illuminating instructions. 'Let every apostle that comes to you be received as the Lord. And he shall stay one day and, if need be, the next also; but if he stays three days he is a false prophet. And when the apostle goes forth, let him take nothing save bread, until he reaches his lodging. But if he asks for money, he is a false prophet.' 'No prophet that orders a table in the Spirit shall eat of it, else he is a false prophet.' 'If he that comes is a passer-by, succour him as far as you can. But he shall not abide with you longer than two or three days unless there is necessity. But if he is minded to settle among you and be a craftsman, let him work and eat. But if he has no trade, according to your understanding, provide that he shall not live idle among you, being a Christian. But if he will not do this, he is a Christmonger: of such men beware' (*Didache*, 11–12). The date of the *Didache* is about AD 100.

Even the early Church knew the constant problem of those who traded on charity.

Matthew 24:1–14

This passage shows the uncompromising honesty of Jesus. He never promised his disciples an easy way; he promised them death and suffering and persecution. There is a sense in which a real Church will always be a persecuted Church, as long as it exists in a world which is not a Christian world. Where does that persecution come from?

(1) Christ offers a *new loyalty*; and again and again he declared that this new loyalty must surpass all earthly ties. The greatest ground of hatred in the days of the early Church was the fact that Christianity split homes and families, when one member decided for Christ and the others did not. Christians are those who are pledged to give Jesus Christ the first place in their lives – and many a human clash is liable to result from that.

(2) Christ offers a *new standard*. There are customs and practices and ways of life which may be all right for the world, but which are far from being all right for Christians. For many people, the difficulty about Christianity is that it is a judgement upon themselves and upon their way of life in their business or in their personal relationships. The awkward thing about Christianity is that anyone who does not wish to be changed is bound to hate it and resent it.

(3) Christians, if they are true Christians, introduce into the world a *new example*. There is a daily beauty in their lives which makes the lives of others ugly. Christians are the light of the world, not in the sense that they criticize and condemn others, but in the sense that they demonstrate in themselves the beauty of the Christ-filled life and therefore the ugliness of the Christless life.

(4) This is all to say that Christianity brings a *new conscience* into life. Neither the individual Christian nor the Christian Church can ever know anything of a cowardly concealment or a cowardly silence. The Church and the individual Christian must at all times constitute the conscience of Christianity – and it is a human char-

acteristic that there are many times when we would wish to silence conscience.

In the days to come, Jesus saw that two dangers would threaten the Church.

(1) There would be the danger of *false leaders*. False leaders are people who seek to propagate their own version of the truth rather than the truth as it is in Jesus Christ, and are those who try to attach others to themselves rather than to Jesus Christ. The inevitable result is that false leaders spread division instead of building up unity. The test of any leader is likeness to Christ.

(2) The second danger is that of *discouragement*. There are those whose love will grow cold because of the increasing lawlessness of the world. True Christians are men and women who hold to their beliefs, when belief is at its most difficult; and who, in the most discouraging circumstances, refuse to believe that God's arm is shortened or his power grown less.

The Third Sunday before Advent
Concerning Those Who Have Died *and* The Fate of the Unprepared

1 Thessalonians 4:13–18

The idea of the second coming had brought another problem to the people of Thessalonica. They were expecting it very soon; they fully expected that they would still be alive when it came, but they were worried about those Christians who had died. They could not be sure that those who had already died would share the glory of that day which was to come so soon. Paul's answer is that there will be one glory both for those who have died and for those who survive.

He tells them that they must not grieve as others do who have no hope. Confronted by death, the world stood around in despair. People met death with grim resignation and bleak hopelessness. The Greek tragedian Aeschylus wrote: 'Once a man dies, there is no resurrection.' The Greek poet Theocritus wrote: 'There is hope for those who are alive, but those who have died are without hope.' Catullus, the Roman poet, wrote: 'When once our brief light sets, there is one perpetual night through which we must sleep.' On their tombstones, grim epitaphs were carved. 'I was not; I became; I am not; I care not.' One of the most moving papyrus letters of sympathy which runs like this. 'Irene to Taonnophris and Philo, good comfort. I was as sorry and wept over the departed one as I wept for Didymas. And all things whatsoever were fitting, I did, and all mine, Epaphroditus and Thermouthion and Philion and Apollonius and Plantas. But nevertheless against such things one can do nothing. Therefore comfort one another.'

Paul lays down a great principle. Those who have lived and died in Christ are still in Christ even in death and will rise in him. Between Christ and all who love him, there is a relationship which nothing can break, a relationship which overcomes death. Because Christ died and rose again, so all who are one with Christ will rise again.

The picture Paul draws of the day when Christ will come is poetry, an attempt to describe what is indescribable. At the second coming, Christ will descend from heaven to earth. He will utter the word of command, and thereupon the voice of an archangel and the trumpet of God will waken the dead; then both the dead and the living will be caught up in the chariots of the clouds to meet Christ; and thereafter they will be forever with their Lord. We are not meant to take with crude and insensitive literalism what is a prophet's vision. It is not the details which are important. What is important is that in life and in death Christians are in Christ – and that is a union which nothing can break.

Matthew 25:1–13

If we look at this parable with western eyes, it may seem an unnatural and a 'made-up' story. But, in point of fact, it tells a story which could have happened at any time in a Palestinian village and which could still happen today.

A wedding was a great occasion. The whole village turned out to accompany the couple to their new home, and they went by the longest possible road, in order that they might receive the glad good wishes of as many as possible. 'Everyone', runs the Jewish saying, 'from six to sixty will follow the marriage drum.' The Rabbis agreed that a man might even abandon the study of the law to share in the joy of a wedding feast.

The point of this story lies in a Jewish custom which is very different from anything we know. When a couple married, they did not go away for a honeymoon. They stayed at home; for a week they kept open house; they were treated, and even addressed, as prince and princess; it was the happiest week in all their lives. To the festivities of that week their chosen friends were admitted; and it was not only the marriage ceremony, it was also that joyous week that the foolish virgins missed, because they were unprepared.

The story of how they missed it all is perfectly true to life. Dr J. Alexander Findlay, Principal of Didsbury Methodist College, Manchester, tells of what he himself saw in Palestine. 'When we were approaching the gates of a Galilaean town,' he writes, 'I caught a sight of ten maidens gaily clad and playing some kind of musical instrument, as they danced along the road in front of our car; when I asked what they were doing, the dragoman [interpreter] told me that they were going to keep the bride company till her bridegroom arrived. I asked him if there was any chance of seeing the wedding, but he shook his head, saying in effect: "It might be tonight, or tomorrow night, or in a fortnight's time, nobody ever knows for certain." Then he went on to explain that one of the great things to do, if you could, at a middle-class wedding in Palestine was to catch the bridal party napping. So the bridegroom comes unexpectedly, and sometimes in the middle of the night; it is true that he is required by public opinion to send a man along the street to shout: "Behold! the bridegroom is coming!" but that may happen at any time; so the bridal party have to be ready to go out into the street at any time to meet him, whenever he chooses to come . . . Other important points are that no one is allowed on the streets after dark without a lighted lamp, and also that, when the bridegroom has once arrived, and the door has been shut, late-comers to the ceremony are not admitted.' There, the whole drama of Jesus' parable is re-enacted in the twentieth century. Here is no made-up story but a slice of life from a village in Palestine.

Like so many of Jesus' parables, this one has an immediate and local meaning, and also a wider and universal meaning. In its immediate significance, it was directed against the Jews. They were the chosen people; their whole history should have been a preparation for the coming of the Son of God; they ought to have been prepared for him when he came. Instead, they were quite unprepared and therefore were shut out. Here in dramatic form is the tragedy of the unpreparedness of the Jews.

But the parable has at least two universal warnings.

(1) It warns us that there are certain things which cannot be obtained at the last minute. It is far too late for a student to be preparing when the day of the examination has come.

It is too late to acquire a skill, or a character, if we do not already possess it, when some task offers itself to us. Similarly, it is easy to leave things so late that we can no longer prepare ourselves to meet with God. When the Queen of England, Mary of Orange, was dying, her chaplain sought to tell her of the way of salvation. Her answer was: 'I have not left this matter to this hour.' To be too late is always tragedy.

(2) It warns us that there are certain things which cannot be borrowed. The foolish virgins found it impossible to borrow oil when they discovered they needed it. We cannot borrow a relationship with God; we must possess it for ourselves. We cannot borrow a character; we must be clothed with it. We cannot always be living on the spiritual capital which others have amassed. There are certain things we must win or acquire for ourselves, for we cannot borrow them from others.

Tennyson took this parable and turned it into verse in the song the little novice sang to Guinevere the queen, when Guinevere had too late discovered the cost of sin:

Late, late so late! and dark the night and chill!
Late, late so late! but we can enter still.

Too late, too late! ye cannot enter now.
No light had we; for that we do repent;
And learning this, the bridegroom will relent.
Too late, too late! ye cannot enter now.
No light: so late! and dark and chill the night!
O let us in, that we may find the light!
Too late, too late: ye cannot enter now.
Have we not heard the bridegroom is so sweet?
O let us in, tho' late, to kiss his feet!
No, no, too late! ye cannot enter now.

There is no knell so laden with regret as the sound of the words
too late.

The Second Sunday
before Advent
Like a Thief in the Night *and* The
Condemnation of the Buried Talent

1 Thessalonians 5:1-11

We shall not fully understand the New Testament pictures of
the second coming unless we remember that they have an Old
Testament background. In the Old Testament, the idea of the day
of the Lord is very common; and all the pictures and apparatus
which belong to the day of the Lord have been attached to the
second coming. For the Jews, all time was divided into two ages.
There was this present age, which was wholly and incurably bad.
There was the age to come, which would be the golden age of
God. In between, there was the day of the Lord, which would be
a terrible day. It would be a day in which one world was shattered
and another was born.

Many of the most terrible pictures in the Old Testament are of
the day of the Lord (Isaiah 22:5, 13:9; Zephaniah 1:14–16; Amos
5:18; Jeremiah 30:7; Malachi 4:1; Joel 2:31). Its main characteristics
were as follows. (1) It would come suddenly and unexpectedly. (2) It
would involve a cosmic upheaval in which the universe was shaken
to its very foundations. (3) It would be a time of judgement.

Very naturally, the New Testament writers to all intents and
purposes identified the day of the Lord with the day of the second coming of Jesus Christ. We will do well to remember that
these are what we might call traditional stylized pictures. They are
not meant to be taken literally. They are pictorial visions of what
would happen when God broke into time.

Naturally, people were anxious to know when that day would come. Jesus himself had bluntly said that no one knew when that day or hour would be, that even he did not know and only God knew (Mark 13:32; cf. Matthew 24:36; Acts 1:7). But that did not stop people speculating about it, as indeed they still do, although it is surely almost blasphemous that we should seek for knowledge which was denied even to Jesus. To these speculations, Paul has two things to say.

He repeats that the coming of the day will be sudden. It will come like a thief in the night. But he also insists that that is no reason why anyone should be caught unawares. It is only the person who lives in the dark and whose deeds are evil who will be caught unprepared. Christians live in the light – and, no matter when that day comes, if they are watchful and sober, it will find them ready. Waking or sleeping, Christians are already living with Christ and are therefore always prepared.

No one knows when God's call will come, and there are certain things that cannot be left until the last moment. It is too late to prepare for an examination when the examination paper is in front of you. It is too late to make the house secure when the storm has burst. An old Scotsman was offered comforting sayings near the end. The old man's reply was: 'I theekit [thatched] ma hoose when the weather was warm.' If a call comes suddenly, it need not find us unprepared. Those who have lived all their lives with Christ are never unprepared to enter his nearer presence.

Matthew 25:14–30

This parable had an immediate lesson for those who heard it for the first time, and a whole series of permanent lessons for us today. It is always known as the parable of the talents. The *talent* was not a *coin*, it was a *weight*; and therefore its value obviously depended on whether the coinage involved was copper, gold or silver. The most common metal involved was silver; and the value of a talent of silver was considerable. It was worth about fifteen years' wages for a working man.

There can be no doubt that originally in this parable the whole attention is riveted on the useless servant. There can be little doubt that he stands for the scribes and the Pharisees, and for their attitude to the law and the truth of God. The useless servant buried his talent in the ground, in order that he might hand it back to his master exactly as it was. The whole aim of the scribes and Pharisees was to keep the law exactly as it was. In their own phrase, they sought 'to build a fence around the law'. Any change, any development, any alteration, anything new was to them anathema. Their method involved the paralysis of religious truth.

Like the man with the talent, they desired to keep things exactly as they were – and it is for that that they are condemned. In this parable, Jesus tells us that there can be no religion without adventure, and that God can find no use for the shut mind. But there is much more in this parable than that.

(1) It tells us that God gives us differing gifts. One man received five talents, another two, and another one. It is not our talent which matters; what matters is how we use it. God never demands from us abilities which we have not got; but he does demand that we should use to the full the abilities which we do possess. Human beings are not equal in talent; but they can be equal in effort. The parable tells us that whatever talent we have, little or great, we must lay it at the service of God.

(2) It tells us that the reward of work well done is still more work to do. The two servants who had done well are not told to lean back and rest on their oars because they have done well. They are given greater tasks and greater responsibilities in the work of the master.

(3) It tells us that those who are punished are the people who will not try. The man with the one talent did not lose his talent; he sim-

ply did nothing with it. Even if he had adventured with it and lost it, it would have been better than to do nothing at all. It is always a temptation for the one talent person to say: 'I have so small a talent and I can do so little with it. It is not worth while to try, for all the contribution I can make.' The condemnation is for anyone who, having even one talent, will not try to use it, and will not risk it for the common good.

(4) It lays down a rule of life which is universally true. It tells us that to those who have, more will be given, and those who have not will lose even what they have. The meaning is this. If we have a talent and exercise it, we are progressively able to do more with it. But, if we have a talent and fail to exercise it, we will inevitably lose it. If we have some proficiency at a game or an art, if we have some gift for doing something, the more we exercise that proficiency and that gift, the harder the work and the bigger the task we will be able to tackle. Whereas, if we fail to use it, we lose it. That is equally true of playing golf or playing the piano, or singing songs or writing sermons, of carving wood or thinking out ideas. It is the lesson of life that the only way to keep a gift is to use it in the service of God and in the service of our neighbours.

The Sunday next before Advent
Paul's Prayer for the Church *and* God's Standard of Judgement

Ephesians 1:15–23

In this passage, we see what Paul asks for a church which he loves and which is doing well.

(1) He prays for the Spirit of wisdom. The word he uses for *wisdom* is *sophia*. *Sophia* is the wisdom of the deep things of God. He prays that the church may be led deeper and deeper into the knowledge of the eternal truths. If that is ever to happen, certain things are necessary.

(a) It is necessary that we should have a thinking people. Religion is nothing unless it is a personal discovery. As Plato wrote long ago: 'The unexamined life is the life not worth living,' and the unexamined religion is the religion not worth having. It is an obligation for thinking people to think their way to God.

(b) It is necessary that we should have a teaching ministry. The seventeenth-century theologian William Chillingworth said: 'The Bible, and the Bible only, is the religion of Protestants.' That is true; but so often we would not think so. The preaching and explanation of Scripture from the pulpit is a first requirement of religious wakening.

(c) It is necessary that we should have a readjusted sense of proportion. It is one of the strange facts of church life that, in official church gatherings a great many hours might be given to the discussion of mundane problems of administration for every one hour given to the discussion of the eternal truths of God.

(2) Paul prays for a fuller revelation and a fuller knowledge of God. For Christians, growth in knowledge and in grace is essential.

Anyone who follows a profession knows that it is a mistake to stop studying. Doctors never think that they have finished learning when they leave university. They know that week by week, and almost day by day, new techniques and treatments are being discovered; and, if they want to continue to be of service to those who are ill and in pain, they must keep up with those advances. It is the same with Christians. The Christian life could be described as getting to know God better every day. A friendship which does not grow closer with the years tends to vanish with the years. And it is the same with us and God.

(3) Paul prays for a new realization of the Christian hope. It is almost a characteristic of the age in which we live that it is an age of despair. The novelist Thomas Hardy wrote in *Tess of the D'Urbervilles*: 'Sometimes I think that the worlds are like apples on our stubbard tree. Some of them splendid and some of them blighted.' Then comes the question: 'On which kind do we live – a splendid one or a blighted one?' And Tess's answer is: 'A blighted one.' On every side, the voice of the pessimist sounds; it was never more necessary to sound the trumpet-call of Christian hope. If the Christian message is true, the world is on the way not to disintegration but to consummation.

(4) Paul prays for a new realization of the power of God. For Paul, the supreme proof of that power was the resurrection. It proved that God's purpose cannot be stopped by any human action. In a world which looks chaotic, it is good to be aware that God is still in control.

(5) Paul finishes by speaking of the conquest of Christ in a sphere which does not mean so much to us today. As the Authorized Version has it, God has raised Jesus Christ 'far above all principality, and power, and might, and dominion, and every name that is named'. In Paul's day, people strongly believed both in demons and in angels; and these words which Paul uses are the titles of different grades of angels. He is saying that there is not a being in heaven

or on earth to whom Jesus Christ is not superior. In essence, Paul's prayer is that we should realize the greatness of the Saviour God has given to us.

In the very last phrase of the chapter, Paul has two tremendous thoughts. The Church, he says, is the essential element in the work of Christ. Just as the ideas of the mind cannot become effective without the work of the body, the tremendous glory which Christ brought to this world cannot be made effective without the work of the Church. This is one of the most tremendous thoughts in all Christianity. It means nothing less than that God's plan for one world is in the hands of the Church.

An illustration perfectly sums up this great truth. There is a legend which tells how Jesus went back to heaven after his time on earth. Even in heaven, he bore upon him the marks of the cross. The angels were talking to him, and Gabriel said: 'Master, you must have suffered terribly for men and women down there.' 'I did,' said Jesus. 'And,' said Gabriel, 'do they all know about how you loved them and what you did for them?' 'Oh no,' said Jesus, 'not yet. Just now, only a few people in Palestine know.' 'What have you done,' said Gabriel, 'to let everyone know about it?' Jesus said: 'I have asked Peter and James and John and a few others to make it the business of their lives to tell others about me, and the others still others, and yet others, until the furthest person on the widest circle knows what I have done.' Gabriel looked very doubtful, for he knew well what poor stuff human beings were made of. 'Yes,' he said, 'but what if Peter and James and John grow tired? What if the people who come after them forget? What if, way down in the twenty-first century, people just don't tell others about you? Haven't you made any other plans?' And Jesus answered: 'I haven't made any other plans. *I'm counting on them.*' To say that the Church is the body means that Jesus is counting on us.

Matthew 25:31–46

This is one of the most vivid parables Jesus ever spoke, and the lesson is crystal clear – that God will judge us in accordance with our reaction to human need. His judgement does not depend on the knowledge we have amassed, or the fame that we have acquired, or the fortune that we have gained, but on the help that we have given. And there are certain things which this parable teaches us about the help which we must give.

(1) It must be help in simple things. The things which Jesus picks out – giving a hungry person a meal, or a thirsty person a drink, welcoming a stranger, cheering the sick, visiting the prisoner – are things which anyone can do. It is not a question of giving away huge sums of money, or of writing our names in the annals of history; it is a case of giving simple help to the people we meet every day. There never was a parable which so opened the way to glory to us all.

(2) It must be help which is uncalculating. Those who helped did not think that they were helping Christ and thus piling up eternal merit; they helped because they could not stop themselves. It was the natural, instinctive, quite uncalculating reaction of the loving heart. Whereas, on the other hand, the attitude of those who failed to help was: 'If we had known it was *you* we would gladly have helped; but we thought it was only some insignificant person who was not worth helping.' It is still true that there are those who will help if they are given praise and thanks and publicity; but to help like that is not to help, it is to pander to self-esteem. Such help is not generosity; it is disguised selfishness. The help which wins the approval of God is that which is given for nothing but the sake of helping.

(3) Jesus confronts us with the wonderful truth that all such help given is given to himself; in contrast, all such help withheld is with-

held from himself. How can that be? If we really wish to bring delight to those who are parents, if we really wish to move them to gratitude, the best way to do it is to help their children. God is the great Father; and the way to delight the heart of God is to help his children, our fellow men and women.

There were two men who found this parable blessedly true. The one was Francis of Assisi; he was wealthy and high-born and high-spirited. But he was not happy. He felt that life was incomplete. Then one day he was out riding and met a leper, loathsome and repulsive in the ugliness of his disease. Something moved Francis to dismount and fling his arms around this wretched sufferer; and in his arms the face of the leper changed to the face of Christ.

The other was Martin of Tours. He was a Roman soldier and a Christian. One cold winter day, as he was entering a city, a beggar stopped him and asked for alms. Martin had no money; but the beggar was blue and shivering with cold, and Martin gave what he had. He took off his soldier's coat, worn and frayed as it was; he cut it in two and gave half of it to the beggar man. That night he had a dream. In it he saw the heavenly places and all the angels and Jesus among them; and Jesus was wearing half of a Roman soldier's cloak. One of the angels said to him: 'Master, why are you wearing that battered old cloak? Who gave it to you?' And Jesus answered softly: 'My servant Martin gave it to me.'

When we learn the generosity which without calculation helps others in the simplest things, we too will know the joy of helping Jesus Christ himself.